THE   GOOD   NEWS
ACCORDING   TO   JESUS

Smyth & Helwys Publishing, Inc.
6316 Peake Road
Macon, Georgia 31210-3960
1-800-747-3016
©2009 by Smyth & Helwys Publishing
All rights reserved.
Printed in the United States of America.

The paper used in this publication meets the minimum requirements of
American National Standard for Information Sciences—
Permanence of Paper for Printed Library Materials.
ANSI Z39.48–1984. (alk. paper)

Library of Congress Cataloging-in-Publication Data

Queen, Chuck.
The good news according to Jesus : a new kind of Christianity
for a new kind of Christian / by Chuck Queen.
p. cm. Includes bibliographical references (p.) and index.
ISBN 978-1-57312-528-4 (pbk. : alk. paper)
1. Jesus Christ—Person and offices.
2. Bible. N.T. Gospels—Criticism, interpretation, etc.
I. Title.
BT203.Q44 2009 232.9'54—dc22 2009003403

The Good News According to

Jesus

A New Kind
of Christianity
for a New Kind
of Christian

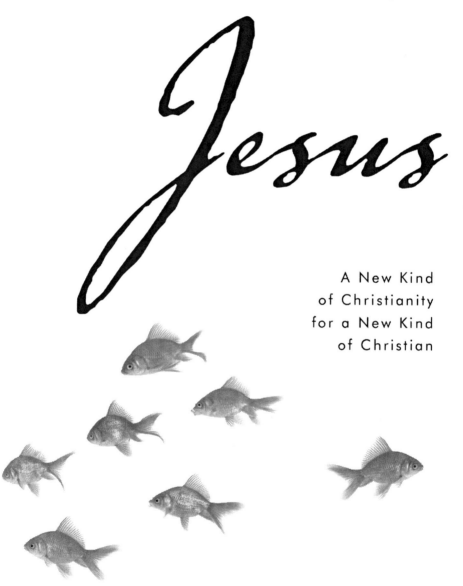

Chuck Queen

Advance Praise for *The Good News According to Jesus*

In *The Good News According to Jesus: A New Kind of Christianity for a New Kind of Christian,* Chuck Queen has given us a book that lives up to the promise of its title. I had planned to skim this book but found myself completely immersed in it. Queen has delivered a thoughtful, intelligent, and scholarly—yet imminently readable—examination of what it can mean, what it can look like, and yes, what it can feel like, to be a Christian in today's world. He begins with the Bible, of course, then reaches out to other writers, philosophers, scholars, theologians, and just plain Christians to hone what can well be called a handbook of Christian understanding and action. I'll go back to this book again and again.

—James A. Autry
Author of *Looking Around for God*
and *The Spirit of Retirement*

If you've ever wrestled with your faith, welcome Chuck Queen, who offers a candid perspective too often neglected by preachers wanting to play it safe. If you have struggled with sincere questions, you will discover a fellow pilgrim who is willing to trust you and invite you into the conversation. Either way, you'll find a caring and honest pastor helping you find Jesus' life-giving good news.

—Mark Johnson
Senior Minister, Central Baptist Church
Lexington, Kentucky

Dedication

To my wife, Melissa,
who, for many years, has been a true partner in the work of the kingdom,
and to our children, Hollie, Julie, and Jordan,
who have brought us great joy and
helped make life an adventure.

To the open minded, wide hearted, deep thinkers of Immanuel Baptist
Church in Frankfort, who are being transformed
by Jesus' vision of a new world.

Acknowledgments

I am grateful to the folks at Immanuel Baptist Church, who have participated in my classes and study/discussion groups, encouraged me with kind, positive words as I preached and taught this material, and have caught a vision of the kingdom of God and the church's mission.

I thank Dr. Greg Earwood, President of Baptist Seminary of Kentucky, for reading some of my earlier work when I first aspired to write, and for offering some helpful advice.

I especially owe a huge debt of gratitude to Jane Brake, Earl Hohman, Bennie League, and Suzie Stivers, members of Immanuel, who read the manuscript, helping with initial corrections and making valuable suggestions.

And I thank Melissa, my wife, for prodding me to write and for sharing my excitement in the book's publication.

Contents

Introduction

The time has come for evangelical Christians to rethink their faith. I grew up with a Christianity that centered mostly on the teachings of Paul; most sermons I heard as a teenager were derived from Paul's letters. If a Gospel text was used, almost invariably it was taken from the Gospel of John. I can't tell you how many sermons I heard from Paul on the subject of being saved by faith and from John on the subject of being born again. I don't think my experience was that unusual. Traditional, evangelical Christianity has typically kept its theological emphasis on Paul or the Gospel of John.

The problem with focusing on Paul is that Paul's letters largely concentrate on the particular problems, issues, questions, and challenges faced by the churches he either founded or planned on visiting at the time. Paul's letters are our earliest New Testament documents, but they are slanted toward the troubling issues in the Pauline churches. Paul shows no interest in expounding on the life and teachings of Jesus in his letters. Pauline scholars explain this in various ways. It is conceivable for Paul to have instructed the churches in his initial, core teaching, or it could be that Paul's interest was elsewhere. A substantial case can be made that Paul gave center stage to the development of a theology of corporate participation in the death and resurrection of Christ.

John's Gospel reflects a kind of theological synthesis of Jewish and Greek ideas and beliefs about Jesus that emerged as Christianity made inroads into the larger world. It contains little of what Jesus actually said and did, reflecting more of what the church, close to a century later (possibly in Ephesus), had come to believe about Jesus. Even a casual reading of John makes obvious that the Jesus of John's Gospel talks and acts differently than the Jesus in the other Gospels. I am not suggesting that the Gospel of John is not true; rather, its truth is in its theological presentation of the Jesus story, not in its historical portrayal of Jesus.

My approach is to focus on the Gospels of Mark, Matthew, and Luke (commonly called the "Synoptic Gospels" because they share much material in common). I will work on the basis of the nearly unanimously accepted thesis that Mark's Gospel was the first Gospel to be written, possibly around AD 70, just prior to or after the destruction of Jerusalem. It is believed that the Gospels of Matthew and Luke were written ten to twenty years after Mark and that their authors used Mark's Gospel as they wrote. It is also believed that Matthew and Luke shared a common written source, as well as having access to their own unique oral and written materials in composing their accounts.

Without question, each of the Synoptic Gospels is unique in their theological presentation of the Jesus story, and yet they share much theology in common. My focus in this book is generally on what they share in common, though it will be necessary from time to time to elaborate on a particular theme or teaching that one Gospel may emphasize over the others or vice versa.

On the whole, the portrait of Jesus in the Synoptic Gospels takes seriously his life, works, and teachings. In fact, in these Gospels, the death and resurrection of Jesus cannot be grasped apart from his life; the life, works, teachings, death, and resurrection of Jesus form one piece. It is my contention that when the good news according to Jesus is drawn from these Gospels, the result is a richer, deeper, healthier, more relevant and holistic gospel than is current in traditional, evangelical Christianity.

I am a Christian minister immersed in the theological and practical questions of common parishioners. I do not profess to be a scholar, nor am I writing for the scholarly community, though I certainly draw from scholarly sources. In the pages that follow, my indebtedness to theologians, biblical scholars, spiritual writers, and pastoral teachers and educators of all persuasions will be apparent. I speak to the common Christian and religious seeker. Some of the questions I address in this book are as follows:

• What was the message and ministry of Jesus really about?
• What does Jesus' practice of an "open table" say about the nature of God's kingdom?
• How should disciples of Jesus Christ relate to people of other religious faiths?
• What kind of God is the God of Jesus, and what difference does it make?
• What are the dynamics of an authentic faith? What are the dynamics of grace and forgiveness?
• In what ways did Jesus turn conventional values upside down?
• What's involved in living in God's new world?
• Why did Jesus have to die?

- How can we understand God's judgment in light of Jesus' teaching on love?
- How should we understand the concept of "hell" today?
- Must Jesus literally return to this earth?

The explanations I offer with regard to these questions are not the standard answers one usually hears from traditional, evangelical Christian preachers and teachers.

The time has come for evangelical Christians to embrace a more credible, reasonable, inclusive, and gracious Christianity—a Christianity that can actually contribute to making this world a better world, or, as I suggest throughout the book, can help transform this world into God's new world.

M. Scott Peck, in his introduction to the twenty-fifth anniversary edition of *The Road Less Traveled*, discusses the timing of his book. He doubts that, had his book been published twenty years previously, it would have been even slightly successful. When his book hit the press, he says, "a large number of women and men in the United States were both psychologically and spiritually sophisticated and had begun to deeply contemplate 'all the kinds of things that people shouldn't talk about.' They were almost literally waiting for someone to say such things out loud."[1]

I believe this is where many in the evangelical community will stand today in relation to the teaching of this book. Evangelical leaders, who are content with the way things are, will not welcome these teachings; they will probably call me a radical and dismiss what I say. But I am convinced that many evangelicals are waiting for someone to say these things out loud. I offer this book with a prayer that it will help contemporary Christians and religious seekers explore a better way of being Christian.

Note

1. M. Scott Peck, *The Road Less Traveled: A New Psychology of Love, Traditional Values, and Spiritual Growth*, 25th anniversary ed. (New York: Simon and Schuster, Inc.), 6.

Chapter 1

The Message of Jesus

In *The Secret Message of Jesus,* Brian McLaren writes,

> I've become convinced that if the good news of Jesus were carried in a newspaper today, it wouldn't be hidden in the religion section (although it would no doubt cause a ruckus there). It would be a major story in every section, from world news (What is the path to peace, and how are we responding to our neighbors in need?) to national and local news (How are we treating children, poor people, minorities, the last, the lost, the least? How are we treating our enemies?), in the lifestyle section (Are we loving our neighbors and throwing good parties to bring people together?), the food section (Do our diets reflect concern for God's planet and our poor neighbors, and have we invited any of them over for dinner lately?), the entertainment and sports sections (What is the point of our entertainment, and what values are we strengthening in sports?), and even the business section (Are we serving the wrong master: money rather than God?). . . .
>
> Jesus echoed and intensified the prophetic message that a new world order was possible and coming. . . . In that new reality, the poor and rejected will be embraced and valued and brought back into the community. In that new era, what will count is what is in the heart—not merely what is projected, pretended, or professed. In that new realm, evil in all its forms will be exposed, named, and dealt with. In that new kingdom, justice, integrity, and peace will overcome. . . .
>
> This revolutionary image of Jesus didn't come to me in Sunday school as a boy. There, Jesus was a nice, quiet, gentle perhaps somewhat fragile guy on whose lap children liked to sit. . . . This revolutionary image of

Jesus didn't come to me in church either. There, Jesus was someone whose main job was to die so my sins could be forgiven and I could go to heaven. . . . Or else he was a teacher whose words would be quoted to condemn people our church or denomination didn't approve of. . . . But Jesus wasn't presented as someone whose message would overturn our thinking as well.[1]

Brian McLaren admits that in the church where he began his Christian journey, Jesus "was someone whose main job was to die so my sins could be forgiven and I could go to heaven." Most evangelicals would echo that same belief and experience. How did the church ever come to this conclusion: that Jesus came mainly to die in order for human beings to go to heaven? Certainly not from the Gospels of Matthew, Mark, and Luke; these Gospels present a much different perspective on the good news according to Jesus. In this chapter my main consideration is the central theme of Jesus' preaching and ministry as it is presented in these Gospels.

The Kingdom of God

I had been in the ministry for several years when I realized I had never delivered a sermon on the foundational theme in the preaching and teaching of Jesus, namely, the kingdom of God. The Gospel of Mark introduces the preaching ministry of Jesus in this manner: "Now after John was arrested, Jesus came to Galilee, proclaiming the good news of God, and saying, 'The time is fulfilled, and the kingdom of God has come near; repent, and believe in the good news'" (Mark 1:14-15).[2] In the Gospels of Matthew and Luke, when Jesus sends out the twelve to engage in a ministry of healing, he charges them with preaching the nearness of the kingdom of God (Matt 10:1, 7; Luke 9:1-2). Matthew substitutes the word "heaven" for God ("kingdom of heaven") with no essential change in meaning in order to avoid speaking of God so directly.

The Jewish people who heard Jesus would certainly have been familiar with the idea of God as king. They spoke of God as king regularly in their worship. The psalmist expresses this theology:

Lift up your heads, O gates!
and be lifted up, O ancient doors!
That the King of glory may come in.
Who is the King of glory?
The LORD, strong and mighty.
the LORD, mighty in battle.

Lift up your heads, O gates!
and be lifted up, O ancient doors!
that the King of glory may come in.
Who is the King of glory?
The LORD of hosts,
he is the King of glory. (Ps 24:7-10)

Jesus embraced the idea of God as sovereign ruler, but the way he spoke of the kingdom was different than the way other Jews used the phrase. As mentioned above, in Matthew and Luke Jesus announces that the kingdom "has come near" or "is at hand" (another possible translation). When Jesus is accused of driving out demons by the power of the evil one, according to Matthew's Gospel he says, "But if it is by the Spirit of God that I cast out demons, then the kingdom of God has come to you" (Matt 12:28). From this perspective the kingdom of God was either present in Jesus or imminent in Jesus (would soon appear). Jesus talks about "receiving" the kingdom and "entering" the kingdom (Mark 10:15, 23-25). He compares the kingdom to seeds growing (Mark 4:26-29); to yeast in a batch of dough (Luke 12:20); and to the discovery of a treasure of such immense value that the one who finds it joyfully gives up everything in order to acquire it (Matt 13:44-46). Jesus tells his disciples to pray, "your kingdom come" (Luke 11:2). This dynamic way of speaking about the kingdom of God makes it virtually impossible to reduce its meaning to a simple or single definition. In some sayings Jesus seems to indicate that the kingdom is here, now, but in other sayings Jesus envisages it as something yet to come, a future reality that is on the verge of arriving. It is "now here" in one sense, and "not yet here, but soon coming" in another sense. So what does Jesus have in mind by the phrase "kingdom of God"?

Jesus is building on a foundation laid by the prophets of Israel. Jesus' contemporaries looked forward to a time when God's people would be nationally restored, spiritually renewed, and at peace. This hope was expressed in diverse ways, but it often included a global and universal dimension. Isaiah 2:2-4 envisions it this way:

In days to come
the mountain of the LORD's house
shall be established as the highest of the mountains,
and shall be raised above the hills;
all the nations shall stream to it.

> Many peoples shall come and say,
> "Come, let us go up to the mountain of the LORD,
> to the house of the God of Jacob;
> that he may teach us his ways
> and that we may walk in his paths."
> For out of Zion shall go forth instruction,
> and the word of the LORD from Jerusalem.
> He shall judge between the nations,
> and shall arbitrate for many peoples;
> they shall beat their swords into plowshares,
> and their spears into pruning hooks;
> nation shall not lift up sword against nation,
> neither shall they learn war any more.

Here the prophet envisions God's peaceable kingdom extending to the nations, though centering in Jerusalem where the law of God goes forth.

The prophets imagined a new ordering of creation. In Isaiah 11:6-9 the prophet says,

> The wolf shall live with the lamb,
> The leopard shall lie down with the kid,
> The calf and the lion and fatling together,
> and a little child shall lead them . . .
> The cow and the bear shall graze,
> their young shall lie down together;
> and the lion shall eat straw like the ox.
> The nursing child shall play over the hole of the asp,
> And the weaned child shall put its hand on the adder's den.
> They will not hurt or destroy
> on all my holy mountain;
> for the earth will be full of the knowledge of the LORD
> as the waters cover the sea.

The language of course is poetic; it is metaphorical and figurative, but without question points to a different kind of world. Destruction and death give way to life and peace.

Jesus' announcement of the kingdom of God must be understood against this backdrop. According to Matthew's Gospel, John, who is in prison, sends messengers to inquire if Jesus is "the one who is to come," that is, the one in and through whom Israel's prophetic hope would be realized.

Jesus responds, "Go and tell John what you hear and see: the blind receive their sight, the lame walk, the lepers are cleansed, the deaf hear, the dead are raised and the poor have the good news brought to them" (Matt 11:4b-5).

In this text the healing miracles and the exorcisms (the driving back of demonic powers) of Jesus signal the future rule of God breaking into the present world through his life and ministry. These works of power (bringing healing and wholeness) function as signs of the inbreaking kingdom of God and mark the beginning of the fulfillment of Israel's prophetic hope for a restored and healed people.

In Luke's Gospel Jesus enters the synagogue in Nazareth on the Sabbath. He is given the scroll of the prophet Isaiah. He unrolls the scroll and reads from Isaiah 61:1-2,

> The Spirit of the LORD is upon me,
> because he has anointed me to bring good news to the poor.
> He has sent me to proclaim release to the captives
> and recovery of sight to the blind, to let the oppressed go free,
> to proclaim the year of the LORD's favor. (Luke 4:18-19)

With all eyes fastened on him, Jesus says to them, "Today this scripture has been fulfilled in your hearing." This is Luke's way of introducing the mission and ministry of Jesus. Luke defines the role of the Messiah as one who brings good news to the poor, sets the prisoners free, restores sight to the blind, and liberates the oppressed as outlined in Isaiah 61, which originally referred to Israel's vocation as the Servant of the Lord to the nations. Jesus claims that the day of fulfillment has dawned; that the age of God's reign has come. In Luke's presentation, Jesus sees himself as fulfilling Israel's role as God's chosen Servant destined to bring liberation and hope to the disadvantaged and marginalized. The new day, anticipated by the prophets, has arrived, and it will mean salvation for the poor and justice for the oppressed.

The prophets believed Israel's vocation involved being the people through whom their God would rescue the world from the forces of evil and put the world to rights. Jesus believed he was bearing Israel's vocation in himself, through his works of mercy and his teachings about a new kind of world where the blessed ones are not the powerful, prominent, and proud, but the poor, broken, and humble. So when Jesus announces the nearness or "soon coming" of the kingdom of God, he is talking about *the practical, effective, dynamic out-working of God's saving presence and power in human and earthly life that has already begun in his ministry and that will one day trans-form the world, bringing peace and justice to all people.*[3]

The Gospels interpret the words and deeds of Jesus as evidence that the future kingdom of God is now present, but not in a final or ultimate sense. It has arrived in the life, teachings, works, death, and resurrection of Jesus, though in a partial and preliminary way. The kingdom of God breaks into this present world in and through Jesus, the Christ, as a foretaste and fore-shadowing of what is to come. By healing the lame, the blind, and the diseased, by expelling the demonic powers that deform and destroy, by teaching the word of God in new, fresh ways, and by giving himself in serv-ice for others, even unto death, Jesus embodied the saving, redeeming, and transforming presence and power of God in the world. By looking to Jesus, we can visualize what the future kingdom is like. God's new world, though not yet here in any final or ultimate sense, is nevertheless realized in Jesus, the Christ.

An Open Table

One of the most poignant ways through which Jesus demonstrated the inclusiveness and graciousness of God's rule in the world was in his practice of table fellowship with "sinners." Mark 2:13-17 describes the open table practice of Jesus that incurred the wrath of some of the religious leaders:

> Jesus went out again beside the sea; the whole crowd gathered around him, and he taught them. As he was walking along, he saw Levi son of Alphaeus sitting at the tax booth, and he said to him, "Follow me." And he got up and followed him.
>
> And as he sat at dinner in Levi's house, many tax collectors and sinners were also sitting with Jesus and his disciples—for there were many who fol-lowed him. When the scribes of the Pharisees saw that he was eating with sinners and tax collectors, they said to his disciples, "Why does he eat with tax collectors and sinners?" When Jesus heard this, he said to them, "Those who are well have no need of a physician, but those who are sick; I have come to call not the righteous but sinners."

In most cultures, eating together signifies mutuality and acceptance, as well as friendship and fellowship. Today, one might imagine a business luncheon or some other formal setting where this would not necessarily apply, but normally, sharing a meal together suggests a healthy, affirming relationship.

In the world of Jesus meal sharing was not only an act of hospitality; it took on a sacred character, expressing religious obligations and sanctions. Purity laws governed not only what could or could not be eaten, but how the food should be prepared. Eating food not prepared according to the purity code rendered one "unclean" or "impure." The religiously "pure" would not think of eating with the "impure." The people with whom one ate reflected the ethos that was deeply embedded in the religious and social climate. Table fellowship was one of the principal ways the religious establishment maintained and enforced the purity system.

Two groups of Jews in particular, the Pharisees and the Essenes, regarded table fellowship with the utmost sensitivity. Many of the Pharisees were scrupulous in adhering to the purity laws regarding food and ceremonial cleansings and made such practices test cases of covenant loyalty and obedience to God. Those who did not measure up to their standard of purity were called "sinners."

"Sinners," therefore, constituted a well-defined social class rejected by many of the religious leaders. Tax collectors were a particularly despised group of "sinners." By their profession they were entitled to decide how much tax to levy in addition to what the Roman government required. It was a profession that attracted the dishonest in Israel, and it required close collaboration with the Roman authorities. Tax collectors, then, were not only considered to be the worst kind of "sinners," but they were also regarded as traitors.

The kind of culture that emerged from this emphasis on purity emphasized "shame and honor." In a shame and honor culture, everything depends on how others see you. There are clearly defined lines and boundaries. In Jesus' culture, the "pure" (those who kept the purification laws) did not associate with the "impure." The "righteous" looked down on the "sinners."[4]

Once a person was identified as a "sinner," he or she, for the most part, was locked into that category with no practical way out. Many of these "sinners" were not sinners intentionally, but labeled as such due to being poor and uneducated. The laws and customs associated with ritual matters were so complicated that it was difficult for the uneducated to know exactly what was expected. Education was a long, expensive process, and purification rites and sacrifices for cleansing were tedious and costly. So the mostly poor folks who made up this class had neither the time nor the money required to become "righteous."[5]

The system was apparently working well until Jesus came along and undercut it. Jesus invited sinners and tax collectors to take part in the rule of God. He said, "It is not the healthy who need a physician, but the sick. I did not come for the righteous, but for sinners" (Mark 2:17). But who is not sick in some way? Who among us are so righteous that they do not need the gracious, saving power and presence of God in their lives? The invitation offered to "the sick" (to "sinners") is an invitation offered to all. This is the good news: Jesus invites all sinners to the table.

Tony Campolo tells about getting off a plane in Honolulu at 3:30 in the morning wanting breakfast. He found a little place that was open, and as he sat at the counter sipping his coffee and eating his donut, eight or nine prostitutes walked in. The talk was loud and crude, and Campolo felt completely out of place. But just as he was about to make his getaway, he overheard a woman say, "Tomorrow's my birthday. I'm going to be thirty-nine." Her friend responded in a nasty and sarcastic tone, "So what do you want from me? A birthday party?" The woman replied, "Why do you have to be so mean? I was just telling you. I have never had a birthday party in my whole life. Why should I have one now?"

After the women left, Campolo asked Harry, the big, rough-looking owner and cook, about the women. Harry informed him that they came in every night at about the same time. The woman who had never had a birthday party was named Agnes. When Campolo brought up the possibility of throwing her one, Harry thought it was a great idea.

Campolo got the decorations, Harry made the cake, and the next evening when the women entered the diner, Agnes was given a surprise birthday party. Agnes cried and was told to cut the cake. She hesitated, looked down at the cake, and said to Harry, "Would it be okay if I keep the cake a while? I mean, is it all right if we don't eat it right away?"

Harry said, "Sure! If you want to keep the cake, keep the cake. Take it home if you want to." And with that, Agnes picked up the cake like it was the Holy Grail and walked right out the door. Everyone else sort of stood there in stunned silence. Finally Campolo said, "What do you say we pray?" And he started to pray for Agnes, asking that her life would be touched by God's love and that God would be good to her. When he finished, Harry leaned over the counter and said, "Hey, you never told me you were a preacher. What kind of church do you belong to?" Campolo answered, "The kind that throws birthday parties for prostitutes at 3:30 in the morning." Harry responded, "No you don't. There's no church like that. If there was, I'd join it. I'd join a church like that."[6]

This is the kind of community Jesus came to create; one that welcomes those that are marginalized and excluded by others. Jesus tells stories (parables) to provoke his hearers to think about God's kingdom. In several of them, Jesus uses the image of a banquet where all people are invited to participate. In Jesus' stories, the meal becomes a vivid symbol depicting the merciful and compassionate nature of God's rule. In Luke 14, Jesus tells a parable about someone who "gave a great dinner and invited many." But when the invitation—"Come; for everything is ready"—went out, those invited began to make excuses. When the excuses were reported to the owner of the house, he said to his servant, "Go out into the streets and lanes of the town and bring in the poor, the crippled, the blind and the lame." Such is the nature of God's rule.

God's new world has come near, and if we have eyes to see, we will find it in places where we least expect it. God's rule knows no race, class, social order, creed, or nationality. All boundaries are shattered, and all are invited to share in it.

The movie *Antwone Fisher* opens with Antwone (Derek Luke), who is enlisted in the Navy, asleep on his bunk. He dreams that he is a little boy standing outside a huge barn. The doors open, and a man escorts him to a wonderful feast. Many people are present; their dress suggests that they span history, and Antwone is the guest of honor. His mother sets before him a big plate of pancakes. Just as he is about to eat, he awakens.

Antwone was born in prison. His father was killed before he was born, and he was placed in an orphanage until his mother could come for him. She never came. He lived a painful childhood. His foster mother beat him and verbally abused him; the daughter in the home sexually molested him when he was six.

Because of his volatile temper, Antwone is sent to the naval psychiatrist, Dr. Jerome Davenport (Denzel Washington), who has a passion to help the young man. The story alternates between the present and Antwone's childhood as Dr. Davenport helps him confront his past. Antwone finally decides to follow the doctor's advice to look for his family. His girlfriend goes with him. He locates an aunt who helps him find his mother. When his mother sees him, she says nothing. Antwone begins speaking gently.

Why did you never come for me? Didn't you wonder where I was? And what I was doing? Or what I became? Even if I was still alive? I've taken care of myself. I've never been in trouble with the law. I've read hundreds of books, written poems, painted pictures. I've traveled the world. I serve my country. I speak two languages and I'm workin' on a third. I've never fathered any children. Never done drugs or even smoked a cigarette.

Then he moves close. He sits down beside her and puts his hand on her shoulder. Still she doesn't respond. He says,

> I use to dream about you. My mother, what you would be like, how you look, your smile, even your scent. For all these years I've wondered about you. I've dreamed about you. Didn't you miss me? I would go to school each day and imagine you were just around the corner and when I'd get there you would be there. And in my mind you were always there, you just couldn't find me. So I'd race to the next corner, and you would be there, I know you would, and you would buy me ice cream, and then would take me home. I'm a good person. I'm a good man.

He kisses her on the cheek, but she remains silent. He gets up and leaves. After he leaves, tears fill her eyes, and she puts her head in her hands. Her life is so broken that she cannot, at least at first, accept his offer of love and for-giveness.

When Antwone returns to his aunt's house, he finds the house full of rel-atives. He is greeted with a smile and a man says, "How you doing? I'm your Uncle Horeb." Another says, "I'm your cousin Jeanette." Someone else says, "I'm your Aunt Anna." He is directed to the doors that open into the dining room, where a table is covered with all kinds of food—even pancakes.

The matriarch of the family places her hands on either side of his face. Then, with grace-filled eyes she says, "Welcome." She turns to the others and says, "All right," and amid joy and laughter the feast begins.[7]

Such is the kingdom of God breaking into the present world. We get a unique revelation of its character and nature in the life and ministry of Jesus, especially his table fellowship with sinners. We do not need to jump through any hoops. There are no gatekeepers to draw boundaries. In sitting at the table with Jesus, we join with all the other sick folks who need the healing grace of the great Physician—sinners one and all.

The Call to Discipleship

The "open table" is a powerful symbol of the graciousness of God's rule, but it is *God's* rule—God's effective, good, benevolent will that heals and trans-forms. God's rule is not static. Once we join Christ at the table, we are then expected to open ourselves to the redeeming power of God embodied in

Jesus' life and teachings. The invitation to participate in God's reign is an invitation to be a disciple of Jesus Christ. It is an invitation to learn from Jesus how to experience and express the redeeming power of God that is meant to reorder and transform the world.

In Mark's Gospel, just after the call of Levi and after Jesus' open meal with tax collectors and sinners, pro-purity adherents ask Jesus why his disciples are not fasting. The disciples of the Pharisees fasted regularly; it was part of their code of holiness. Even the disciples of John the Baptist fasted, but Jesus' disciples were not fasting and the Pharisees couldn't understand why. Jesus said, "The wedding guests cannot fast while the bridegroom is with them, can they? As long as they have the bridegroom with them, they cannot fast. The days will come when the bridegroom is taken away from them, and then they will fast" (Mark 2:19-20).

Jesus is not denouncing the practice of fasting in this passage. In fact, he suggests that there will eventually be an appropriate time for his disciples to fast, but instead of linking the practice to a system of purity laws and holiness codes, Jesus connects it to himself. The decision to fast is determined by a relationship to Jesus.

The imagery of the Jewish wedding is significant. A wedding was a time of great joy and celebration, characterized by music, processions, and festivity. It was not a time to be concerned about the rigid application of purity laws. New Testament scholar Lamar Williamson observes that the depiction of Christ as bridegroom "connotes . . . joy in the presence of the Lord and celebration of the 'already' dimension of the Kingdom of God."[8]

Robert Fulghum tells about a wedding produced on an epic scale by a mother of the bride—an eighteen-piece brass and wind ensemble; gift registries spreading across most of the continental United States; twenty-four bridesmaids, groomsmen, flower-petal throwers, and ringbearers. Fulghum says, "Looking back, it seems now that the rehearsal and dinner on the evening before the great event were not unlike what took place in Napoleon's camp the night before Waterloo. Nothing had been left to chance. Nothing could prevent a victory on the coming day. Nobody would *ever* forget this wedding."

The great day came. The plans went smoothly—until the climactic moment of the processional. Fulghum writes,

> Ah, the bride. She had been dressed for hours if not days. No adrenaline
> was left in her body. Left alone with her father in the reception hall of the
> church while the march of the maidens went on and on, she walked along

the tables laden with gourmet goodies and absentmindedly sampled first the little pink and yellow and green mints. Then she picked through the silver bowls of mixed nuts and ate the pecans. Followed by a cheeseball or two, some black olives, a handful of glazed almonds, a little sausage with a frilly toothpick stuck in it, a couple of shrimps blanketed in bacon, and a cracker piled with liver pate. To wash this down—a glass of pink champagne. Her father gave it to her. To calm her nerves. What you noticed as the bride stood in the doorway was not her dress, but her face. White. For what was coming down the aisle was a living grenade with the pin pulled out. The bride threw up. Just as she walked by her mother. And by "threw up," I don't mean a polite lady-like urp into her handkerchief. She puked. There's just no nice word for it. I mean, she hosed the front of the chancel—hitting two bridesmaids, the groom and ringbearer, and me. . . . Only two people were seen smiling. One was the mother of the groom. And the other was the father of the bride.[10]

Fulghum explains how they pulled themselves together for a quieter ceremony in the reception hall. "Everybody cried, as people are supposed to do at weddings, mostly because the groom held the bride in his arms through the whole ceremony. And no groom ever kissed a bride more tenderly than he."[11]

Ten years later, everyone was invited back for another party—thrown by the mother of the bride—to celebrate the disaster. They watched it on three TV sets. In spite of the ceremony disaster, the bride and the groom were united in marriage, and that's all that mattered. The *relationship* mattered.

In his practice of an open table, in his healing and liberating ministry, and in his preaching and teaching about the rule of God, Jesus acted not only for God, but also with and in God. Jesus made the invisible God visible, making available to others the same kind of life in God, with God, and for God that he experienced. The invitation to know this dynamic reality is an invitation to be in relationship with God; it's the call to be a disciple and learn from Jesus how to experience and express the reality and power of God's rule. We learn from Jesus how to embody God's purpose in the world; how to love God, love others, and love all creation. Philosopher and theologian Dallas Willard states,

Jesus came among us to show and teach the life for which we were made. He came very gently, opened access to the governance of God with him, and set afoot a conspiracy of freedom in truth among human beings. Having overcome death he remains among us. By relying on his word and presence we are enabled to reintegrate the little realm that makes up our life into the infinite rule of God. And that is the eternal kind of life. Caught up in his active rule, our deeds become an element of God's eternal history. They are what God and we do together, making us part of his life and him a part of ours.[12]

Jesus' vision of a transformed world captured his imagination and fueled his mission and ministry. Disciples of Jesus share his vision of a world bathed in God's love and grace, a world of justice, compassion, and peace. The extent to which we can actualize this vision now is the degree to which we, like Jesus, can experience "already" what is "not yet."

Some years ago, Larry Walters, who was thirty-three years old at the time, went down to the local army surplus store and purchased forty-two used weather balloons, which he filled with helium. That afternoon he strapped himself to a lawn chair and had several of his friends attach some of these balloons to his chair. He took along a six-pack of beer, a peanut-butter-and-jelly sandwich, and a BB gun, figuring he could shoot the balloons one at a time when he was ready to land. He guessed that the balloons would lift him about 100 feet, but he did not figure on soaring to 16,000 feet right into the middle of the air traffic pattern of the Los Angeles International Airport. He had just started shooting the balloons when he lost his grip on the gun. He was airborne for more than two hours. When he safely landed, the police cited him and reporters interviewed him. After he confessed that he was scared and vowed never to do it again, he was asked why he did it. He answered, "Because you can't just sit there."

Jesus could not just sit there, gripped by the prophetic vision of a new world. What about us? Can we dream new dreams? Can we imagine a world made whole? The capacity to think new thoughts and imagine life with God in charge will inevitably lead us into a process of change. When we decide to be in relationship with Jesus Christ, to live as his disciple, we submit to a conversion process that realigns and reshapes our values and priorities. Disciples of Jesus dance to the beat of a different drummer.

According to Mark's Gospel, when Jesus announces that "the time is fulfilled" and that "the kingdom of God has come near," he issues a call to "repent and believe the good news" (Mark 1:15). The call to repent is a call to turn from a life governed by our ego needs. This involves a radical centering in God's will and immersion in God's ways that will sometimes run directly counter to the aspirations and values of our culture.

The decision to abide with Jesus in a relationship of commitment and trust in order to learn from him how to live in communion and cooperation with God both simplifies and complicates life. It simplifies life in that disciples of Jesus have a center around which everything else revolves. Disciples of Jesus are singularly and wholeheartedly committed to the way of Christ in the world—the way of compassionate service to others and the pursuit of justice, especially for the marginalized and downtrodden. However, living this out in a world dominated by greed and violence is complicated and often risky. In fact, Jesus warns his disciples that in the world, they will face opposition and persecution. When he sends them out to proclaim the good news of the kingdom, he warns them that they will be like sheep among wolves (Matt 10:16-31).

Undoubtedly, the call of these first disciples to follow Jesus came as an enormous disruption in their lives and families. Just after Jesus announces the nearness of the kingdom and calls his hearers to repent and believe the message, Mark says,

> As Jesus passed along the Sea of Galilee, he saw Simon and his brother Andrew casting a net into the sea—for they were fishermen. And Jesus said to them, "Follow me and I will make you fish for people." And immediately they left their nets and followed him. As he went a little farther, he saw James son of Zebedee and his brother John, who were in their boat mending their nets. Immediately he called them; and they left their father Zebedee in the boat with the hired men, and followed him. (Mark 1:16-20)

This would have come as a major disruption of life, not only for the individual who said yes to the call, but for the family as well. There is mention in the text of "hired men," so the business of the fishermen was obviously productive, but the departure of the two sets of brothers could easily have put the welfare of their families and their fishing businesses at risk. The whole family would have shared the burden of the call.

Many "Christians" fall short in our commitment to follow the radical life and teachings of Jesus and instead settle for the Jesus of our denomination or the Jesus of popular religion—the Jesus who takes away the guilt of sin and grants the assurance of heaven without demanding that we alter our vision and way of life. Steve Chalke, in his book titled *The Lost Message of Jesus*, wrote,

Our thinking in the twenty-first century has become rather dualistic. So much of the "gospel" we peddle is all about the future tense, not the present reality. We live with the idea that the gospel's chief aim is to make us fit for heaven, when in reality Jesus' message is focused on making us citizens and recipients of the Kingdom of God today. Too often we present Christianity as a faith to die by, asking questions such as, "If you were to die tonight, where do you think you would spend eternity?" However, Jesus' message is about a faith to live, love, work and play by, today. And it's not just personal and it's definitely not private, but rather it is public and corporate.

Too often it is the thought of our heavenly reward that motivates us to take action rather than the spiritual and social deprivation and injustice that we see around us. Our goal is not to store up treasures in heaven; to rack up spiritual brownie points in order to build the heavenly mansion we'll live in after death, and of course, to get other people there as well. But such attitudes are a travesty. If we think of the gospel only as a means by which people get to heaven, then we are misrepresenting and missing the major thrust of the message of Jesus.[13]

The Jesus of popular Christianity may ask us to give a tithe of our income and some of our time to support the church program but says little against our need to accumulate more possessions than we could ever use, our need to compare and compete for top titles and accolades, and our need to be successful at any cost. Most of us live with a comfortable commitment that shapes our Christianity to fit our lifestyle, but the call to discipleship asks us to relinquish our hold on these former things and be formed anew in the way of Christ.

The story is told about a simple, illiterate man who was changed through the work of the Salvation Army. He went regularly to their meetings. One day he came home rather sad. His wife asked, "What's the matter?" He said, "I've just noticed that all the people in the Salvation Army wear red sweaters, and I don't have a red sweater." She said, "I'll knit you one." So she knitted him a red sweater.

The next Sunday, he was still unhappy. She asked, "What's wrong now?" He said, "I just noticed that all their red sweaters have yellow writing." They were both illiterate, but she said, "Don't worry about it. I'll embroider some writing on it for you."

The motto printed on the sweaters read "Blood and Fire." Since the woman couldn't read, she decided to copy a sign from a store window across from their home. She embroidered these words onto her husband's red sweater. When he came home the next Sunday, she asked, "Did they like your sweater?" He replied, "They loved my sweater. Some of them said they liked my sweater better than their sweater."

What neither of them knew was that the sign on the store window—and the new yellow words on his sweater—read, "This Business Under New Management."

The invitation to be a disciple of Jesus is an invitation to bring our lives under new management. The early Christians confessed at their baptism, "Jesus is Lord," words that had both personal and political implications. Jesus scholar Marcus Borg points out that the language and titles used to refer to Caesar were reemployed by Christ's first followers to refer to Jesus. Titles such as "Son of God," "Savior," "King of Kings," and "Lord of Lords" were applied to Caesar as the supreme ruler of the empire. Borg mentions that the familiar affirmation, "Jesus is Lord," which today is practically a Christian cliché, originally challenged Caesar's claim to be lord and still challenges all systems that claim ultimate allegiance.[14] Disciples of Christ believe that living in the way of Jesus is God's plan for the world, and they are firmly committed to learn from Jesus how to live compassionately, mercifully, justly, and humbly with God and with all humanity and creation.

Pursuing the way of Christ in the world may mean swimming upstream against the current of prevailing political, economic, and even religious systems and conventional wisdom. When we decide to live as disciples of Jesus Christ, our lives will possibly be turned upside down. The irony is that only when our world is turned upside down are we in a position to live right side up. The message of the "open table" extends the invitation to anyone and everyone. We come as we are, but we don't stay that way. Discipleship to Christ is a transformative relationship.

In my church, we have a banner ministry team that creates beautiful banners to adorn our sanctuary and entryways. They recently made two banners that read, "Come as You Are" and "Discover Whose You Are." Now we need a third that reads, "Become What You Were Meant to Be." Come as you are—no need to change in order to be welcomed at the table. God's love is an unconditional love. Discover whose you are—that you are loved and forgiven, a daughter or son of God, chosen and called to be the salt of the earth and the light of the world. Become what you were meant to be—a representative and agent of God's saving, redeeming, whole-making power and presence (God's kingdom), a disciple of Jesus Christ, embodying his love, compassion, concern for justice, humility, goodness, and grace.

Mark presents the call of the first disciples in an abrupt, decisive manner, highlighting the authority of Christ as God's redemptive agent of the kingdom. They found Jesus' challenge so compelling that "immediately they left their nets and followed him"; "they left their father Zebedee in the boat with the hired men, and followed him." We don't know historically if the break was as decisive as the story suggests, since through the next eight chapters of Mark's Gospel Jesus remains in the vicinity of Galilee, and boats are constantly available (one of the brother's fishing boats?) when they need them. In Luke's version, the call comes later after they have witnessed Jesus' ministry for a time (Luke 5:1-11). In addition, in Luke it is not so much Jesus the preacher of the kingdom who evokes their commitment as it is Jesus the transcendent, compelling Christ whose power draws them.[15]

The call can come to us in a variety of ways and through diverse means. Some experience the call to discipleship as a decisive turning around and can pinpoint the day and hour they made the decision; others come to it more gradually. But however we embrace the relationship, the living Christ uproots old ways of thinking, reacting, and relating and implants his mind and heart in us.

Jesus employs an image from fishing: "Follow me and I will make you fish for people."[16] Most likely this means something like, "I will teach you how to enlist people for the kingdom; I will show you how to persuade others to join my cause in the world." There is some question as to whether Jesus is speaking specifically about the ministry of the twelve or more broadly about the task of all disciples. Later, Jesus sends the twelve to do what he was doing—heal the sick, expel the evil spirits, and preach the good news of the kingdom of God (Mark 3:13-19; Matt 9:35-10:16; Luke 9:1-6). In Luke's Gospel, Jesus also sends out "seventy others" (Luke 10:1-12). At the conclusion of Matthew's Gospel, the risen Christ charges the eleven (now without Judas) who have gathered at the mountain to "make disciples of all nations" (Matt 28:18). Does this apply to all disciples or only those with an apostolic call? Either way, it is the mission of the church to make disciples of Christ, perhaps with more specific responsibility resting on those with a special apostolic gift.

So how do we go about this? I suspect Jesus utilized the fishing image in this context because he called fishermen. But we have to be careful how we apply it. I like the story about the preacher who was invited by one of his parishioners to go fishing. When the boat stopped, the preacher started rummaging through his tackle box for a lure. His friend said, "You won't need any of that today." Then he lit a stick of dynamite and threw it over the side. Kaboom! Fish started floating to the surface. The preacher was in shock. "Man, what are you doing? You can't do that! We'll go to jail!" While the preacher was still ranting and raving, his friend lit another stick of dynamite and tossed it to him. "Preacher, are you going to talk all day or are you going to fish?"

The friend's fishing method reminds me of ways I've seen Christians evangelize over the years: "We have the truth, and you'd better accept it or else. Repent or kaboom!" This approach is patterned more after John the Baptist than Jesus. Is it arrogant to assume that we as Christians have a corner on the truth and that our mission is to convert people into our way of believing and practicing the Christian faith?

I believe in Christian particularism, but not exclusion. There is a particularism to Christian faith that confesses Jesus of Nazareth as the incarnation of God's nature and purpose. We believe Jesus embodies God's character and will in a unique way as the Christ. Christians can confess their belief that Jesus is the ultimate revelation of God and still hold to an inclusive position that God is great enough and gracious enough to accommodate God's self to people of other religious faiths and traditions. For Christians, Jesus is the way of redemption; to encounter and experience Christ is to encounter and experience God. But for those outside the witness of Christian revelation, surely God can meet them through their own unique religious experiences and beliefs.

I believe the kingdom of God is much larger and greater than our particular understanding of the gospel. Who am I to say who has or does not have an authentic experience of God? Who am I to say to whom God speaks or doesn't speak? Who am I to claim sole possession of the truth?

The church must not assume a superior position over and against other religious worldviews and perspectives. We must listen and notice how God is working with people who may not share our faith convictions. Gandhi never claimed to be a Christian (he said at least once that he might have become a Christian if it were not for the Christians), but his life certainly embodied and demonstrated the way of Jesus and God's new world.

We should ask, "What does the world need from us to bring genuine hope and help to those on the brink of despair? How can we share with others a vision of a world made whole, redeemed, restored, and put to rights without assuming that we have all the answers? How can we respect other religious perspectives and still share our understanding of Jesus and the new world he announced and embodied?"

There are no easy answers or solutions, but in our age of religious pluralism we must enter into dialogue in ways that are respectful of our differences. By engaging other worldviews in a spirit of friendship and mutuality, we are less likely to assume a position of superiority over others and more likely to meet them as fellow pilgrims and seekers of the truth. We must come together as friends in search of truth together. No matter how firmly we hold to our own beliefs, we must converse in a spirit of humility, willing to concede that we could be wrong. Without such humility, no genuine dialogue can occur.

We must show humility also when we share our faith with those who have no religious background. If we approach nonreligious people with humility, honesty, authenticity, and a willingness to concede that we have more questions than answers, we may find dialogue partners who in time will be open to an invitation to discipleship.

Questions for Reflection and Discussion

1. What aspects of life must we be concerned about if we are to be agents of the kingdom of God proclaimed and embodied by Christ?
2. Jesus' practice of an open table demonstrated God's welcome, acceptance, and inclusion of people who were excluded by a law-dominated religious system. What types of religious systems exclude people today? What kinds of people in our culture would Jesus welcome to his table? What can the church do to break down walls of exclusion and share the hospitality of Christ with the marginalized and disadvantaged?
3. The movie *Antwone Fisher* powerfully portrays the dynamics of exclusion and embrace that permeates our society. Consider watching the movie and reflecting on the ways the film addresses our need for acceptance and belonging.
4. What elements are involved in a relationship of authentic discipleship to Christ? How does discipleship simplify one's life? How does it complicate life?
5. Reflect on the meaning and implications of the following statements: Come as You Are; Discover Whose You Are; and Become What You Were Meant to Be.
6. Do you find the image of "catching people" for God's kingdom positive or negative? Should all Christians engage in this work or only those so gifted

and called? Should disciples of Christ try to convert or win over adherents of other faiths? Do you agree with the approach of mutual dialogue suggested in this chapter?

7. Discuss your agreement or disagreement with my position of "Christian particularism, but not exclusion."

Notes

1. Brian D. McLaren, *The Secret Message of Jesus* (Nashville: W Publishing Group, 2006), 10–11, 23, 33.

2. Unless otherwise indicated, all Scripture quotations are from the NRSV.

3. Jesus most likely imagined the kingdom coming soon, perhaps shortly after his death. If he indeed felt it was being manifested through his own life and works, it is likely that he would have expected its full arrival as imminent. He may have understood his death to be the event that would trigger the crisis signaling the arrival of the kingdom (see Matt 24:34 and Matt 16:27-28). I think it likely that Jesus considered his approaching death to be the sign and seal of God's new covenant with his people (Mark 14:24), a covenant that would result in the fulfillment of the prophetic hope of a world pervaded by peace and justice.

4. Marcus Borg, *Meeting Jesus Again for the First Time: The Historical Jesus and the Heart of Contemporary Faith* (New York: HarperSanFrancisco, 1994), 50–53.

5. Albert Nolan, *Jesus Before Christianity* (Maryknoll NY: Orbis Books, 1976), 27–36.

6. Tony Campolo, *The Kingdom of God Is a Party* (Dallas: Word Publishing Co., 1990), 3–9.

7. *Antwone Fisher*, dir. Denzel Washington, written by Antwone Fisher, 20th Century Fox, 2002.

8. Lamar Williamson, Jr., *Mark*, Interpretation: A Bible Commentary for Teaching and Preaching (Louisville: John Knox Press, 1983), 69.

9. Robert Fulghum, *It Was on Fire When I Lay Down on It* (New York: Ivy Books, 1989), 9.

10. Ibid., 10–11.

11. Ibid., 12.

12. Dallas Willard, *The Divine Conspiracy: Rediscovering Our Hidden Life in God* (New York: HarperSanFrancisco, 1998), 27.

13. Steve Chalke and Alan Mann, *The Lost Message of Jesus* (Grand Rapids MI: Zondervan, 2003), 35–36.

14. Marcus J. Borg, *The Heart of Christianity: Rediscovering a Life of Faith* (New York: HarperSanFrancisco, 2003), 136.

15. Fred Craddock, *Luke*, Interpretation: A Bible Commentary for Teaching and Preaching (Louisville: John Knox Press, 1990), 69.

16. In Luke, "from now on you will be catching people" (5:10).

Chapter 2

Imagining God

A man was traveling to his cabin by the lake, and just as he was crossing the bridge four miles from his destination, his car broke down. He managed to coast off the bridge and pull to the curb. Since his cell phone did not work in this remote area, he decided to walk the remaining distance to his cabin where he could use the local telephone service. Halfway into the walk, a storm blew in. With no available cover, he pressed on, fighting the wind and rain. As he turned down his street toward home, a lightning bolt came firing out of the sky, hit his cabin, and in minutes consumed the building in flames. He leaned against a tree in tears and exclaimed in exasperation, "Why God, why?" At that moment, a voice rang out of the heavens: "Some people just tick me off!"

Some people conceive of God as a cosmic killjoy—whimsical, capricious, ready to pounce upon humans and make us pay for our sins. How we imagine God is critical in determining how we relate to God and to others. Both hard and soft images of God are inadequate. If we conceive of God as an unmoved lawgiver who arbitrarily sets rules, keeps records of offenses, and punishes offenders, or if we conceive of God as a controlling sovereign who predetermines every detail of our world and our lives, then there is a fair chance that our spiritual life will reflect legalistic or fatalistic qualities. On the other hand, if we perceive of God as a cosmic Santa Claus rewarding the obedient with prosperity, success, and health, or as a divine genie who makes no demands and grants our every wish, then there is a good possibility that our spiritual life will reflect the character of our consumerist culture. It will become a way to use God to endorse our plans, to get what we want and make us successful, while isolating and insulating us from our suffering world.

Perhaps the most destructive image of all is that of a vengeful God, full of wrath and needing to be placated. A common human failure in religion is the tendency to project our fears onto God. Week after week, a man kept telling his therapist that God was punishing him for all his sins. He despaired under the weight of guilt and self-condemnation. One day the therapist said, "Doesn't God ever say anything nice to you?" If we are neurotic, there is a strong possibility that we will project our neurosis onto God. What we fear becomes our guiding image of God.

As pointed out in the previous chapter, in Luke 4 we are introduced to the mission of Jesus and the focus of his ministry. Jesus is the hometown boy coming back to Nazareth as a prophet. He is recognized as such by the leaders of the synagogue and given the opportunity to read from the Scripture and speak to the worshipers. He reads from Isaiah 61 and defines his ministry according to the prophet's sense of God's call—proclaiming good news to the poor, liberating the captives, restoring sight to the blind, and setting free the oppressed. The initial reaction to Jesus is mixed. Some are doubtful and incredulous: "Is this not Joseph's son? We know his family; his mother and brothers and sisters are all here. We watched him grow up. Is he anyone special?"

In Mark's and Matthew's account of Jesus' visit to his hometown, the emphasis falls on the people's lack of faith and their inability to see how Jesus could be God's prophet and messenger (Mark 6:1-6a and Matt 13:54-58). Luke's version is more subtle and nuanced. Some initially doubt, but others have high expectations that Jesus will do mighty works in their midst. They have heard reports about his works in Capernaum and expect even greater works among his own people. Perhaps when Jesus says, "Today, this is fulfilled in your hearing," they interpret that to mean he will give them special attention and do many mighty works among them. Luke says the people spoke well of him.

By the time Jesus finishes his teaching, however, there is a mob reaction. Luke says they "were filled with rage" and sought to kill him. What happened to turn the tide against him? What happened to turn Jesus' hometown crowd into a raging mob that attempted to throw him off a cliff? Jesus was one of their own. Why would they want to kill him?

Jesus recalls a couple of Bible stories from the Scriptures, stories I'm sure they wished weren't in their Bible, stories they probably wished they had conveniently forgotten. There was the time when it hadn't rained for three and a half years and a severe famine ravaged the land. Many widows in Israel were in great need, but Elijah wasn't sent to any of them. God sent Elijah to a Gentile woman who lived in the region of Sidon. Also, in the time of Elisha, there were many lepers in Israel, but Elisha was not sent to any of them. Rather, he was sent by God to heal Naaman, the Syrian (Luke 4:25-27).

Obviously, when Jesus talked about his mission as a ministry of bringing good news to the poor and setting free the oppressed, the folks at Nazareth were thinking in terms of their own poor and oppressed—those in Nazareth and in Israel. "God Bless Israel" was their motto. It gave them a sense of privilege and security. But then, from the Hebrew Scriptures, Jesus announced that God is larger and greater and more gracious than the tribal God they claimed for themselves. God wants to bless all people; God is no respecter of persons. God's forgiveness, mercy, grace, and blessing know no boundaries— God is not limited by nationality, ethnic identity, social class, gender, or any other humanly imposed barrier that separates, divides, and excludes.

Their attempt to murder Jesus was an out-of-control reaction to Jesus' assault on their theology of God. If they had been more clear-headed, they could have responded by challenging Jesus' reading and interpretation of Scripture. They could have found many Bible verses to support their position. They could have turned to the passage where God chose Isaac and rejected Ishmael. They could have appealed to those passages where Israel is praised as the apple of God's eye. They could have quoted the psalms that call down curses upon God's enemies. They could have drawn from the stories where God drove out the inhabitants of the land and gave them military victory after victory, even commanding the complete annihilation of whole cities and tribes. They could have quoted the Scripture that says to Israel, "Come out from among them and be separate, says the Lord." They had access to sufficient biblical material to counter Jesus' reading.

Some years ago, I, along with three other pastors, tried to change the policy in our local Baptist association. As the policy stood, women could not speak publicly to any issue up for vote at the semi-annual meetings. In pressing for the change, I talked about how Jesus broke tradition and developed an egalitarian approach to ministry by calling women disciples. I talked about the great vision of Paul in Galatians 3:28 where "there is neither Jew or

Gentile, neither slave or free, neither male or female, for all are one in Christ"—Paul at his best. I pointed out how Paul had women coworkers and partners in the gospel who served as ministers, teachers, and prophets in the early churches.

Do you know what happened? Those opposed to the change quoted Scripture too. They quoted 1 Corinthians 14:34, which says, "Women should be silent in the churches. For they are not permitted to speak, but should be subordinate, as the law also says. If there is anything they desire to know, let them ask their husbands at home. For it is shameful for a woman to speak in church." Someone asked, "What if they don't have husbands at home?" The response was, "They need to get husbands!" Then those opposed quoted the equally oppressive text in 1 Timothy 2 that says a woman should learn in submission and be quiet because Adam was created first, and the woman was deceived. "It's in the Bible," they said. "God said it, we believe it, and that settles it."

So our proposed change was voted down, 3 to 1. I wasn't ready to kill anyone, but I was upset. They say the pen is mightier than the sword, and so I wrote a letter to the editor and it was published in the *Ashland Daily*. I wanted everyone to know about the backward ideas of our particular Baptist association.

You can imagine what happened after that. For two months there were letters to the editor—pro and con, arguing the points, back and forth. There was more excitement in the churches than we had experienced in a long time.

The people in the synagogue at Nazareth could have done that; they could have quoted Scriptures to support their prejudice against the Gentiles. But they were so incensed that they rushed to kill Jesus, and Luke gives the impression that they would have succeeded, except it was not Jesus' time in the outworking of God's redemptive purpose.

This is certainly not an isolated incident. The history of religion and the history of the church in America are littered with this sort of thinking. Fred Craddock, former professor of New Testament and Preaching at Candler School of Theology in Atlanta, tells an applicable story. When he was getting started in ministry, he lived in Tennessee in a remote community with few houses. Violence erupted nearby. He was asked to try to intercede; he was told that if he didn't stop it, someone would get killed. So he went. Men stood behind trees aiming rifles and shotguns into a one-room mountain cabin. Fred didn't know who was in the cabin. He raised his hand toward the gunmen and walked toward the cabin. Looking back, he says he wasn't brave, just stupid.

He went to the door, and when it cracked a little he found himself starring into the barrel of a gun. The voice of a woman said, "Who are you and what do you want?" He looked at the gun and had trouble remembering his name. He told her who he was and why he had come. Finally she said, "Come in."

The inside of the house was peppered with gunfire. A calendar hanging on the wall had bullet holes instead of numbers. The shooting had been going on all night.

Fred asked, "What's the quarrel?

She said, "I have no quarrel."

"How long have you lived here?"

"A week."

"Where are you from?" Fred wondered.

"Western New York," the woman replied.

"Do you know any of these people shooting?"

"No."

"I'm a minister of a church in town. Are you in church?"

"Yes, we're Roman Catholic." From behind the chairs and the couch emerged six beautiful, frightened children. She and six children were being pelted with gunfire.

Two of the shooters were members of the little church where Fred was preaching. Fred asked them to meet with him, and they got the others together. Fred asked, "Do you know who she is?"

"No, but they say she is from up north."

"Do you know what church she belongs to?"

"We don't know, but they say she's Roman Catholic."

"Is that it? What has she done?"

"We don't want that kind in this community."

"What kind?"

"Her kind!"

It went on and on. "Finally," said Fred later, "I realized I was on the wrong track. I stopped talking about North and South, protestant and catholic, foreigners and locals, insiders and outsiders. No more of that. I started talking about God."

Fred went directly to the leader of the shooters. "Red, tell me about your God."

"It was pitiful," Fred later said. "The God they worshiped was so mean." Then Fred told them about the God he worshiped: "Fellows, we have a problem about God. Not about the woman, not about me, not about you, but about God." And for the rest of the time that Fred preached there, he talked about one thing—God. Fred explained afterward, "They believed in a God deeply for whom they would kill. And the woman believed in a God for whom she would be killed. What kind of God do you believe in?"[1]

In Luke 4 Jesus calls into question a deeply ingrained religious belief used by his contemporaries to justify their exclusion of certain people. Their God played favorites, and their God was a vengeful God.

A person may not consciously make this connection between belief and practice, but the kind of God one believes in is reflected in the way that person lives. Anyone who says theology isn't important doesn't understand what motivates people at a spiritual, even unconscious level. The religious people who wanted to kill Jesus had a different kind of God than the God of Jesus.

Jesus didn't begin with Scripture and from Scripture derive his understanding of God. Israel's sacred Scripture offered rather diverse perspectives on the nature of God, a tension of paradox and contradiction. Israel's God ordered the complete destruction of tribes and peoples—men, women, children, and all living things—and yet people worshiped this God and proclaimed him "merciful and gracious, slow to anger and abounding in steadfast love" (compare Josh 6:17-21 with Ps 103:8). In the book of Jonah, God is pictured as having great compassion and concern for a pagan, godless people that oppressed Israel. Scripture can support both images of God—a tribal God who loves Israel more than others, or a universal God who enters into covenant relationship with Israel in order to bless all the people of the earth. Philosopher and theologian Peter Rollins describes it this way:

> In the Bible we find a vast array of competing stories concerning the character of God that are closely connected to the concrete circumstances of those who inhabit the narrative. . . . The Bible itself is a dynamic text full of poetry, prose, history, law, and myth all clashing together in a cacophony of voices. We are presented with a warrior God and a peacemaker, a God of territorial allegiance and a God who transcends all territorial divides, an unchanging God and a God who can be redirected, a God of peace and a God of war, a God who is always watching the world and a God who fails to notice the oppression against Israel in Egypt.[2]

Jesus didn't start with Scripture. Jesus began with his personal experience of God's character and then filtered his reading and interpretation of Scripture through the funnel of his experience. Jesus' grasp of the nature and character of God became the lens through which he read Scripture. In the rest of this chapter, we will try to probe the heart of Jesus' perception and understanding of God. I believe the most important question in religion, and indeed in life, is this: What kind of God is your God?

The God of Compassion

Compassion is both a feeling and a way of being that flows out of that feeling. In the English etymology, *passion* comes from the Latin word that means "to feel," and the prefix *com-* means "with." Compassion means, "to feel with." To show compassion is to feel the hurt or pain of someone else and then, on the basis of that feeling, to do something, to act on the person's behalf.[3] Religious scholar Bryan Stone argues that compassion includes "this twin ability, both to receive and to give, both to suffer with and to heal, both to hear the cry of the oppressed and to offer liberation, that characterizes the God of compassion and defines the compassion of God."[4]

The event that most clearly defined Israel as the people of God was the exodus, God's liberation of Israel from Egyptian slavery and oppression. As a prelude to the liberation event, the biblical writer describes the situation: "The Israelites groaned under their slavery, and cried out. . . . God heard their groaning, and God remembered his covenant with Abraham, Isaac, and Jacob. God looked upon the Israelites, and God took notice of them" (Exod 2:23-24). God is portrayed as identifying with Israel's suffering and then acting on their behalf to bring deliverance and hope, thus demonstrating the two critical components of compassion.

The Hebrew word for compassion in its singular form means "womb." When the Hebrew Bible speaks of God as compassionate, it does so with reference to the "womb." Jesus scholar Marcus Borg wrote,

> As an image for the central quality of God, it is striking. To say that God is compassionate is to say that God is "like a womb," is "womblike," or, to coin a word that captures the flavor of the original Hebrew, "wombish." What does it suggest to say that God is like a womb? Metaphoric and evocative, the phrase and its associated image provocatively suggest a number of connotations. Like a womb, God is the one who gives birth to us—the mother who gives birth to us. As a mother loves the children of her womb and feels for the children of her womb, so God loves us and feels

for us, for all of her children. In its sense of "like a womb," *compassionate* has nuances of giving life, nourishing, caring, perhaps embracing and encompassing. For Jesus, this is what God is like.[5]

This dual capacity to identify with those suffering and then engage the suffering in order to bring relief and hope is fully expressed in the life and ministry of Jesus.

In Mark 6 the twelve gather around Jesus, having returned from their mission of healing and announcing the good news of the kingdom of God. Jesus says to them, "Come away to a deserted place all by yourselves and rest for a while." Mark notes that "many were coming and going, and they had no leisure even to eat." They needed solitude and silence in order to recharge emotionally, physically, and spiritually. They departed by boat, but somehow the crowd arrived there ahead of them, along with many others from nearby towns. Jesus had every right to be upset with them; surely they knew his intentions. But Mark says, "As he went ashore, he saw a great crowd; and he had compassion for them, because they were like sheep without a shepherd; and he began to teach them many things." Facing clinging throngs of people when we desperately need rest would cause most of us to throw our hands up in frustration, but Jesus stretches out his hands in compassion. He sees them not through the weariness of his body and spirit, but through the compassion of his heart; he sees them as sheep without a shepherd—aimless, confused, and lost.

All the ways Jesus ministered to people (his proclamation of God's kingdom, his practice of an open and inclusive table, his eating with "sinners," his reaching out to the poor and marginalized, his works of healing, his teaching the people), were concrete demonstrations of God's compassion. In fact, these actions of compassion were more than spontaneous expressions; they constituted an intentional effort. Marcus Borg describes it this way,

> For Jesus, compassion was more than a quality of God and an individual virtue [though it was indeed that]: it was a social paradigm, the core value for life in the community. To put it boldly: compassion for Jesus was political. He directly and repeatedly challenged the dominant sociopolitical paradigm of his social world and advocated instead what might be called a *politics of compassion.*[6]

Jesus understood his mission as one of bringing good news to the poor. Jesus believed that championing God's cause meant caring for and standing up for the poor and downtrodden. Here Jesus stands squarely in the best of Israel's prophetic tradition. New Testament scholar James D. G. Dunn describes the poor in Israel:

> In the Old Testament "the poor" are of course the *materially impoverished.* In the agricultural economies of the ancient Near East, ownership of the land was the basis of economic security. Poverty might be the result of any one or more of a number of factors: bad harvests caused by natural disaster, enemy invasion and appropriation, indolence and bad management, malpractice by powerful neighbors, or entrapment in a cycle of debt at extortionate interest. The poor, then, were those who lacked a secure economic base. Like widows, or orphans, and aliens, they were in an especially vulnerable position, without any means of self-protection.[7]

Poverty then, as today, was not simply the result of personal laziness and mismanagement; it was and is a social condition with social causes. Often it is the result of greed and manipulation on the part of those who wield power. The poor are vulnerable, powerless, easily victimized, and pushed to the margins of society, thus making it difficult for them to break free from a culture of poverty.

The prophets railed against the oppression of the poor by the wealthy and powerful. Read Isaiah's denunciation of the rulers in Israel who were taking advantage of the poor:

> The LORD enters into judgment
> with the elders and princes of his people:
> It is you who have devoured the vineyard;
> the spoil of the poor is in your houses.
> What do you mean by crushing my people,
> by grinding the face of the poor? Says the Lord God of hosts. (Isa 3:14-15)

A common theme in the prophets is a call to active concern and care for one's neighbor. Faithful obedience to ritual and religious practice is worthless if it is not accompanied by compassionate care for the poor.

In Isaiah 1, the prophet rails against Israel for meticulously keeping the rituals, feasts, and ceremonies of the law while neglecting justice and mercy. They have "forsaken the Lord" and "despised the Holy One of Israel." God cries out against them, "I have had enough of burnt offerings of rams and the fat of fed beasts. . . . I cannot endure solemn assemblies with iniquity. Your new moons and your appointed feasts my soul hates." Though they say many prayers, God will not listen. God calls for repentance: "wash your-selves; make yourselves clean . . . cease to do evil, learn to do good." And what is the good they are to do? The prophet is clear: "seek justice, rescue the oppressed, defend the orphan, plead for the widow."

Jesus is firmly planted in this tradition. It fell to the non-poor to make provision for the poor; Israel's Law required it (Deut 15:7-11; 24:10-15; 24:19-22). One could not be faithful to the covenant and in a right relation-ship with God without expressing and demonstrating compassionate, active helpfulness and care on behalf of the poor and marginalized of society.

Jesus' concern for the poor and his compassion for all people were derived not simply from his understanding of the Old Testament but from his experience of God. As stated earlier, Jesus' experience of the nature of God provided the lens through which he read Scripture. Marcus Borg offers this explanation:

> It is implausible to see his perception of God as compassionate and the pas-sionate courage with which he held to it as simply a result of the intellectual activity of studying the tradition, or to assume that based on some other grounds he decided it was a good idea. Rather, it is reasonable to surmise that he spoke of God as compassionate—as "like a womb"— because of his own experience of the Spirit.[8]

This is confirmed too by the way in which Jesus related to God as a loving Parent.

Jesus spoke of God in the most intimate way as a compassionate Father. Jesus was not alone in Israel in his intimate experience of God, and certainly the concept of God as a "compassionate Father" was not unique to Jesus or the Judaism of Jesus' world. For example, a Jewish prayer from this general time period reads, "Our Father, merciful Father, thou who are ever compas-sionate, have pity on us and inspire us to understand and discern, to perceive, learn and teach, to observe, do, and fulfill gladly all the teachings of thy Torah."[9] Obviously, others experienced God as a merciful Father. However, the unique form of the Aramaic word Jesus chooses when referring to God (the colloquial *Abba* that in some contexts can mean something like "Daddy") and the consistency with which he speaks of God as a compassion-ate Parent suggests that Jesus related to God in a different way than most of his contemporaries did.

We know this from the way the word comes to us in the Greek New Testament. In several places, the Aramaic form used by Jesus is first transliterated (written the way it sounds) and then translated. For example, in Mark 14:36 Jesus is in prayer in Gethsemane. The text reads, "He said, Abba, Father, for you all things are possible; remove this cup from me; yet not what I want, but what you want." Before the word is translated, it is transliterated. Paul does this twice in his letters. One passage reads, "For you did not receive the spirit of slavery to fall back into fear, but you have received a spirit of adoption. When we cry, 'Abba! Father!' it is that very Spirit bearing witness with our spirit that we are children of God" (Rom 8:15; see also Gal 4:6). This way of addressing God goes back to Jesus, and it came to have such a special place in the Greek-speaking churches that the Aramaic form was preserved. It was an expression of tenderness, warmth, intimacy, and endearment that meant something special to the early Christian communities.

The image of God as "Father" should not, however, be understood in a gender-specific way. The image is not about the maleness of God, for God is neither male nor female. Rather, it speaks to the personhood and parenthood of God; God is like the most loving parent that can be imagined, a parent intimately engaged with his or her children.

The earlier quotation from Marcus Borg points out that the Hebrew word for compassion in its singular form means "womb." It is a word that conveys the feminine side of God. God is the life-giver—the source and sustainer of life. This picture of motherly nurturance and care of an infant is a poignant image of the compassion of God. It is somewhat surprising that such images of God are found in Scripture, given the pervasive patriarchal culture out of which Scripture arose. Isaiah uses this image to assure God's people that they have not been forgotten: "Can a woman forget her nursing child, or show no compassion for the child of her womb? Even these may forget, yet I will not forget you" (Isa 49:15). All God language is metaphorical, non-literal language. The language we use to talk about God is simply a way of trying to imagine and relate to God; it is personal, interactive language. We need the feminine language and imagery to talk about God as much as we need the masculine language and imagery.

I suspect that some readers, like myself, come from an evangelical tradition and have not been taught, encouraged, or conditioned to speak of God as mother. When we first start to use this language, we may feel uneasy. Jesus would have been conditioned in the male-dominant culture of his society to think of God in male terms, and yet he uses a word that refers to God in a way that transcends masculine and feminine categories. The image conveyed by the word *Abba* is not about gender, but about compassion. God is not male or female, masculine or feminine, man or woman, but we can only think about and imagine God in personal terms. The point is that God is like a compassionate parent. Two stories illustrate this.

A Raisin in the Sun is a play, as well as a movie, by Lorraine Hansberry. It is about the dreams and struggles of an African-American family in 1950s Chicago. The son, Walter, gets cheated out of a large sum of money. He accepts a buyout of their new home by a white community association that didn't want the African Americans moving into their neighborhood.

The sister, Beneatha, is beside herself. In the movie version, she tells her mother, "He's no brother of mine. That individual in that room from this day on is no brother of mine."

The mother rebukes her daughter. "I thought I taught you to love him." Beneatha retorts, "Love him? There's nothing left to love."

The mother responds,

> There's always something left to love. Have you cried for that boy today? Now, I don't mean for yourself and for the family because we lost the money. I mean for him, and what he's gone through! God help him, what it's done to him. Child, when do you think is the time to love somebody the most? When he's done good and made things easy for everybody? Oh no. It's when he's at his lowest and he can't believe in himself because the world done whipped him so. When you start measuring somebody, measure them right, child. You make sure you take into account the hills and valleys he's come to, to get to wherever he is.[10]

Richard Foster tells about a friend who was in a shopping mall with his two-year-old son. His son lost control and began shrieking. This father, instead of shaking or scolding his son, picked him up and began singing an impromptu love song as he made his way to the car. He told the child over and over how much he loved him and how special he was. By the time they reached the car, his son was completely calm. When the dad placed him in the car seat, his son reached out his arms to his father and said, "Sing it to me again, Daddy."

God is like this mother and father. God is not literally a mother or father, but God relates to us the way a compassionate mother or father would relate to her or his child. These stories or images of compassionate parents serve as windows through which we look to grasp something of the nature and character of God. God is like this mother who feels deep hurt and love for her son; God is like this father who responds to his screaming child with a love song.

Jesus likens the care of the Divine Parent to the providential care provided for the birds of the air and the lilies of the field. God feeds the birds and clothes the flowers. Do we not mean more to God than the birds and the lilies? Will God abandon God's children? Certainly not! We are free to focus on first things; we are free to seek the kingdom of God and God's kind of justice and goodness (Matt 6:25-33; also Luke 12:22-34). God is trustworthy, generous, and gracious. No crisis can overwhelm us, for God is with us and for us and will never abandon us. The God of Jesus, the God who is a Compassionate Parent, commends trust that can instill a peace deeper than the confusion and chaos created by the storms of life.

Unhealthy religion tends to play on our fears, which we then project onto God, but with *Abba* there is no need to be afraid. An ancient Jewish tradition taught that no one could see God and live. Originally, it may have been used to evoke a sense of respect and awe for God, but in the tradition it is more often interpreted in a negative way. God's presence is something to be feared. This is evident in many biblical stories where either God or one of God's angelic messengers appears to human beings. In almost every incident, the recipient of the revelation is terrified. Trust in the Compassionate Parent drives out fear, because there is no fear in love (1 John 4:16-18).

Cal Ripkin, Jr., known as the "Iron Man," gives credit for his success in baseball and in life to the example and teaching of his father, Cal Ripkin, Sr., who coached with the Baltimore Orioles organization for many years in the minor league. During the 1996 season, Ripkin, Sr., was inducted into the Orioles hall of fame. After he delivered his acceptance speech, his son came to the microphone. In his book, *The Only Way I Know,* Cal Ripkin, Jr., writes about that experience:

> I hadn't prepared anything beyond a couple of notes scribbled on a paper napkin. I wasn't even certain I wanted to speak—or put it this way: I knew I wanted to speak, but I didn't know if I could say what I wanted to say. It's difficult for me to talk about my father and what he means to me. So I started with a few stories and jokes, took advantage of the opportunity to needle my brother Billy, who was in the audience, and then referred to my own children, Rachel, six years old at the time, and Ryan, three. They'd been in a bickering mode for weeks, and I explained how one day I heard Rachel taunt Ryan, "You're just trying to be like Daddy." I wanted to break things up but also put some kind of positive spin on the situation. That's

the parent's job, right? After a few moments of indecision I turned to Rachel and asked, "What's wrong with trying to be like Dad?" When I finished telling this story at the banquet, I added, "That's what I've always tried to do."[11]

Jesus' experience of the love and compassion of God compelled him to be just like his merciful Father/Mother. Jesus sets before his followers the same expectation. Jesus instructs his disciples to love their enemies, to do good to those who hate them, and to pray for those who would harm them. By actively loving those who seek our harm, we will live as "children of the Most High; for he is kind to the ungrateful and the wicked." Jesus says, "Be merciful [or compassionate], just as your Father is merciful [compassionate]" (Luke 6:35b-36). Disciples of Jesus learn from him how to live as God's "beloved" children in a relationship of intimacy and trust, in which they depend on God, their compassionate Father and Mother, to sustain, nurture, and equip them for life in the kingdom of God.

Compassion is often trivialized in our culture. Suffering with others is deemed a waste of time and dismissed as unprofitable. In our competitive culture, compassion is often regarded as a sign of weakness or ineptness instead of being considered a mark of human dignity and strength. In God's kingdom, it is redemptive; it is what matters.

In the movie *Life as a House,* George, a forty-something employee at an architectural firm, loses his job and discovers that he has cancer and only a few months to live. He spends the remaining weeks of his life building the house of his dreams. With the help of his estranged son and his ex-wife, he tears down his shack and builds a beautiful home on the California coast. The restoration of the house is a metaphor for the restoration of George's life. He learns compassion and yearns to make restitution to those he has hurt.

During this process, George tells his son, Sam, about how his alcoholic father (Sam's grandfather) caused an accident in which a woman was killed and her small child paralyzed. George aches over the injustice his father caused. He tells Sam, "Twenty-nine years ago my father crossed a double line and changed my life and that of a little girl forever. I just can't stop thinking about it."

George's final days are lived compassionately and have a redemptive influence on the family. He bequeaths his newly built home to Sam, who knows in his heart what he needs to do. He tracks down the paralyzed girl in a trailer park. He and his mother encounter the woman in a wheelchair, hanging laundry on a clothesline. Sam says to the woman, "Excuse me. Would you mind if we sit a moment and talk? My father built you a house."[12] Anyone open to the experience of compassion discovers that it has redemptive power—in one's own life as well as in the lives of others.

True compassion is as unbiased as Jesus in his love for the poor, the oppressed, and the despised. It is unconditional. It does not divide people into those who deserve it and those who do not. It is creative and cannot be regulated by rules or laws or contained within strict boundaries. I heard about two teenagers of a small town who were killed in a car accident. Since they were best friends, the parents held a joint wake and funeral service. Many people attended, some waiting hours to greet the family. One man stood by himself in line for more than three hours. When he finally greeted the families, he said, "I didn't know your children and I have never met you. But I had a son who died two years ago. I know how this feels. In the days ahead, you will go through every emotion you can imagine. I just want you to know I'm here for you, if you ever need to talk." Then he pressed his card into their hands and walked away. I'm sure it was painful for him to relive his own son's death and reenter the world of grief and suffering. He didn't know these people, but he was moved by compassion.

We often fail at expressing compassion because we are too quick to try to "fix" things. We want to stop a person's suffering, so we try to offer comfort, when they actually need us to acknowledge their pain. The great spiritual teacher and writer Henry Nouwen recalls a time when he visited a woman who suffered a devastating loss after a hurricane and flood swept through her neighborhood. Nouwen found her alone, staring desperately at the damage done to her house. She felt meaningless and unneeded, a burden to herself and her family. She said to herself, "There is only one thing left for me to do: to die." Though Nouwen knew her as a talkative and outgoing woman, she hardly recognized him. Nouwen said to her, "You have no reason to be depressed. You have children who love you and like to visit you. You have charming grandchildren who are happy to have a grandmother to spend time with them. Your son already plans to fix your house. Besides, few people in this neighborhood fared as well as you in the storm." He did not help her with these words. In fact, it made her more depressed, for now she was haunted by guilt for not facing her world with a smiling face. His words came more as accusation than consolation. Nouwen says, "When I left, I went from a woman feeling more sad than before, more burdened because I had not even acknowledged I had heard her. I did not give her permission to feel sad in a sad moment."[13]

When we try to fix or rescue people without giving them time to process their grief or without entering into their painful experience, we show a lack of compassion. Instead of helping, we can actually be the cause of feelings of guilt and defensiveness. Why do we do this? It could be that we do not want others to hurt because *we* do not want to hurt. When we act in compassion, we join those who are suffering and share their pain; we form a bond of solidarity with the hurting and grieving. We hurt along with them.

In order to experience and express compassion, we must die to our egocentric tendencies. If I crave acceptance, then I am likely to be motivated to help, not out of compassion, but out of the need to find my identity and sense of self in the praise and approbation of those I serve. If I am driven by a spirit of competitiveness, the need to be first, to be the best, to achieve honor and recognition for my service, I am not free to be compassionate. If I engage in works of service thinking that if I do enough good things for others I can earn God's acceptance and favor, then once again I will not be free to express authentic compassion. When my own unmet needs are at the center of my works of mercy, then compassion is not possible, for while I am doing for others, I am really doing for the sake of myself.

As long as we feel that we have to prove ourselves, compete with others, or do something relevant in order to be accepted and loved, we are incapable of compassion. We reduce Christianity to our particular brand of worship, our set of beliefs, our way of interpreting Scripture, or our kind of righteousness. Unable to show real compassion, we turn lesser things into idols and make them priorities so that we will not have to admit to failing in the one thing that really matters.

Egocentricity can also take the form of self-rejection. It may be a deflated ego, rather than an inflated one, that hinders our experience of compassion. Brennan Manning, a popular Christian writer, says, "the evangelical [read as "missional"] enterprise is the awareness that we ourselves are the primary target. It is not 'they' who are poor, sinful, and lost. It is ourselves."[14] Even so, compassionate people do not wallow in their sinfulness. They are more aware than most of the dark side of their humanity, but it does not debilitate or demoralize them. Manning expresses it this way:

> In returning to ourselves, in contemplating the compassion of Jesus and realizing that "This means me," we come under the Mercy and qualify for the nametag "blessed." In urging us to compassionate caring for others,

Jesus invites us to have compassion for ourselves. The measure of our compassion for others lies in proportion to our capacity for self-acceptance and self-affirmation. When the compassion of Christ is interiorized and appropriated to self, the breakthrough into being for others occurs. In a win-win situation, the way of compassionate caring for others brings healing to ourselves, and compassionate caring for ourselves brings healing to others. Solidarity with human suffering frees the one who receives and liberates the one who gives through the conscious awareness "I am the other."[15]

Compassionate people are secure in God's acceptance and love. This revelation of God's love generates an overflowing source of gratitude for life. Grateful for our inclusion in God's family and sure of our identity as God's "beloved," we are free to enter more readily into the suffering of others. This is why our perception and understanding of God and our relationship to God are so important. If we are secure in ourselves as God's "beloved," then we are free to be vulnerable. Authentic compassion requires a kind of vulnerability that leaves us unguarded and open to suffering. When we share in the hurts of others, we also share our own hurts that may have been buried for some time. We can only bear such exposure by being absolutely convinced of and grateful for God's unconditional love that embraces us and provides for us, in our darkness, an ever-present source of light. We are held up by Love, and Love will never let us go.

A little girl approaches her father, who is typing a report on his computer. At first he doesn't notice her, but when she clears her throat, he looks over and says, "Honey, what do you want?" She says, "Daddy, it's my bedtime. Mommy said that if I come and stand beside you, you'd give me a hug and a kiss." "All right." The father reaches down and gives her a hug and kiss. "Now, off to bed." He goes back to his computer. A minute later he looks away from his computer and his daughter is still there. He says, "Honey, I gave you a hug and kiss. What more do you want?" She says, "Daddy, you gave me a hug and kiss, but you weren't in it." You can give a hug and kiss and not be in it. I can preach a sermon or do a good deed for someone and not be in it. The compassion of God evokes a nearness and closeness that enables us to be "in" the words we speak and the service we render to others.

Lost and Found

Luke 15 has been called "the gospel within the gospel." That which is lost is found. The lost sheep is returned to the flock, the lost coin is recovered by its owner, and the lost son is restored to his father. You could say that God is better at finding than we are at getting lost, and that is good news. One of the central themes in the biblical story that describes God's relationship with God's people is that of exile and homecoming—a pattern of going away and coming home again.

When we read these stories, most of us imagine ourselves at the receiving end. Fred Craddock reminisces about playing hide-and-seek as a child on the farm:

> My sister was "It." When my sister was "It," she cheated. Well, she started off honestly enough; she would say, "One, two, three, four, five, six, seven, ninety-three, ninety-four." But I had a place under the porch and under the steps of the porch. Because of my size I could get under there, and I knew she'd never find me. "Ninety-nine, one hundred. Here I come, ready or not." Here she came, in the house, out of the house, in the weeds, in the trees, down to the corncrib, in the barn. She couldn't find me. I almost gave myself away, down under there just snickering to myself, *She'll never find me here, she'll never find me here.* Then it occurred to me . . . she'll never find me here. So after awhile I would stick out a toe. When she came by and saw my toe, she said, "Uh oh, I see you," and she'd run back and touch the base three times and say, "Ha ha, you're it, you're it." I would come out brushing myself off and saying, "Oh shoot, you found me." What did I want? What did I really want? The very same thing as you.[16]

This is a poignant image of the spiritual longing in each of us. It is a feeling that runs deep into the human spirit. We experience it as alienation, loneliness, disconnection, fragmentation, emptiness, sadness, and homesickness. Who can forget the scene in *E. T.* when the little extraterrestrial, left all alone on this strange planet, separated from his family, feeling lost and lonely, extends his long, pointed finger into the sky, and with a sigh of homesickness says, "E.T. phone home."

We all feel it. On a spiritual level, all our longings for home and place and belonging reflect a deeper longing for God, even though we may not consciously be aware of our need. These feelings are meant, I think, to drive us to God, to find belonging, family, and community in a relationship with God that automatically gives us many sisters and brothers in a family of faith. Of course, living together as family is always challenging. So the pattern repeats itself many times, in our relationship with God, and with our brothers and sisters in the faith community.

There is another way, however, to read these stories of being lost and found. In Luke's narrative introduction to these parables, the Pharisees and scribes were grumbling, "This fellow welcomes sinners and eats with them." In response to their complaints, Jesus invites the religious leaders, not merely to imagine themselves as a lost sheep or lost coin or lost son, but to imagine themselves as the shepherd who diligently seeks the lost sheep, the woman who tirelessly searches for the lost coin, and the father who patiently waits for the son's return. Jesus asks them to change their feelings about the people they have come to despise and disdain, the ones they have excluded and rejected. Jesus asks them to love those people so much that they would leave the safety and security of their sacred traditions and laws in order to mingle and mix with "sinners," accepting them as brothers and sisters.

The story about the shepherd is particularly relevant.

> So he told them this parable: "Which one of you, having a hundred sheep and losing one of them, does not leave the ninety-nine in the wilderness and go after the one that is lost until he finds it? When he has found it, he lays it on his shoulders and rejoices. And when he comes home, he calls together his friends and neighbors, saying to them, 'Rejoice with me, for I have found my sheep that was lost.' Just so, I tell you, there will be more joy in heaven over one sinner who repents than over ninety-nine righteous persons who need no repentance." (Luke 15:3-7)

It's much easier to focus on the good sheep that don't wander off; there's no risk in the safety of the fold. But the shepherd takes the risk, leaving the sheep in the open country, defenseless, in order to find the lost one. It's not logical. It's not good shepherding. But he loves the lost one so much that he is willing to take the risk in order to find it. Barbara Brown Taylor may speak for all of us when she says honestly, "I want to concentrate on the good people, the one who wants to be found, or who are busy finding others. I think about heaven ignoring those good folks in favor of one sinner who finally says, 'I'm sorry,' and I want to sue God for mercy."[17]

Fred Craddock tells about being in Oklahoma when an approaching tornado was announced. Fred and his family stood in the front yard and watched; the weatherman was right—it was coming. They thought it was going to change direction, then realized almost too late that it was headed straight for them. They needed to move quickly. They started the car to go west of town, but then someone screamed, "Oh, no! Where's Gretchen?"

Gretchen was an aged dachshund—nearly at the end of her life. Yet here comes a tornado, and the family takes time to go back in and get Gretchen.[18]

The shepherd leaves the others and wanders off looking for the lost one. It doesn't make sense. It's just one sheep. Some people would call the shepherd's action stupidity. Some would call it foolishness. I like to call it God.

Unconditional Forgiveness

The parable in Luke 15 that is often called the "Parable of the Prodigal Son" is possibly the most widely known and best loved of all Jesus' parables.

> Then Jesus said, "There was a man who had two sons. The younger of them said to his father, 'Father, give me the share of the property that will belong to me.' So he divided his property between them. A few days later the younger son gathered all he had and traveled to a distant country, and there he squandered his property in dissolute living. When he had spent everything, a severe famine took place throughout that country, and he began to be in need. So he went and hired himself out to one of the citizens of that country, who sent him to his fields to feed the pigs. He would gladly have filled himself with the pods that the pigs were eating; and no one gave him anything. But when he came to himself he said, 'How many of my father's hired hands have bread enough and to spare, but here I am dying of hunger! I will get up and go to my father, and I will say to him, "Father, I have sinned against heaven and before you; I am no longer worthy to be called your son; treat me like one of your hired hands."' So he set off and went to his father. But while he was still far off, his father saw him and was filled with compassion; he ran and put his arms around him and kissed him. Then the son said to him, 'Father, I have sinned against heaven and before you; I am no longer worthy to be called your son.' But the father said to his slaves, 'Quickly, bring out a robe—the best one—and put it on him; put a ring on his finger and sandals on his feet. And get the fatted calf and kill it, and let us eat and celebrate; for this son of mine was dead and is alive again; he was lost and is found!' And they began to celebrate." (Luke 15:11-24)

Perhaps it would be better to call this story the "Parable of the Waiting Father." The son is drawn away by the lure of "a distant country." He thinks it offers freedom, but it results in bondage. The father knows this, but lets him go. The son expresses great contempt for the father in requesting his inheritance early—a complete disregard for common tradition and practice.

The father knows his son is making a huge mistake, but he also knows that he cannot make his son love or respect him. Power may compel conformity, but it cannot create love. Because the father loves his son, he turns him loose. Many parents struggle with this.

Joe Garagiola, former major league baseball star and TV personality, tells about the time when Stan Musial came up to the plate in a critical game. Musial, a super hitter, was at the peak of his career. The opposing pitcher was a rookie, young and nervous. Garagiola, the catcher, called for a fastball. The young pitcher waved it off. Next, he signaled for a curve. Again, the pitcher shook his head. Garagiola then asked for one of his specialty pitches. Once more, the pitcher hesitated. So Garagiola called "Time" and walked out to the pitcher's mound. "I've called every pitch in the book; what do you want to throw?" "Nothing," said the pitcher, "I want to hold on to it as long as I can." Parents are sometimes like that, but there comes a time when we have to say to our children who become young adults, "You are free."

Our children were never intended to be an extension of ourselves. They are not ways for us to achieve immortality, nor are we to live vicariously through them. They are their own persons, and there comes a time when as parents we must say "you are free," even if we do so with uncertainty and reluctance.

God took a great risk in giving us freedom; God made God's self vulnerable. The process of human redemption has brought and continues to bring God immense pain and suffering. We were created to have a glorious destiny—to be God's friends and partners, to have a share in God's creative work, to know God's love and radiate God's love throughout the earth. But love cannot be forced or coerced, demanded or manipulated; it must be received and personally experienced. We live in an open universe, and we are free to receive or reject God's love. If condemnation rests upon any one of us, it is self-inflicted, because God sent Jesus into the world not to condemn the world, but to save it. Our destiny is ours to choose.

Perhaps in time all people will see the beauty and glory of God's love, freely embracing God's forgiveness and sincerely obeying God's benevolent will. Richard Rohr suggests that in order for God's love to be truly victorious, it must eventually win out in every person's life. Rohr views life as a great school of love, asserting that "God's love is so great that God will finally teach it to all of us. We'll finally surrender and God will finally win. That will be God's 'justice,' which will swallow up our lesser versions."[19]

Philip Gulley and James Mulholland's passionate book, *If Grace Is True: Why God Will Save Every Person*, states their belief in universal salvation. They tell about a man named Tony "who personified evil . . . was self-centered, verbally and physically abusive to his family, lazy, and alcoholic."

> I once thought Tony and I had been presented with the same gift—one I accepted and he rejected. Now I know none of us are as free as we believe and that some are more bound than others. God's grace came to me wrapped in shiny paper, tied in a bow, with a tag bearing my name. My decision to unwrap God's gift came easily. When grace was offered to Tony, his life experiences led him to fear even touching the box. His fears were legitimate. As a young child, he'd watched his father pour hot grease on his mother's arm when breakfast wasn't ready. After all the times Tony had yearned for love, only to be disappointed when it exploded in his face, how could he easily embrace it?
>
> The day will come when Tony will unwrap the gift and know what it means to love and be loved. His fear and resistance are not the final word. Once he truly experiences God's grace, his resistance will end. I hope he will cease resisting on this side of the Jordan, but I am confidant he will one day respond. No one who truly understands God's grace will reject it. To do so would be a sign not of freedom but of insanity.[20]

Perhaps in time all will come to repent of their evil ways and embrace the God who loves everyone unconditionally.

Luke tells us that the son left his father's provision and authority, but he never left his father's love. You would think the father would say, "If you want to go, go! Don't come crawling back when you get in trouble!" But instead, the father waits and watches. When he sees his son a long way off, he runs to meet him. He embraces him, kisses him, and throws him an extravagant welcome-home party. The father never stopped loving his son.

God's love is an unconditional love unlike what we find in most human interactions. Generally the love we express to one another is qualified in some way. It is love with an "if"—if you love me back, if you meet my requirements, if I find you attractive, if you are interesting, intelligent, humorous, hard-working, etc. God loves us. Period.

John Ortberg tells a story about a rag doll named Pandy. It was his sister's favorite doll, and it wasn't always in rags. It was originally a carefully selected Christmas gift plucked from the window of Marshall Fields in Chicago by a cherished aunt. John's sister loved Pandy with a love too strong for Pandy's own good. Pandy was literally loved to death—taken to bed, to lunch, even into the bath. Ortberg writes,

> By the time I knew Pandy, she was not a particularly attractive doll. In fact, to tell you the truth she was a mess. She was no longer a very valuable doll; I'm not sure we could have given her away. But for reasons that no one could ever quite figure out, in the way that kids sometimes do, my sister Barbie loved her as strongly in the days of Pandy's raggedness as she ever had in the days of her great beauty.[21]

Once the Ortberg family took a vacation to Canada. They had nearly returned to their home in Rockfield, Illinois, when they realized that Pandy had not come back with them. So John's father turned the car around, and they drove from Illinois all the way back to Canada. Pandy was found in the laundry room of the hotel, about to be washed to death. Ortberg says, "The measure of my sister's love for that doll was that she would travel all the way to a distant country to save her."[22] Ortberg concludes that we are all rag dolls, but we are God's rag dolls, and that makes the difference.

God's love precedes all desertions and betrayals and will continue faithfully after all desertions and betrayals have taken place. Henry Nouwen describes it this way: "It is the fountain of all true human love, even the most limited. Jesus' whole life and preaching had only one aim: to reveal this inexhaustible, unlimited motherly and fatherly love of his God and to show the way to let that love guide every part of our daily lives."[23]

Dennis, Sheila, and Matthew Linn have written an excellent book that aims to help people heal their hurtful images of God. Dennis Linn was at one time a priest. One day a woman named Hilda came to him because her son had tried to commit suicide for the fourth time. She told Dennis that he was involved in prostitution, drug dealing, and murder. She ended the list by saying that her son had no interest in God. She wanted to know what would happen to her son if he committed suicide without repenting.

Dennis didn't have much hope for her son, but he knew better than to say that. His theological training had taught him what to do in such situations. He said, "What do you think?" She said, "I think that when you die, you appear before the judgment seat of God. If you have lived a good life, God will send you to heaven. If you have lived a bad life, God will send you to hell." She concluded, "Since my son has lived such a bad life, if he were to die without repenting, God would certainly send him to hell."

Dennis then said to her, "Close your eyes. Imagine that you are sitting next to the judgment seat of God. Imagine also that your son has died with all these serious sins and without repenting. He has just arrived at the judgment seat of God. Squeeze my hand when you can imagine."

When she had it in her mind, she squeezed his hand. He asked her, "Hilda, how does your son feel?" She said, "My son feels so lonely and empty." Dennis next asked her what she wanted to do. She said, "I want to throw my arms around my son." She lifted her arms and began to cry as she imagined holding her son tightly.

Finally, when she stopped crying, Dennis asked her to look into God's eyes and imagine what God wanted to do. She imagined God stepping down from his throne and embracing her son. And the three of them, Hilda, her son, and God, cried together and held one another. Dennis says, "I was stunned. What Hilda taught me in those few minutes is the bottom line of healthy Christian spirituality. . . . God loves us at least as much as Hilda loves her son. . . . God loves us at least as much as the person who loves us the most."[24]

Jesus' experience of the compassion and love of God informed and shaped his reading and interpretation of Scripture; it must also inform and shape ours. Gulley and Mulholland write,

> Weighing Scripture is discerning which Scriptures accurately reflect God's character. If all Scripture is equally inspired and authoritative, God is as likely to swallow us up in an earthquake or drown us in a flood as God is to forgive our sin and take us into his arms. The reported behavior of God in the Bible is erratic at best and nearly schizophrenic in some instances. God rescues the Jewish people from the oppression of Egypt in one chapter and a few chapters later has to be convinced by Moses not to destroy them.
>
> Weighing Scripture allows for the possibility that some descriptions of God and his behavior are inaccurate. It is not merely counting how many Scriptures say "this" about God and how many Scriptures say "that" about God and believing whichever one receives the highest score. Weighing Scripture is what Jesus taught when he was asked, "What is the greatest commandment in the law?"
>
> If Jesus believed that all Scriptures were of equal worth, he would have answered, "All the commandments are equally important." Instead, he replied, "Love the Lord your God with all your heart, and with all your soul, and with all your mind. This is the first and greatest commandment.

And the second is like it: Love your neighbor as yourself" (Matthew 22:37-39).

Then Jesus added a pivotal footnote. He said, "All the law and the prophets hang on these two commandments" (Matthew 22:40). In other words, these two verses exalting love are as heavy as the rest of the Bible. Jesus tipped the scales irrevocably in favor of love.

Love is the core message of the Bible. . . . If in our examination of every chapter and verse of Scripture we miss the primacy of love, we strain out a gnat and swallow a camel. . . .

The primacy of love means I can't accept Joshua's claim that God commanded the genocide of his neighbors in Canaan. A God of love doesn't murder his children. A God who has commanded me to love my neighbor doesn't demand that I kill the same neighbor. It is out of character. Weighing this story on the scales of grace finds it wanting.

Weighing Scripture has allowed me to avoid the all-or-nothing approach to the Bible so prevalent in Christianity. I often hear people say, "If there is one error in the Bible, how can we trust any of it?" I no longer understand that statement. It suggests the only choices are uncritical acceptance or complete rejection. To reject the Bible completely is to miss its proclamation of God's love, but to accept it uncritically is to support some ugly notions about God.[25]

Peter Rollins declares that "the religious idea of truth demands that we should have a prejudice when reading the text: a prejudice of love. The Bible itself teaches us that we must not enter into any situation in a neutral and objective manner, even the reading of scripture, but always with the eyes of love."[26] This, contends Rollins, was "the central interpretive tool that Jesus employed when interpreting the scriptures"—the prejudice of love.[27] All our readings and interpretations of Scripture are influenced by a number of factors: cultural context, intellectual and psychological make-up, educational background, church tradition, etc. We do need an interpretative grid, a set of guidelines to keep us within the appropriate limits of what is possible. For Christians Jesus sets the limits and possibilities in the way he experienced God, interpreted Scripture, and embodied the unconditional love of God.

Returning to the story of the prodigal son, two things make reconciliation possible: the father's unconditional forgiveness and the son's repentance. The son comes to the end of himself. He squanders his money "in dissolute living" and has no provision for the difficult days of famine. He finds himself in dire need—hungry, destitute, and impoverished. Then "he came to himself"; another translation says, "he came to his senses." He makes a wise choice. The son says to himself, "How many of my father's hired hands have bread enough and to spare, and here I am dying of hunger!" So he turns back toward home with the intention of confessing his sin and striking a bargain, to say to his father, "I am no longer worthy to be called your son; treat me like one of your hired hands." He knows he will be better off as a hired hand in his father's house; at least there he will find a warm, safe place to sleep and enough to eat. The son, however, is still thinking of himself, not his father. He is not thinking of how he disregarded and disgraced the father, how he treated the father with contempt. He is thinking about his own self-preservation. His confession is more of a bargaining tool than a genuine acknowledgment of his betrayal of the father's love and trust.

Perhaps this is the first step toward redemption—having enough sense to know that the path we are on leads to destitution and self-destruction, fragmentation and alienation. At some point, however, if we are to enter fully into the redemptive process and experience full reconciliation with God and others, we must move beyond the mere need for self-preservation to an experience of God's motherly and fatherly love.

The father sees him "still far off." To see him at such a distance means that the father was watching, waiting, and hoping for the son's return. The father runs to meet him "filled with compassion," throws his arms around him, kisses him, and lavishes his son with love and forgiveness before the son can even offer to strike a bargain.

The son is won over by this display of forgiveness. There is no bargaining now, only a simple confession: "Father, I have sinned against heaven and before you; I am no longer worthy to be called your son." What began as a reasonable decision at self-preservation now develops into a "broken and contrite heart" (Ps 51:17). The son is overwhelmed by the father's love.

Awareness and admission of guilt are important, but acknowledgment of guilt alone is not likely to produce lasting change. We can never become the persons God created us to be through guilt or fear. Certainly guilt or fear may cause us to modify our behavior. But these feelings are incapable of forming us into more loving persons. For that we need a grand and glorious vision of the goodness and love of God. Dennis, Sheila, and Matthew Linn write,

> We can scare people into changing their behavior through fear of hell or of
> losing love. In fact, fear may have to be used occasionally on an emergency
> basis. For example, a family might tell their alcoholic father that unless he
> changes they are going to leave in order to protect themselves from his

behavior. By appealing to his fear of not belonging, this family might get the alcoholic to stop drinking. But unless the alcoholic's fear is eventually replaced with a deep sense of love and belonging, he will replace drinking with other addictions. Through fear we can temporarily change a person's behavior, but only love and belonging can ultimately change the person.[28]

We are inspired to love to the extent that we are able to grasp and experience the beauty and greatness of God's love that holds us in its grip and never lets us go. This experience changes us in the core of our being. Thomas Merton's prayer reflects the kind of change God wants in our lives:

> My Lord God, I have no idea where I am going. I do not see the road ahead of me. I cannot know for certain where it will end. Nor do I really know myself, and the fact that I think I am following your will does not mean that I am actually doing so. But I believe that the desire to please you does in fact please you. And I hope I have that desire in all that I am doing. I hope that I will never do anything apart from that desire. And I know that if I do this, you will lead me by the right road, though I may know nothing about it. Therefore I may seem lost and in the shadow of death. I will not fear, for you are with me, and you will never leave me to face my perils alone.[29]

The kind of sincerity and desire reflected in this prayer cannot be produced by guilt or fear. Only the unconditional forgiveness, acceptance, and love of God can produce such a response to God. There is no greater gift.

I think all of us long to experience this kind of love. Ernest Hemingway wrote a story about a Spanish father whose son rebelled and left home. The father never stopped searching. Finally, in Madrid, Spain, in a last desperate attempt to find his son, the father put an ad in the local newspaper: "PACO, MEET ME AT HOTEL MONTANA NOON TUESDAY. ALL IS FORGIVEN, PAPA." Paco is a common name in Spain, and when the father went to the square he found eight hundred young men named Paco waiting for their fathers.[30]

Years ago during wartime, military personnel might stay away from their families for several years. I heard about a Marine who left for duty when his wife was expecting a child. His beautiful little girl was born. For years, though the child never saw her father, the mother talked about him every day and shared photos. When their daughter was four years old, she was playing in the front yard one afternoon. A man came to the gate. She looked up into his eyes and he looked into hers. Then she screamed with delight, "Daddy, you are really for real!"

The God who sustains all of life is a gracious Father and Mother who loves unconditionally. God's grace knows no limits. All is forgiven. God calls and waits. God is ready to shower us with love; God is ready to throw a great welcome-home party.

Why would anyone want to remain in the far country?

The Powerless Almighty

Many who have heard the story of the prodigal son's homecoming do not realize that there is more to the story. The father in Luke 15 has two sons.

> Now his elder son was in the field; and when he came and approached the house, he heard music and dancing. He called one of the slaves and asked what was going on. He replied, "Your brother has come, and your father has killed the fatted calf, because he has got him back safe and sound." Then he became angry and refused to go in. His father came out and began to plead with him. But he answered his father, "Listen! For all these years I have been working like a slave for you, and I have never disobeyed your command; yet you have never given me even a young goat so that I might celebrate with my friends. But when this son of yours came back, who had devoured your property with prostitutes, you killed the fatted calf for him!" Then the father said to him, "Son, you are always with me, and all that is mine is yours. But we had to celebrate and rejoice, because this brother of yours was dead and has come to life; he was lost and has been found."

In the context of Luke's narrative, there is no doubt that the "elder son" represents some of the scribes and Pharisees who were grumbling because of Jesus' table fellowship with "sinners" (Luke 15:1-2). In other contexts, Jesus demonstrates tough love by boldly confronting their self-righteousness and hypocrisy; here, however, he conveys the tenderness of God's love for them. As self-righteous as they are, God loves them. The father loves both sons. As soon as he becomes aware that his elder son is not present at the celebration, he seeks him and pleads with him to join them. The father's love is inclusive. He says to his alienated son, "You are always with me, and all that is mine is yours." The father is grieved that his elder son is bitter and angry.

Both sons resist grace. The elder son, from all appearances, is the obedient son. He did all the father had asked of him: "For all these years I have been working like a slave for you, and I have never disobeyed your command." But he cannot do the one thing the father desires the most, the one thing the father desires more than all his slavish obedience; he cannot share the father's compassion and joy in the return of his younger brother. The elder brother, resentful and unforgiving, wants nothing to do with him, identifying him as "this son of yours," severing all connections. Outward conformity to religious rules, rituals, and practices is no guarantee that in our hearts we share the character and nature of God. Outwardly we can be faultless, but inwardly devoid of compassion and love.

The elder brother in us resists grace. The elder brother in us is more at home with a system that dispenses rewards and punishments based on comparisons and competition—a merit system in which we earn our way. In a world governed by giving scores and providing statistics, rewarding the achievers, honoring the successful, and distributing trophies to the winners, grace is hard to take, especially when we are the ones receiving the trophies and earning the rewards. When grace celebrates the loser, the winner in us becomes resentful and bitter. Henry Nouwen confesses,

> It is strange to say this, but, deep in my heart, I have known the feeling of envy toward the wayward son. It is the emotion that arises when I see my friends having a good time doing all the sorts of things that I condemn. I called their behavior reprehensible or even immoral, but at the same time I often wondered why I didn't have the nerve to do some of it or all of it myself.
>
> The obedient and dutiful life of which I am proud or for which I am praised feels, sometimes, like a burden that was laid on my shoulders and continues to oppress me, even when I have accepted it to such a degree that I cannot throw it off. I have no difficulty identifying with the elder son of the parable who complained: "All these years I have slaved for you and never once disobeyed any orders of yours, yet you never offered me so much as a kid for me to celebrate with my friends." In this complaint, obedience and duty have become a burden, and service has become slavery.[31]

Robert Roberts tells about a fourth grade class that played "balloon stomp." A balloon was tied to each child's leg, and the object was to pop everyone else's balloon while protecting one's own. The last person with an intact balloon would win. The game is rooted in the philosophy of "survival of the fittest."

The moment the game began, it was instant mayhem. Balloons were relentlessly targeted and destroyed. A few of the children hung shyly on the sidelines, and their balloons were among the first to go. The game was over in a matter of seconds. Only one balloon was still inflated, and its owner was the most disliked kid in the room.

But then, says Roberts, a second class was brought into the room to play the game; only this time it was a class of mentally challenged children. They too were each given a balloon. They were given the same instructions as the other group, and the same signal to begin the game. This time, however, the game proceeded differently. The instructions were given too quickly and misunderstood. In the confusion, the one idea that sank in was that the balloons were supposed to be popped. But instead of fighting each other off, these children got the idea that they were supposed to help each other pop balloons. One little girl knelt and held her balloon carefully in place while a little boy stomped it flat. Then he knelt and held his balloon still for her to stomp. On and on it went, with all the children helping one another in the great stomp. When the last balloon was popped, everybody cheered.[32]

This is what the father in the parable hopes: that the elder son will celebrate the truth that we are all winners. The elder son, however, refuses to let go of his anger and resentment. Life as the elder brother is joyless. If we are constantly worrying over comparisons that provoke rivalry and repeatedly fretting over a sense of being cheated, we cannot celebrate when grace is given to one who is undeserving. As long as I am trying to earn my way and compete with others for places of privilege, I can never rejoice when grace is poured out in lavish fashion on my competitors.

The same freedom granted to the younger son is granted to the elder son. The father does not demand or coerce, but pleads with the son to share his joy. New Testament scholar Eduard Schweizer calls this "Luke's parable of the powerless omnipotent."[33] Because the father loves both sons, he is absolutely powerless to demand that they share his love and be subject to his will. Schweizer observes that Jesus did not merely tell this parable; he lived it. Jesus allowed himself to be led to the cross powerless to prevent it because he had decided to love.

> It is Jesus who has told and lived the parable of the powerless almighty father, Jesus who knows his father in heaven better than anyone else knows him. Should it not be true that this his father in heaven is to be found, first of all, where the father stands at the end of the parable—out in the dark where the rebels are fighting against him? The New Testament says that he is to be found on the cross, and this means there where his limitless love is waiting and suffering and inviting until all people return—not forced, not even persuaded, but out of a heart that has been really moved—to the one

who loves them. . . . The God of the New Testament is, first of all, the powerless man nailed to the cross, and only when we have found God there shall we experience his power of loving and helping, his real omnipotence.[34]

Because of love, the almighty God becomes vulnerable and powerless and must suffer the rejection of his children. Yet, God doesn't give up. After enough rejections, we would probably write people off as unredeemable, but God persists, which means God continues to suffer. The cross of Jesus becomes the ultimate representation of that suffering.

In light of such love and compassion, why would anyone not want to celebrate with God when God's wayward children return home? When I hear God say to me, "All that is mine is yours," how can I remain bitter toward anyone? How can I remain distant and detached, alienated and estranged, when the God of this universe includes me in everything he is doing?

Questions for Reflection and Discussion

1. The people's attempt to murder Jesus in Luke 4 was a hostile reaction to Jesus' assault on their exclusivist theology of God. When you are confronted with an image of God that goes against your belief and image of God, how do you respond?

2. This chapter presents the view that Jesus did not first derive his understanding of God from Scripture, but from his own personal experience of God, which then informed and shaped his reading and interpretation of Scripture. Where should Christians start in forming their images and beliefs about God?

3. What are the characteristics of a compassionate life? Reflect on the ways the two essential components of compassion were brought together in the life of Jesus of Nazareth. Why are both elements essential? What can an individual do personally and the church do corporately to nurture compassion in the faith community and in the world outside the church? What hinders a life of compassion?

4. How do you resolve the tension of the contradictory images of God portrayed in the Scriptures?

5. Reflect on the parable of the Prodigal Son in Luke 15. While Jesus' parables provide a window through which we can see God's world, the window also serves as a mirror in which we see a reflection of ourselves. Can you see yourself in the characters of the story (the father, the younger

son, and the elder son)? What are the positive and negative ways you identify with the characters? What keeps the elder son from joining the party?

6. Complete the following statement: If God loves me at least as much as the
person who loves me the most, then . . . . What are the implications of
this kind of love? Does this provide a basis for the belief that in time God
will eventually redeem all of God's wayward, rebellious children?

7. What's the difference between forgiveness and reconciliation?

8. Do you agree with the assessment that guilt and fear are incapable of pro-
ducing lasting change? Why or why not?

9. In what sense is God "the Powerless Almighty"?

Notes

1. Fred Craddock, *When the Bible Makes Me Angry*, Fred Craddock collection, part 1 (Marietta GA: Bell Tower Production).

2. Peter Rollins, *How (Not) to Speak of God* (Brewster MA: Paraclete Press, 2006), 12–13.

3. Marcus Borg, *Meeting Jesus Again for the First Time: The Historical Jesus and the Heart of Contemporary Faith* (New York: HarperSanFrancisco, 1994), 47.

4. Bryan P. Stone, *Compassionate Ministry: Theological Foundations* (Maryknoll NY: Orbis Books, 1996), 56.

5. Borg, *Meeting Jesus Again*, 48.

6. Ibid., 49.

7. James D. G. Dunn, *Jesus' Call to Discipleship: Understanding Jesus Today* (Cambridge: Cambridge University Press, 1992), 36–37.

8. Borg, *Meeting Jesus Again*, 61.

9. James H. Charlesworth, *Jesus Within Judaism: New Light from Exciting Archaeological Discoveries,* The Anchor Bible Reference Library (New York: Doubleday, 1988), 133.

10. Lorraine Hansberry, screenplay and Daniel Petrie, director, *A Raisin in the Sun* (Columbia Pictures, 1961).

11. Cal Ripkin, Jr., and Mike Bryan, *The Only Way I Know* (New York: Penguin Books, 1997), 25.

12. *Life as a House*, dir. Irwin Winkler, written by Mark Andrus, New Line Cinema, 2001.

13. Henry Nouwen, *Turn My Mourning into Dancing* (Nashville: W Publishing Group, 2001), 68–69.

14. Brennan Manning, *A Glimpse of Jesus: The Stranger to Self-hatred* (New York: HarperSanFrancisco, 2003), 134.

15. Ibid., 134.

16. Fred Craddock, *Craddock Stories,* ed. Mike Graves and Richard F. Ward (St. Louis: Chalice Press, 2001), 34.

17. Barbara Brown Taylor, *The Preaching Life* (Cambridge: Cowley Publications, 1993), 153.

18. Craddock, *Craddock Stories*, 96.

19. Richard Rohr, *Everything Belongs: The Gift of Contemplative Prayer*, rev. and updated ed. (New York: Crossroad Publishing Company), 133.

20. Philip Gulley and James Mulholland, *If Grace Is True: Why God Will Save Every Person* (New York: HarperSanFarnacisco, 2003), 92, 107.

21. John Ortberg, *Love Beyond Reason* (Grand Rapids: Zondervan Publishing House, 1998), 11–12.

22. Ibid., 13–14.

23. Henry Nouwen, *The Return of the Prodigal Son: A Story of Homecoming* (New York: Doubleday, 1992), 109.

24. Dennis Linn, Sheila Fabricant Linn, and Matthew Linn, *Good Goats: Healing Our Image of God* (Mahwah NY: Paulist Press, 1994), 8–11.

25. Gulley and Mulholland, *If Grace Is True*, 51–53.

26. Rollins, *How (Not) to Speak of God*, 59.

27. Ibid., 61.

28. D. Linn, S. F. Linn, and M. Linn, *Good Goats,* 46.

29. Quoted in Philip Gulley and James Mulholland, *If God Is Love: Redisovering Grace in an Ungracious World* (New York: HarperSanFrancisco, 2004), 45–46.

30. Quoted in Philip Yancey, *What's So Amazing about Grace?* (Grand Rapids: Zondervan Publishing House, 1997), 37. Original source: Ernest Hemingway, "The Capitol of the World," in *The Short Stories of Ernest Hemingway* (New York: Scribner, 1953), 38.

31. Nouwen, *Return of the Prodigal Son*, 70.

32. As told by John Ortberg, *Love Beyond Reason*, 150-52. Original source is Robert Roberts, *Taking the Word to Heart* (Grand Rapids: Eerdmans, 1993), 156. Ortberg writes, "The question you have to ask is, who got the game right, and who got the game wrong? The question you have to answer is, which game are you going to play?"

33. Eduard Schweizer, *Luke: A Challenge to Present Theology* (Atlanta: John Knox Press, 1982), 78.

34. Ibid., 81.

Chapter 3

The Dynamics of Faith

In the Gospels, Jesus engages in works of healing and exorcism. The Gospels mention a number of different kinds of healings, such as healings from fever, leprosy, paralysis, blindness, and muteness—even restoration to life. The Gospels also contain a number of accounts where Jesus casts out demons. However we choose to explain and understand such phenomena, there is no doubt that Jesus and his contemporaries believed evil spirits could possess people. Their worldview took for granted the existence of such spirits, and they assumed a close connection between disease and the demonic. Jesus shared this worldview, though he clearly rejected the sickness-as-punishment theology of many of his contemporaries. Jesus also rejected the strategy of attracting followers by dazzling people with miracles, even for the good and benefit of others (Matt 4:4-5 and Luke 4:9-12).

The most common word employed in the Gospels to describe Jesus' works or miracles of healing is *dynamis*, which depicts them as acts of power. New Testament scholar R. E. Brown says, "The acts of power were weapons Jesus used to claim people and the world from the dominion of evil. When Jesus healed the sick or resuscitated the dead, he was breaking satanic power that manifested itself in illness and death."[1] While we may not share the ancient worldview of Jesus and his first followers, we must not treat their perspective as a pre-scientific stage of religion with no value for us. Modern physics is shattering the old conceptions that once carefully segregated the physical and immaterial worlds. It's all one world, and God's rule encompasses both the physical realm as well as the spiritual dimensions of life.

In the Gospels, these works of power (healings and exorcisms) function as signs of the transforming presence and power of God breaking into the world in a fresh new way through the ministry of Jesus. According to Luke's Gospel, when religious leaders asked Jesus when the kingdom of God would appear, Jesus responded, "The kingdom of God is not coming with things that can be observed; nor will they say, 'Look, here it is!' For, in fact, the kingdom of God is among you" (Luke 17:20-21).[2] In the person of Jesus, the dynamic, whole-making presence of God was in their midst.

Jesus' miracles were not intended to dazzle for show, but to represent the redeeming, renewing reality that characterizes God's new world; a divine presence and power that can heal wounded psyches, restore physical, mental, and spiritual wholeness, reconcile fragmented and fractured relationships, reorder and transform political, economical, social, and religious systems, and bring harmony and balance to the whole cosmic order of things. Theologian Harvey Cox puts this in perspective:

> He [Jesus] made it clear that sick people were not responsible for their diseases, but at the same time taught that sickness was not part of God's intention for the natural order. He saw it as the result of some kind of structural disarray in the cosmos. Using the language of the day, he linked disease to demons or Satan or the power of evil. In other words, there was a flaw, a malevolent energy at work in the universe itself. St. Paul later referred to the same idea when he spoke of the creation as "subject to decay." These toxic forces manifested themselves in illness, injustice, and oppression. But Jesus saw himself as the emissary of a Benevolent Power who was engaged in a struggle with this antihuman nemesis, and would eventually triumph over it. Jesus' healings were not attention-grabbing dazzlers. They were an integral part of his message, signs of the dawning of God's eventual victory, an enticing aperitif of the banquet to come.[3]

God's redemptive purpose encompasses the whole of everything—the physical, spiritual, and social; the individual, communal, and global dimensions of life. The life-giving and life-enhancing power of God's new world drives back the forces of destruction and evil wherever they are found, bringing harmony and wholeness to persons, relationships, organizations, and whole communities.

Faith in God's Whole-making Power

The healing stories in the Gospels are often connected to faith. Faith is not mentioned in each story, but it is certainly close at hand—if not in the one who is healed, then surely in Jesus. Albert Nolan makes the perceptive observation that Jesus' success at liberating people from their suffering must be attributed to the power of his faith, which he wanted for others. Nolan writes, "What he wanted to do most of all was awaken the same compassion and the same faith in the people around him. That alone would enable the power of God to become operative and effective in their midst."[4]

Back in the days of house calls, a doctor and his nurse responded to the anguished plea of a farmer whose wife was desperately ill. The doctor, with his familiar black bag, and the nurse were ushered upstairs where the wife lay sick. The farmer and his family waited downstairs in the parlor. After a few minutes, the doctor came down with a worried look on his face and asked for a screwdriver. After a few more minutes passed, the nurse asked for a can opener. Soon after that, the doctor reappeared, tense and visibly upset, and asked for a hammer and chisel. By this time, the distraught farmer couldn't contain himself any longer. "Tell me, Doc, what's wrong with my wife?" The doctor retorted, "Don't know yet. I can't get my black bag open." In the way the doctor's healing capacity was linked to opening his bag of medical tools, so the whole-making power of God is linked to the opening of our minds and hearts to God in faith. For instance, in Mark's account of Jesus' rejection in his hometown of Nazareth, the writer tells us Jesus could do few works of healing there because of their lack of faith (Mark 6:1-6a).

This close connection between the whole-making power of God's reign and faith can be seen in the healing stories of the woman with a hemorrhage and the restoration to life of a young girl in Mark 5:21-43. This story is actually a story within a story—two miracle stories woven together, with one bracketing the other. Common features unite the stories. In both, the individuals made whole are beyond medical help, and Jesus overturns sacred taboos by touching those pronounced "unclean."

> When Jesus and his disciples crossed over the Sea of Galilee, a great crowd gathered around him. Jairus, one of the leaders of the synagogue, came to Jesus, fell at his feet and begged him repeatedly, "My little daughter is at the point of death. Come and lay your hands on her, so that she may be made well, and live." So Jesus went with him.
>
> And a large crowd followed him and pressed in on him. Now there was a woman who had been suffering from hemorrhages for twelve years. She had endured much under many physicians, and had spent all that she had; and she was no better, but rather grew worse. She had heard about Jesus, and came up behind him in the crowd and touched his cloak, for she

said, "If I but touch his clothes, I will be made well." Immediately her hemorrhage stopped; and she felt in her body that she was healed of her disease. Immediately aware that power had gone forth from him, Jesus turned about in the crowd and said, "Who touched my clothes?" And his disciples said to him; how can you say, "Who touched me?" He looked all around to see who had done it. But the woman, knowing what had happened to her, came in fear and trembling, fell down before him, and told him the whole truth. He said to her, "Daughter, your faith has made you well; go in peace and be healed of your disease."

While he was still speaking, some people came from the leader's house to say, "Your daughter is dead. Why trouble the teacher any further?" But overhearing what they said, Jesus said to the leader of the synagogue, "Do not fear, only believe." He allowed no one to follow him except Peter, James, and John, the brother of James. When they came to the house of the leader of the synagogue, he saw a commotion, people weeping and wailing loudly. When he had entered, he said to them, "Why do you make a commotion and weep? The child is not dead but sleeping." And they laughed at him. Then he put them all outside, and took the child's father and mother and those who were with him, and went in where the child was. He took her by the hand and said to her, "Talitha cum," which means, "Little girl, get up!" And immediately the girl got up and began to walk about (she was twelve years of age). At this they were overcome with amazement. He strictly ordered them that no one should know this, and told them to give her something to eat. (Mark 5:24b-43)[5]

It is interesting to observe the contrast in Jesus' responses to these two miracles. The woman with the menstrual disorder attempted to keep her condition and healing secret, but Jesus brings it out in the open. On the other hand, the resuscitation of the child who died would have been the talk of the town, but here, Jesus attempts to keep it quiet. New Testament scholar Morna Hooker perceptively observes,

Although the reaction of Jesus in the two stories is so different, it is possible that Mark assumes a common underlying motive; the danger in both cases is of detaching the miracle from the wider context of what is happening in Jesus. The woman could easily treat Jesus as a magician-healer, and the friends of the family babble about his ability to raise the dead; but these things must only be spoken of in the context of faith in Jesus and must not be detached from his proclamation of God's kingdom.[6]

Jesus was indiscriminate in the exercise of God's whole-making power. Of particular significance is his compassionate response to the woman who suffered from vaginal bleeding. Jeffery John, dean of St. Albans Cathedral in Hertfordshire, England, has this insightful word:

> As evidence of Jesus' attitude to women, the healing of the hemorrhaging woman can hardly be overstated. In very many cultures and religions menstruation is still superstitiously understood as a cause of defilement, and as an excuse for the denigration, subjugation or exclusion of women. In the Jewish and Christian religions the pernicious understanding of menstruation as the curse of Eve has been used to justify the worst excesses and abuses of patriarchy and worse still has contributed to lodging in the minds of countless women a belief in the badness of their own body and the moral inferiority of their sex.[7]

As a mediator of God's healing power Jesus, was no respecter of persons, but he certainly had a special regard for those who were suffering on account of sickness, oppression, or exclusion.

In this story, faith is obviously more than belief in a doctrine about Jesus, and yet many Christians understand faith primarily in terms of what beliefs one adopts. As we have seen, what one believes is important, but a dynamic faith is much more than belief. Brennan Manning writes, "If we could free ourselves from the temptation to make faith a mindless assent to a dusty pawnshop of doctrinal beliefs, we would discover with alarm that the essence of biblical faith lies in trusting God."[8]

Ethicist John Kavanaugh spent three months "at the house of the dying" in Calcutta. At the time he was seeking a clear answer as to how to best spend the rest of his life. On the first morning there, he met Mother Teresa. She asked, "And what can I do for you?" Kavanaugh asked her to pray for him.

"What do you want me to pray for?" she asked.

He said, "Pray that I have clarity."

She replied, "No, I will not do that." Of course he wanted to know why. She responded, "Clarity is the last thing you are clinging to and must let go." When Kavanaugh commented that she always seemed to have the clarity he longed for, she laughed and said, "I have never had clarity; what I have always had is trust. So I will pray that you trust God."[9] This is the essence of faith—trust in God.

Neither Jairus, who sought Jesus out, nor the woman who fought through the crowd to get to Jesus trusted a doctrinal belief system. They exercised trust in a real, live person who claimed to know how to access the power and grace of God. In these stories, faith involves trusting the real person of Jesus, who acts as agent and mediator of the inclusive, unconditional mercy and whole-making power of God. Trust is what constitutes the core of a loving relationship between an individual and God and between members of the faith community. Faith is more about falling in love with God and being faithful to God than assenting or ascribing to a set of theological constructs.

Jesus is the human face of God for Christians; the one who makes transparent the nature of God and makes available the presence of God. To have faith *in* Jesus is to personally trust Jesus as the mediator and ambassador of God's healing presence. This includes emulating the pattern or way of life he lived and obeying the teachings he passed on to his disciples. To have the faith *of* Jesus is to be able to trust God in the way and manner in which Jesus trusted God. This involves living in complete reliance upon God to provide for our needs and to transform our deepest self.

It has little to do with being right or correct. The woman's faith bordered on the superstitious and the magical. Apparently she thought of Jesus' clothing as being an extension of his person. She reasoned that if she could simply touch his garment, healing power would be channeled to her. And it was! God honored her immature, superstitious faith. She knew only that God was at work through Jesus, and she believed enough to act on her faith. To act is to trust. Dietrich Bonhoeffer, the German theologian and pastor who was martyred under the Nazis, puts it this way: "For faith is only real when there is obedience, never without it, and faith only becomes faith in the act of obedience."[10]

The call to faith is an invitation to trust God with one's whole heart and in the totality of life. We have no guarantee that God is going to fix all that is broken in our lives or solve all our problems. We must be careful lest we interpret these miracle stories to mean that God will miraculously intervene in our desperate situations to change the circumstances or restore good fortune. God may indeed give us a miracle, but it may be of a different kind than what we want or expect. We can never presume to know the form or expression in which the whole-making power of God will come to us.

Author, poet, and former business executive James Autry offers intriguing reflections in his book, *Looking Around for God: The Oddly Reverent*

Observations of an Unconventional Christian. He shares how he desperately pursued a miracle for his son, who at the age of two was diagnosed with autism. His operating philosophy has been "anything is worth a try." His family tried visualization therapy, diets, megavitamin therapy, special medicine, psychic healing, and even horseback therapy. The boy received the best of traditional medical and educational services. Autry writes,

> With all that we tried, I believe we'll never know what worked and what didn't. Maybe none of it. Maybe all of it. I do know that at some point while chasing after the one big miracle, I finally recognized the real miracle workers and realized that miracles are happening almost every day, one person at a time, one teacher, one friend, one family member, one coach, one music teacher, one ranch-hand wrangler, and one parent at a time.[11]

Faith lays hold of the claim of Jesus that God is near even when we cannot sense or feel God's presence. We have no guarantee that we will be spared suffering or victimization. Trusting Jesus is not an immunization against the pain of life. Jesus was not spared from the cruel hate of the religious leaders or the bitter contempt of the Roman soldiers, and he told his followers to be prepared for the same treatment.

When we find ourselves engulfed in darkness, faith (trust in God) enables us to keep going in the hope that light will one day break through. The story is told of a missionary family home on furlough and staying at the lake house of a friend. One day, Dad was puttering in the boathouse, Mom in the kitchen, and the three children, ages 4, 7, and 12, were on the lawn. Four-year-old Billy escaped from his sister's watchful eye and wandered down to the wooden dock. The shiny aluminum boat caught his eye, but unsteady feet landed him in eight foot water.

When the twelve-year-old screamed, Dad came running. Realizing what had happened, he dove into the murky water. Frantically he felt for his son, but twice, out of breath, he had to return to the surface. Diving down once more he found Billy clinging to a wooden pier several feet under. Prying the boy's fingers loose, he bolted to the surface with Billy in his arms.

Safely ashore, his father asked, "Billy, what were you doing down there?" The little one replied, "Just waitin' on you Dad, just waitin' on you."[12]

Our situation may be such that all we can do is wait. When the darkness is so thick that we can't see to move forward, we trust and wait for God to illuminate a path through it. Richard Rohr reminds us, "The way through is always much more difficult than the way around. Cheap religion gives us the way around. True religion gives us the way through. Cheap religion denies the darkness. True religion steps right into it."[13]

Contrary to some of today's popular Christian teaching, faith is not at odds with human effort, but presupposes it. Jesus said, "Seek first the kingdom of God" (Matt 6:33; Luke 12:31).[14] Earnest seeking requires deliberate, intentional effort. It's not, however, about attaining spiritual greatness or a level of morality that makes one superior. It's not about rewards and punishments or earning and achieving. It's about being ready. We do not have to attain to the presence of God, for we are already in the presence of God, but we can learn to discern God's presence. We cannot manipulate or force this experience. The active presence (the Spirit) of God is like wind; it cannot be controlled.[15] We can, however, be ready to receive God's presence and participate with God in his work to transform the world. This requires an intentional effort of making ourselves ready. The disciplines of the spiritual life—worship, theological reflection, contemplation, service, involvement in justice issues, etc., are designed to help us catch the spirit of Jesus who is in us, with us, among us, and for us.[16]

Life in the fast lane can keep us so distracted that most of our effort is wasted on insignificant things. We are not likely to drift into faith. A magnetic current within society always pulls us toward temporal security through the accumulation of possessions and the pursuit of power and prestige. It works against faith by linking our future solely to our own ability to create that future. The fast track often leads to a life of worry and anxiety, which, according to Jesus, is the opposite of faith (Matt 6:24-34).

Effort is necessary, and yet faith is not something we can magically conjure up or possess by simply trying harder. We can nurture faith by aligning ourselves with the counter-cultural Christ who calls us to a life of humble and compassionate service to others. Following Christ into a life of self-giving for the good of others can break the hold of materialism and ego.

One of the great tragedies of American Christianity in both conservative and liberal forms is that we have modified it to blend into our consumerist culture. Christian faith is tagged onto "life as usual," making little difference. I am reminded of the guy who called 911 and said, "Quick, send an ambulance. My son just swallowed my fountain pen!" The operator, trying not to panic, said in a calm voice, "I am dispatching one now. But what are you doing in the meantime?" He said, "I'm using a pencil." Life cannot proceed as usual when we attach ourselves as apprentices to Jesus in a relationship of trust. To trust and follow Jesus is to participate in God's new world. Life cannot remain the same for those who embark on this journey.

Many versions of contemporary Christianity emphasize the worship of Jesus as the God figure who endorses a domesticated faith thoroughly saturated in the conventional wisdom of the culture. This allows us to avoid real transformation while feeling good about getting the doctrine right. But Jesus, as teacher and prophet, challenged the conventional wisdom of securing oneself in the world and modeled a radical trust in God, even though it led him to the cross. I personally find the human Jesus more a catalyst for personal and world transformation than the divine Jesus. James Autry offers perceptive thoughts:

> We Christians are always professing that we want to be "Christ-like" in our lives. Yet in a way, Jesus as God gives us an out, a readymade excuse when we fall short. After all, Jesus was divine, perfect, right? Thus how can we mere mortals be expected to be Christ-like? How can we be expected to live a life of goodness and compassion every day? It's not "human."
>
> But in my view, this presents the great Christian challenge. If we think of Jesus as human, as a man rather than God, it takes away the "God" excuse. And in a way, it liberates us to examine our place in the world, our relationship to the human condition, and our role in healing whatever we can in this world.
>
> I love the man that Jesus was. I love the way he treated his friends, how he shared his wisdom with everyone who would listen, how he always stuck up for the poor, the disabled, the children, the weak, and the disenfranchised. He embodied goodness and compassion and in doing so showed us how to embody the love that can reveal the divine in us, even as it did in him."[17]

Mark's Gospel says the woman had consulted all the "authorities"—exhausting her resources and suffering much from their so-called remedies. I suspect that many of us have invested time and money seeking cures, looking for happiness, peace, and meaning in our lives, searching for solutions and answers to life's perplexing problems, but often in the wrong places and from the wrong people. The woman, like many of us, had come to the end of herself. The same was true for Jairus.

When Jesus arrives at the home of Jairus, he steps into the commotion associated with great loss—"people weeping and wailing loudly." But with the arrival of Jesus, hope is born. Jesus says, "The child is not dead, but asleep." Mark observes that "they laughed at him." There will always be those who scoff at persons of faith, and sometimes these will be the people in our churches and religious organizations. Those who scoffed at Jesus were not bad people; they were religious people, but they didn't share Jesus' faith in God's nearness and availability.

Certainly both stories highlight the power of Christ to restore life, but in the raising of Jairus's daughter in particular, there is a clear allusion to resurrection. When Jesus says, "Little girl, I say to you get up," the word translated "get up" is the normal word for resurrection in other contexts. Also, "sleep" was a common euphemism for death adopted by the early Christians. The story points beyond the obvious to proclaim that Christ is the one who is able to mediate eternal life, life with and in God, life that transforms individuals and communities.

This particular story is an example of how the healing and miracle stories in the Gospels function almost like parables to proclaim the good news of the living Christ. The living Christ has the power to give meaning to life and bring hope and new possibilities to those at the brink of despair. This wholeness of life, however, lies outside our awareness and experience until our spiritual eyes are opened and we are awakened from our sleep. The gospel of Christ relates as much to the present as to the future. Now is the day of salvation; now is the whole-making power of God's new world present among us. Unfortunately many of us would rather fantasize about what is not than live with what is, because the present moment doesn't seem all that momentous. We are asleep to God's vibrant presence. But when we wake up, when we become aware of God's presence in the present moment, it teems with meaning. Richard Rohr says,

> The contemplative secret is to learn to live in the now. The now is not as empty as it might appear to be or that we fear it may be. When we're doing life right, it means nothing more than it is right now, because God is in this moment in a nonblaming way. When we are able to experience that, taste it and enjoy it, we don't need to hold on to it. The next moment will have its own taste and enjoyment.[18]

The life of faith compels us to trust God one day, one hour, and one moment at a time. When faith awakens us to God's whole-making power, we discover the courage to face every human predicament and problem. The living Christ is saying to us at this moment, "Don't be afraid; just believe."

Faith Is a Matter of Seeing

Matthew's Gospel presents the following account of Jesus being tested by certain religious leaders,

> The Pharisees and Sadducees came, and to test Jesus they asked him to show them a sign from heaven. He answered them, "When it is evening, you say, 'It will be fair weather, for the sky is red.' And in the morning, 'It will be stormy today, for the sky is red and threatening.' You know how to interpret the appearance of the sky, but you cannot interpret the signs of the times. An evil and adulterous generation asks for a sign, but no sign will be given to it except the sign of Jonah." Then he left them and went away. (Matt 16:1-4)

The healing miracles of Jesus do not supply incontrovertible proof or evidence for faith. Jesus engaged in many "works of power," healing sick and broken people, but here, certain religious leaders come seeking a greater "sign." They want Jesus to do a spectacular feat to prove with indisputable evidence that he is of God. I think most of us would like to have this kind of "sign."

Richard Rohr has said that there are three basic ways to see Reality (Reality with a capital "R"). One possibility is that the Divine Reality is against us. God is hostile toward us. God is out for God's self. God reacts on a whim and takes sadistic pleasure in making us squirm. Another possibility is that God is aloof, indifferent, and distant. God is apathetic toward us, and so we are basically on our own. The third possibility is that God is benevolent, good, and compassionate. God deeply cares for the creation and is for us, rather than against us or indifferent to us. Most of us want some indication that God is there and that God cares. We look for a "sign," an unmistakable, indisputable display of God's love for us.

In the movie *Signs*, Mel Gibson plays Graham Hess, an Episcopal priest who loses his faith when his wife, out taking a walk, is hit and killed by a drunk driver. One morning the family wakes up to find a 500-foot crop circle in their backyard. As they watch the news, they discover that crop circles are found all over the world and gradually realize that their world is being invaded. In a gripping conversation between Graham and his brother Merrill (Joaquin Phoenix), who has come to live with them and help with the two children, Graham says,

People break down into two groups when they experience something lucky. Group number one sees it as more than luck, more than coincidence, they see it as a sign, evidence that there is someone up there, watching out for them.

Group number two sees it as just pure luck, a happy turn of chance. You can be sure that the people in group number two are looking at those fourteen lights in a very suspicious way. For them, their situation is fifty-fifty. Could be bad, could be good. But deep down, they feel that whatever happens they're on their own. And that fills them with fear.

But, there are a whole lot of people in group number one. When they see those fourteen lights, they're looking at a miracle, and deep down they feel that whatever's going to happen, there will be someone to help them. And that fills them with hope. So you have to ask yourself: What kind of person are you? Are you the kind that sees signs, and sees miracles? Or do you believe that people just get lucky? Or look at the question this way. Is it possible that there are no coincidences?[19]

There are no clear, indisputable "signs" that prove, beyond any doubt, that God is there and that God cares. Faith is a matter of interpretation; it is a way of seeing Reality.

Some folks constantly grasp for something tangible or visible that proves their faith. Philip Gulley, in his novel *Home to Harmony*, has a chapter titled "The Shroud of Harmony." The Friendly Women's Circle of the Harmony Friends Meeting have a quilt sale each year at their Chicken Noodle Dinner in order to raise money for Brother Norman's shoe ministry to the Choctaw Indians. They are approaching their twenty-fifth anniversary of quilt making. Fern Hampton, who originated the idea twenty-five years ago, is the group's president. She tells the ladies, "We want this one to shimmer. Fifty years from now, we want people to think back on this quilt and quiver. Let's aim for the heavens."

The quilt was indeed a piece of meticulous craftsmanship. They hung it from the wall at the front of the church meeting room. As they sat in worship in the Quaker silence, people looking at the quilt, Fern suddenly screamed out, "I see Him! He's in the quilt!" People looked. Right there on the quilt, they saw a man. It looked like Jesus. Then he was gone.

Word got out. The Associated Press picked up the story. People came from all over to see "The Shroud of Harmony," hoping to see Jesus. And when the light hit the quilt just right he seemed to appear. In the meeting house they noticed that things started disappearing—hymn books, cardboard fans from the Mackey Funeral Home, and even pieces of the pews.

One day Miriam Hodge, longtime member of the Friendly Women's Circle, came to see Pastor Sam Gardner. She was deeply troubled and had to confess. She said to Sam, "I came by one evening when we were finishing up the quilt. I wanted to finish a section. I was drinking coffee and spilled it all over the quilt. I took it home and cleaned it as best I could and brought it back the next morning. Sam, that's not the Lord we've been seeing—that's Maxwell House."[20]

Does this mean there are no "signs"? No, but it is a matter of interpretation; it all comes down to how you "see." What are we looking for when we seek a "sign"? Do we want God to make faith easy for us? Would it even be faith if God worked a dazzling miracle to win us over? Do we want God to conform to our agenda and cater to our demands? Are we looking for a quick excuse? "I asked God to reveal himself to me, but God didn't show up." Maybe God did show up; maybe God is already here, but we do not have eyes to see.

Just after these religious leaders demand a sign from Jesus, Matthew (following Mark's Gospel) includes this story:

> When the disciples reached the other side, they had forgotten to bring any bread. Jesus said to them, "Watch out, and beware of the yeast of the Pharisees and Sadducees." They said to one another, "It is because we have brought no bread." And becoming aware of it, Jesus said, "You of little faith, why are you talking about having no bread? Do you still not perceive? Do you not remember the five loaves for the five thousand, and how many baskets you gathered? Or the seven loaves for the four thousand, and how many baskets you gathered? How could you fail to perceive that I was not speaking about bread? Beware of the yeast of the Pharisees and Sadducees!" Then they understood that he had not told them to beware of the yeast of bread, but of the teaching of the Pharisees and Sadducees. (Matt 16:5-12)

When Jesus used metaphorical language to warn the disciples about the teaching of some of the religious leaders, they did not "perceive"; they did not see or understand. They also did not perceive the spiritual meaning behind Jesus' supply of bread for the multitudes. The meaning of a "sign" is all in how we perceive (see) it.

In Mary Chase's classic play *Harvey* (later a film starring Jimmy Stewart), Elwood P. Dowd is an eccentric drinking man whose closest friend is an enormous rabbit called Harvey, who is, of course, invisible to everyone except Elwood. Elwood's family hires a psychiatrist, Dr. Chumley, to cure Elwood and rid the family of Harvey's embarrassing presence. But in a strange twist of events, Dr. Chumley becomes a believer. Dr. Chumley exclaims, "Flyspecks. I've been spending my life among flyspecks while miracles have been leaning on lamp posts on Eighteenth and Fairfax." We keep looking for God in the spectacular and the sensational, when miracles are occurring daily in ordinary events and relationships, pointing us to the God who loves us and is for us. It's all a matter of "seeing."

Some of the difficulty may be in the way we think about and define a miracle. We usually think in terms of a supernatural intrusion or intervention into our natural world. But the truth is that it's all one world. God's world and our world intersect and interlock. The supernatural world and the natural world are not separate worlds, but one world, God's world. Episcopal priest and professor of religion Barbara Brown Taylor describes her belief in the immanence of God in creation:

> At this point in my thinking, it is not enough for me to proclaim that God is responsible for all this unity. Instead, I want to proclaim that God *is* the unity—the very energy, the very intelligence, the very elegance and passion that make it all go. This is the God who is not somewhere but everywhere, the God who may be prayed to in all directions at once. This is also the God beyond all directions, who will still be here (wherever "here" means) when the universe either dissipates into dust or swallows itself up again. Paul Tillich's name for this divine reality was "the ground of all being." The only thing I can think of that is better than that is the name God revealed to Moses: "I Am Who I Am."[21]

I am not suggesting that God is the creation; God is "more" than the universe, but God fills or inhabits the universe. Everything is in God and God is in all that is, but God is not diffused into many things. God remains the personal God. The theological way to talk about this is to say that God is both transcendent ("more" or "other" than the creation) and immanent ("within" and "part of" creation, as the very life force that sustains it). God is all around us, within us, a part of us, and yet distinct from us as a separate Divine Being. If we have "eyes to see," we can discern the presence of God everywhere since the Divine Reality inhabits both the physical and spiritual dimensions of life. Faith lays hold of a gracious, generous, and good God who wants the best for creation, especially his daughters and sons. Faith "sees" God at work in vast, numerous ways for the good of the creation, while acknowledging the presence of evil forces that are opposed to the work of God in the world.

Desperation as a Context for Faith

A missionary from America invited some African pastors to his native land for a meeting. In their free time, they asked to do some sightseeing. The missionary gave them his cell phone in case they got lost. In less than an hour, he received a call. "Help," said the voice, "we're lost." The missionary told his friend to go to the street corner and find the names of the two streets on the signs. After a minute or two, the lost pastor exclaimed, "I'm at the corner of 'Walk' and 'Don't Walk.'" Have you ever been there—not sure where to go or who to believe, not knowing how to read the signs? It may take this kind of desperate situation for faith to be born in us.

Fred Craddock tells a wonderful story about arriving at a hospital to make a pastoral visit, but in the corridor he saw a woman. Her forehead pressed against the door, she pounded with her fists: "Let me in, let me in, let me in!" As Fred drew closer, he saw that it was the chapel door.

Fred stopped a worker and said, "This chapel is locked."

The worker said, "We have to keep it locked. There were some kids that trashed it and we had to get all new furniture. We can't afford to keep doing that, so we have to keep it locked."

Fred said, "Well, find someone with a key." The worker returned with a woman who opened the chapel. Fred and the woman who was banging on the door went in.

Fred noticed that the woman had come to the hospital suddenly; she wore no makeup, her hair was not combed, and it was obvious that she pulled on her clothes with no thought. She wore a look of desperation. She said, "I know he's going to die, I know he's going to die, I know he's going to die."

"Who?" asked Fred.

"My husband."

"What's the matter?"

"He's had a heart attack."

"Can I get you some water?"

"No," she said.

Fred told her who he was and asked if he could pray. She said, "Please."

Fred started to pray for her and her husband, but she interrupted; in fact, she took over. She started praying herself. Fred was too quiet or slow or saying the wrong thing or something, but she took over. Fred wasn't getting through, and she knew it.

She said,

> Lord, this is not the time to take my husband. You know that better than I do, he's not ready. Never prays, never goes to church or anything. He's not ready, not a good time to take him. Don't take him now. And what about me? If I have to raise these kids, what I am going to do? I don't have any skills, can't find any work. I quit school to marry him. If I'd have known you were going to take him, I'd have stayed in school . . . And what about the kids? They don't mind me now with him around. If he's gone, they'll be wild as bucks. What about the kids? This is not the time to take my husband.[22]

She was talking to God.

Fred stayed that day as long as he felt useful. He went back the next morning and saw that the woman wore a dress and makeup and looked nice. She was in the hallway outside intensive care. Before Fred had time to ask, she said, "He's better." She smiled and said, "I'm sorry about that crazy woman yesterday."

Fred said, "Well, you weren't crazy."

She said, "I guess the Lord heard one of us."

"He heard you."

Fred writes, "She had God by the lapels, with both hands and was screaming in God's face: 'I don't think you're listening!' That's desperation."[23]

Maybe it takes a kind of desperation to awaken us to our need of God. In Mark 1:40-42 Mark tells about a man who was desperate: "A leper came to him begging him, and kneeling he said to him, 'If you choose, you can make me clean.' Moved with pity, Jesus stretched out his hand and touched him, and said to him, 'I do choose. Be made clean!' Immediately the leprosy left him, and he was made clean."

Leprosy was a disease that inflicted much mental and physical anguish. According to the Levitical code, "The person with leprosy must wear torn clothes, let his hair hang loose, cover the lower part of his face and cry out, 'Unclean! Unclean!' As long as he has the disease he remains unclean. He must live alone; he must live outside the camp" (Lev 13:45-46, NIV). Lepers were excluded from social and religious life. In the time of Jesus, they were pushed aside in colonies of seclusion, out of sight and out of mind. In the popular theology of Jesus' world, leprosy was symptomatic of the demonic. Lepers felt the judgment of God and the condemnation of the community; they lived on the brink of despair.

Undoubtedly, this leper felt that he was at the end of his rope. In the pit of despair and desperation, he reached out to Jesus. Sometimes faith born in such circumstances does not last; other times, however, it does last and develops into a more complete faith. We have to start somewhere. It may be that in a situation of desperation we discover that the faith we grew up with and that was passed on to us is no longer sufficient; it simply doesn't work anymore in light of the contradictions and difficulties of life. We need not grieve too long for the loss of such faith. It is our opportunity to develop a more mature faith, a faith with more substance to it. Life experiences have a way of stripping back the superficial layers of a faith that seeks easy answers.

The Quaker educator, writer, and activist Parker Palmer, in his book *Let Your Life Speak*, tells about his descent into the dark woods called clinical depression. He describes it as the ultimate state of disconnection between people, between mind and heart, and between one's self-image and public mask.

Parker says that after many days and hours of listening, his therapist offered him an image that eventually helped him reclaim his life. The therapist said to Parker, "You seem to look upon depression as the hand of an enemy trying to crush you. Do you think you could see it instead as the hand of a friend, pressing you down to ground on which it is safe to stand?"[24] Going down into the depths of our being and laying them open before God is a frightening experience, but it is potentially liberating.

Parker also shares an experience he had while engaged in a course called Outward Bound at Hurricane Island off the coast of Maine. One of his tasks, a task that he feared the most, was to rappel down a 110-foot cliff. As he slowly made his way down the cliff face, he came to a deep hole in the rock. Realizing he couldn't go around it, he became suddenly paralyzed by fear. He hung there in silence for what seemed like a long time. Finally, an instructor shouted, "Parker, is anything wrong?" In a high, squeaky voice he replied, "I don't want to talk about it."

At that moment the second instructor chimed in, "It's time that you learned the Outward Bound motto." Palmer thought, *I'm about to die, and she's going to give me a motto.* But then she shouted ten words that have had lasting impact on his life: "If you can't get out of it, get into it."[25]

When we come to the place where we are immobilized by fear, when we can no longer hide the contradictions of our lives (what we appear to be on the outside is not what we know ourselves to be on the inside), when we struggle with feelings that we cannot control, when there is a rage inside of us that we cannot contain, when the darkness is so thick we feel as though we are suffocating in it, when we are rendered powerless and stripped of all pretenses and defenses, when our deep questions about God are shrouded in mystery, when we are brought low in humiliation, as strange as it may seem, we are then in a place where transformation can occur. We are in a place of healing; a place where we can become more real, more authentic; a place where we can lay hold of God by faith and discover the true self God created us to be. Annie Dillard writes,

> In the deeps are the violence and terror of which psychology has warned us. But if you ride these monsters deeper down, if you drop with them farther over the world's rim, you find what our sciences cannot locate or name, the substrate, the ocean or matrix or ether which buoys the rest, which gives goodness its power for good, and evil it's power for evil . . . .[26]

Many would flee the monsters or try to destroy the monsters; few, I think, are willing to ride them into the depths.

One of the characteristics of popular Christianity (in all its forms) is its offer of quick fixes and simple solutions in place of the mystery, paradox, and ambiguity that surround God and the human condition. It's like the guy who went to a psychologist for therapy. He said, "Doctor, you have got to help me. I haven't slept in days. I wake up in the middle of the night and see monsters crawling out from under my bed. They walk around the room scaring the stew out of me." After months of therapy and getting nowhere, finally the therapist was ready to recommend someone else. Then one afternoon the man entered her office with the announcement, "I'm cured. Been sleeping like a baby. My brother came to visit and cured me." Amazed, she asked, "Is your brother a therapist?" "No." "Is he a psychiatrist or a psychologist?" "No, he's a carpenter. He sawed the legs off my bed." Many want simple answers. It's risky riding the monsters into the depths.

In Mark's story, something gave the leper hope. Something compelled him to break with custom and convention, to risk the judgment and condemnation of his community in boldly confronting Jesus. Something inspired him to reject despair, to act against his fears and all the pressures of his society to stay put and keep quiet. That something was the hope of being healed by Jesus.

The Spirit of Jesus still inspires hope and courage. The living Christ enables us to stop denying our failures and compels us to move out against our fears, to risk embarrassment and looking foolish in order to avail ourselves of the whole-making power of God.

Brennan Manning tells about a lawyer who was an alcoholic but would not admit it and get help. One evening he overheard a conversation between his wife and son. His wife asked the boy, "Vince, why don't you and the other kids play in the pool anymore?" Vince hesitated. "I guess I'm frightened. I never know what Dad will be like, and I don't want the other boys to see him drunk." Hearing those words from his son was like being stabbed in the heart. At that moment he put down his drink, called Alcoholics Anonymous, and began the twelve steps that opened the door to a new way of life. It was painful, but the pain saved his life and his family. Should you find yourself in a desperate situation, then the soil is fertile for the seed of faith to spring to life.

There is an interesting variant here in the textual tradition. The NRSV reads, "Moved with pity, Jesus stretched out his hand and touched him"; but the footnote calls attention to an alternate reading that many textual scholars believe is authentic. Some reliable manuscripts read "anger" instead of "pity" or "compassion." It seems more likely that a scribe would change "anger" to "compassion" rather than the other way around. If "anger" is the correct reading, how might we make sense of it? Jesus surely is not angry with the leper for crying out to be healed of this horrendous disease. Perhaps Jesus is angered by the ravages of disease and by the human anguish experienced by those who suffer. It could be prophetic anger at the societal structures that reduce a human being to a state of self-loathing and despair. I suspect both compassion and anger moved Jesus to respond. Mark tells us that in direct violation of the purity law forbidding contact with lepers, Jesus reached out and touched him and made him whole.

I think the anger Jesus displays here is God's anger at the devastation and suffering caused by disease and evil. Christ's act of touching and healing the leper reflects God's continual compassion for those desperately suffering in our world. In Christ, God draws near to us—whether through the pain of infants or adolescents or young adults or middle adults or senior adults; the pain of unemployment, estrangement from family, physical disease, psychological turmoil, mental illness, whatever. There is no human suffering that is not in some way part of God's experience. Whenever we partake of the bread and the cup in Holy Communion, we enter into this great and wonderful mystery and worship a God who chose not to remain outside our pain, but took on our suffering and bore it even unto death on a cross.

In touching the leper, Jesus did not merely risk catching a highly contagious illness; he also made himself unclean according to the stipulations of Mosaic Law. From Mark's perspective, though, a reversal occurs. Instead of Jesus being made unclean, the leper is made clean. The defiling power of leprosy is rendered impotent before Jesus. It is not the desecrating, destructive power of leprosy that is contagious, but the healing, restoring power of Jesus.

The Question of Faith: Who's in Charge?

I live in Frankfort, Kentucky, situated between Lexington and Louisville. In my congregation are sports fans of both the University of Louisville and the University of Kentucky—huge rivals in our state. Rick Pitino has held the distinction of being the head basketball coach of both schools, formerly at UK and now at Louisville. He was asked in an interview to explain the major difference between the teams in their perception of the big game. He commented that while the fans at Louisville get as excited as the UK fans, once it's over, it's over for the Louisville fans, while the UK fans live out the game all season long. It has been reported that some UK fans actually bleed blue.

In a basketball game between these two schools held at Rupp Arena (UK), an elderly lady was sitting alone beside an empty seat. When someone asked her about it, she explained that it was her late husband's and that they had been season ticket holders for twenty-eight years. The individual asked, "Couldn't you have offered the seat to a friend or a relative so they could enjoy the game with you?" Some UK fans would consider keeping an empty seat at Rupp Arena equivalent to a criminal act. The widow responded, "Well, I would have, but they are all at my husband's funeral." That's taking one's commitment seriously.

Many of the stories and teachings of Jesus in the Gospels invite the reader to think about his or her commitment to his message and cause. One such story is found in Matthew 21:28-32:

> "What do you think? A man had two sons; he went to the first son and said, 'Son, go and work in the vineyard today.' He answered, 'I will not'; but later he changed his mind and went. The father went to the second and said the same; and he answered, 'I go, sir'; but he did not go. Which of the two did the will of his father?" They said, "The first." Jesus said to

them, "Truly I tell you, the tax collectors and the prostitutes are going into the kingdom of God ahead of you. For John came to you in the way of righteousness and you did not believe him, but the tax collectors and the prostitutes believed him; and even after you saw it, you did not change your minds and believe him."

Matthew links the story to its application in Jesus' ministry context. Some of the religious leaders, like the second son, give assent to God's will expressed through the law and prophets and claim faithful obedience to God, but they rejected John, the greatest of the prophets. On the other hand, the "tax collectors and the prostitutes," the "sinners" in Israel, who had carelessly ignored the demands of their religion, had received the witness of John regarding Jesus, and hence they take their place in God's kingdom ahead of these religious leaders.[27] This reminds us that the purpose and ways of God are not always evident to those who claim to know them. New Testament scholar Arland J. Hultgren remarks,

> What is so intriguing is that God often gets a hearing and response in the lives of people whom the righteous despise. These are people who make no claims of being righteous or religious, but who carry on daily tasks given them by God. Precisely when people do not try to be religious, but simply do the will of God through the normal course of living, they respond to God's call.[28]

The first son appears initially to be the biggest problem. When instructed to go work in the vineyard, he blatantly answers, "No, I will not." This son gives the father indigestion at breakfast, but ends up being a joy at supper because he repents and ends up in the vineyard. The second son, on the other hand, is a joy at breakfast and tells the father just what we wants to hear, but he never makes it into the vineyard, so he is a problem at supper. The second son comes across as the faithful, obedient son (not unlike the elder brother in Luke 15), but in reality he is the disobedient one.

Some years ago in the days of the local drugstore, a young man went inside and bought three one-pound boxes of chocolates. The drugstore owner commented that it would be cheaper to buy one three-pound box. The young man explained his strategy. He said, "If my date tonight lets me sit close to her, she gets one box. If she lets me put my arm around her, she gets a second box. If she lets me kiss her, she will get the third box." That night he was having dinner at her house, and he asked her father if he could say a prayer before dinner. He prayed the most fervent prayer. After dinner, on the way to the movie, his date said, "I didn't know you were so religious." He said, "Well, I didn't know your dad owned the drugstore." Appearances can be deceiving.

The son who tells the father what he wants to hear never really meets his father; he avoids him. It's always a tragedy when those within a relationship never truly meet. A girl went home after school with a friend. The friend and her mother got into an argument, and it became so heated that the girl decided to leave. Later, her friend called and apologized. The girl said, "I love the way you and your mother fight. My mom lets me have it and then walks away before I can say anything. Your mother listened to every word and cared enough to tell you why she felt the way she did. Your mother takes you seriously." The second son in the parable doesn't take the father seriously. He tells the father what the father wants to hear to avoid conflict, but has no intention of obeying the father's instruction. The real tragedy is that he doesn't end up in the vineyard doing the father's work.

In the postscript, which applies the story to Jesus' ministry, the word for faith occurs three times: "For John came to you in the way of righteousness and you did not *believe* him, but the tax collectors and the prostitutes *believed* him; and even after you saw it, you did not change your minds and *believe* him." Matthew makes this an issue of faith.

Jesus' question speaks to the nature of faith: "Which of the two did the will of his father?" Faith is about doing the will of God. The response of the son, "I go, sir," is actually "I go, Lord"; it recalls Jesus' words at the end of the body of teaching commonly known as Jesus' Sermon on the Mount: "Not everyone who says to me, 'Lord, Lord,' will enter the kingdom of heaven, but only the one who does the will of my Father in heaven" (Matt 7:21; see also Matt 12:46-50; 25:35-40). This son is all words, but no deeds, and does not do the will of his father. From Matthew's perspective, faith is about doing the will of God.

In a Christian devotional magazine, the writer tells about pulling up at an intersection behind a woman in a station wagon with a bumper sticker that read, "Honk if you love Jesus." So she decided to honk. The lady in the station wagon leaned out of her window and screamed at the top of her lungs, "You dummy, can't you see the light is red!" Then as soon at it turned green, she screeched her tires, scattering a group of teenagers crossing the road. Her bumper sticker said one thing; her actual life said something quite different. Faith is more than words on a bumper sticker or in a confession; faith is also faithfulness to God's will.

In Matthew's narrative prior to this parable, Jesus performs three prophetic acts—he enters Jerusalem claiming to be the one to bring peace in fulfillment of Zechariah 9:9; he stages a protest in the temple; and he pronounces judgment on a fig tree—all authoritative, prophetic acts representing God's word to the religious authorities who had rejected the way of peace and justice. Some of the chief priests and elders confront Jesus in the temple and want to know by what authority he does these things. "Who gave you this authority?" they ask. Within this context, Jesus shares the parable about the two sons, words that convey his authority to act and speak as God's representative on earth, heralding judgment and salvation.

The postscript to the parable points out that John the Baptist had testified to the "way of righteousness," the way of conformity to God's will and purpose, pointing beyond himself to Jesus as the anointed one. Christian faith involves hearing the word of Jesus and responding to that word in trust and in obedience. The faith issue is an authority issue: Who's in charge?

The question of faith is, Who or what has ultimate authority in my life? Will I run my life according to the ways in which I have been socialized by my culture? Will I make decisions and develop relationships based on appearance, achievement, and affluence? Will I seek to secure myself by seeking honor and status, by accumulating possessions, and by making sure I look good to the people who can ensure my success? Or will I die to my ego, to my selfish ambition and greed, to my pursuit of position and power, and trust fully in the provision of God's grace, following Jesus in the way of forgiveness, humility, sacrifice, service, and compassion for all people? Who's in charge? Am I in charge or is Christ in charge?

Questions for Reflection and Discussion

1. Do you agree with the depiction of Jesus' miracles in the Gospels as "acts of power" that signify the inbreaking of God's kingdom into the world? Do you think it is necessary for disciples today to share the ancient worldview regarding the demonic? How might we apply this language today? How might we understand "miracles" today?

2. How important is it to have a "correct" belief? In what ways do our "beliefs" make a difference? In what ways do our "beliefs" not make much difference? How is faith as trust related to what we believe? How would you describe an invitation to faith?

3. How does faith help us when our life is engulfed in darkness?

4. How can we think of faith as both a gift from God and as a human activity demanding human initiative and effort? What can we do to nurture faith?

5. Do you believe in "miracles"? How do you define a miracle? What kind of "signs" do you need to be convinced that God loves you?

6. Is desperation a legitimate context for the nurturing of faith? What might a desperate faith look like today? What form might it take?

7. Why do some people settle for religion that offers quick fixes and easy solutions? How can we move beyond a shallow and superficial faith to one that has substance and depth? How difficult is it to "ride the monsters" down into the darkness in order to find solid ground on which to stand? Can you share a personal experience?

8. If Jesus' attitude toward suffering reflects God's attitude toward suffering, why does God not intervene in human affairs to rectify the wrongs and heal the sick?

9. Life in this world can be so all-consuming that we can practically lose interest in God's new world. What can we do to remain faithful and cultivate a daily, vibrant faith?

Notes

1. Raymond E. Brown, *An Introduction to New Testament Christology* (New York: Paulist Press, 1994), 64.

2. It is possible to translate the phrase as "the kingdom of God is within you"; but in the context Jesus is addressing Pharisees who were antagonistic toward him and his teaching, so the most likely rendering is "among you" or "in your midst."

3. Harvey Cox, *When Jesus Came to Harvard: Making Moral Choices Today* (New York: Houghton Mifflin Company, 2004), 181.

4. Albert Nolan, *Jesus Before Christianity* (Maryknoll NY: Orbis Books, 1976), 44.

5. This passage forms a climax to a unit of miracle stories in Mark that begins at 4:35. In 4:35-41 Jesus exercises power over the wind and waves. In 5:1-20 Jesus wields authority over demons. And here in 5:21-43 Jesus demonstrates power over disease and death.

6. Morna Hooker, *The Gospel According to Saint Mark,* Black's New Testament Commentaries, ed. Henry Chadwick (London: Hendrickson Publishers, 1991), 151.

7. Jeffery John, *The Meaning in the Miracles* (Grand Rapids: William B. Eerdmans, 2004), 105.

8. Brennan Manning, *Ruthless Trust: The Ragamuffin's Path to God* (New York: HarperSanFrancisco, 2000), 6.

9. Ibid., 5.

10. Dietrich Bonhoeffer, *The Cost of Discipleship* (New York: Simon and Schuster Inc., 1995), 64. See Bonhoeffer's excellent discussion of faith in the context of the call to discipleship, 57–78.

11. James A. Autry, *Looking Around for God: The Oddly Reverent Observations of an Unconventional Christian* (Macon GA: Smyth & Helwys Publishing, Inc., 2007), 55.

12. Manning, *Ruthless Trust*, 95–96.

13. Richard Rohr, *Hope Against Darkness: The Transforming Vision of Saint Francis in an Age of Anxiety* (Cincinnati OH: St. Anthony Messenger Press, 2001), 169.

14. The writer to the Hebrews says, "And without faith it is impossible to please God, for whoever would approach him must believe that he exists and that he rewards those who seek him" (Heb 11:6).

15. See John 3:1-8.

16. See Paul's great exposition of "God for us" in Romans 8:31-39.

17. Autry, *Looking Around for God*, 136.

18. Richard Rohr, *Everything Belongs: The Gift of Contemplative Prayer*, rev. and updated ed. (New York: Crossroad Publishing Company), 60–61.

19. *Signs*, dir. and written by M. Night Shyamalan, Touchstone Pictures, 2002.

20. Philip Gulley, *Home to Harmony* (New York: HarperSanFrancisco, 2002), 213–20.

21. Barbara Brown Taylor, *The Luminous Web: Essays on Science and Religion* (Cambridge MA: Cowley Publications, 2000), 55.

22. Fred Craddock, *Craddock Stories*, ed. Mike Graves and Richard F. Ward (St. Louis: Chalice Press, 2001), 110–11.

23. Ibid.

24. Parker Palmer, *Let Your Life Speak: Listening for the Voice of Vocation* (San Francisco: Jossey-Bass, 2000), 66.

25. Ibid., 84.

26. Quoted by Parker Palmer, *The Active Life: A Spirituality of Work, Creativity, and Caring* (San Francisco: Jossey-Bass, 1990), 30.

27. Arland Hultgren notes that the word translated as "going . . . ahead of you" in the NRSV normally refers to a temporal or spatial sequence (to precede, to go before) rather than exclusion. "Therefore the door is left open for the Pharisees finally to repent and enter the kingdom—but they shall be at the end of the line" (Arland J. Hultgren, *The Parables of Jesus: A Commentary* [Grand Rapids: William B. Eerdmans Pub. Co., 2000], 222).

28. Hultgren, *Parables of Jesus*, 224–25.

Chapter 4

Stories of Grace and Hope

Jesus, as a teacher of wisdom, drew lessons from nature and everyday life: "Do not worry about your life. . . . Look at the birds of the air; they neither sow nor reap nor gather into barns, and yet your heavenly Father feeds them. Are you not of more value than they?" (Matt 7:25-26). He was the master of the short, one-liner that evoked the imagination in a variety of ways and elicited thoughtful reflection. Some of these sayings are like riddles that thrive on paradox: "The first shall be last and the last shall be first"; "The one who seeks to save his life will lose it, but the one who loses his life will find it." Others are even more enigmatic and cryptic: "Leave the dead to bury the dead." Still others are intended to shock, making vivid use of personification and hyperbole: "If your right eye causes you to sin, tear it out . . . if your right hand causes you to sin, cut it off." These sayings "tease the imagination into activity, suggest more than they say, and invite a transformation in perception."[1]

Jesus also taught in parables. Some parables are rather simple comparisons and analogies, not much different than the aphorisms (short, memorable sayings) just mentioned: "You are the light of the world. A city built on a hill cannot be hid. No one after lighting a lamp puts it under the bushel basket, but on the lampstand, and it gives light to all in the house. In the same way, let your light shine before others, so that they may see your good works and give glory to your Father in heaven" (Matt 5:14-16).

Jesus' most famous parables are his stories that are true, but not factual. In a preface to one of his books, storyteller Philip Gulley says, "I am a storyteller, not a historian. History is about facts; stories are about truth. It's important to know the difference. If I were a historian, every memory in this book would be precisely factual. Since I'm a storyteller I don't have to labor under that burden."[2] Jesus' stories are not historical accounts, but they are true; they illustrate and reveal truth about life in God's new world, as we have already demonstrated by means of the Luke 15 parables in chapter 2. Jesus' stories are like sacred myths; stories "about the way things never were, but always are."[3]

Paradoxically, they also conceal truth. In Jesus' life setting, his opponents were continually looking for ways to discredit and entrap him. Rome would quickly squelch any message that might arouse militaristic or political aspirations among the Jews. Jesus' opponents would have been quick to twist his words to cause him trouble with the Roman authorities.[4] While his stories evoke thought about God's new world, they do so in a somewhat veiled way.

Most of Jesus' stories have a down-to-earth, real-life character to them and are drawn from common, everyday observations and experiences of life. Yet the truth Jesus sought to reveal by these stories is not necessarily self-evident. In other words, the stories often mean something different than what we might think at first, and they may have a jarring effect on the mind and heart. Episcopal priest Robert Capon observes that with Jesus, "the device of parabolic utterance is used not to explain things to people's satisfaction but to call attention to the unsatisfactoriness of all their previous explanations and understandings."[5]

Jesus' stories have a way of disarming the listener so that truth can slip in through the back door. Eugene Peterson writes,

> As people heard Jesus tell these stories, they saw at once that they weren't about God, so there was nothing in them threatening their own sovereignty. They relaxed their defenses. They walked away perplexed, wondering what they meant, the stories lodged in their imagination. And then, like a time bomb, they would explode in their unprotected hearts. An abyss opened up at their very feet. He *was* talking about God; they had been invaded![6]

My purpose here is to highlight a few of Jesus' parables that have the potential to open our eyes to see God's grace anew and to inspire hope in God's new world.

Surprised by Grace

In Matthew 20:1-16 Jesus says,

> For the kingdom of heaven is like a landowner who went out early in the morning to hire laborers for his vineyard. After agreeing with the laborers for the usual daily wage, he sent them into his vineyard. When he went out about nine o'clock, he saw others standing idle in the marketplace; and he said to them, "You also go into the vineyard, and I will pay you whatever is right." So they went. When he went out again about noon and about three o'clock, he did the same. And about five o'clock he went out and found others standing around; and he said to them, "Why are you standing here idle all day?" They said to him, "Because no one has hired us." He said to them, "You also go into the vineyard." When evening came, the owner of the vineyard said to the manager, "Call the laborers and give them their pay, beginning with the last and then going to the first." When those hired about five o'clock came, each of them received the usual daily wage. Now when the first came, they thought they would receive more; but each of them also received the usual daily wage. And when they received it, they grumbled against the landowner, saying, "These last worked only one hour, and you have made them equal to us who have borne the burden of the day and the scorching heat." But he replied to one of them, "Friend, I am doing you no wrong; did you not agree with me for the usual daily wage? Take what belongs to you and go; I choose to give to this last the same as I give to you. Am I not allowed to do what I choose with what belongs to me? Or are you envious because I am generous? So the last will be first, and the first will be last."

What is your initial reaction to this story? Suppose the story came from someone other than Jesus; would you like it? The workers who put in the most time and effort and who bore the heat of the day are paid the same wage as those who worked only one hour. If we could transport this scenario into a modern setting, we might imagine lawsuits and picket lines with signs reading, "Management Unfair to Labor." They have a good case, don't they?

We learn to protest at an early age. One Sunday a pastor decided to use the children's sermon to teach the children about inequality. He first invited only the children with blond hair to come forward. He told them how special they were and gave them each several M&Ms. Then he asked the rest of the children to come forward and stand to the other side. They expected positive words and certainly candy, but they received neither. In fact, the pastor announced that he had nothing for them. An awkward period of silence followed. Then the pastor asked the children if they noticed anything unfair. A feisty blond-haired girl, pointing her finger at a little blond-haired boy, blurted out, "It's not fair. You gave him three M&Ms and only gave me two." In our culture, protest is almost a way of life. Of course, if you were among the workers who worked only one hour and got an entire day's wage, you might see the situation from a different perspective. One's perspective has a lot to do with where one stands.

It is illuminating to situate this parable in its context in Matthew's Gospel. Jesus has just informed the twelve that they will have a special role in judging the twelve tribes of Israel. Then he says, "And everyone who has left houses or brothers or sisters or father or mother or children or fields, for my name's sake, will receive a hundredfold, and will inherit eternal life" (Matt 19:29). This promise is a response to Peter's reaction after the rich young official walks away when Jesus asks him to give his wealth to the poor and become a disciple. Peter says, "Look, we have left everything and followed you. What then will we have?" (Matt 19:27). Obviously, Peter is thinking, What reward will we receive for making this kind of sacrifice?

The parable of the workers follows this interchange. After sharing the story, Jesus predicts his death, and a power struggle ensues between the disciples as they jostle for seats at the head table. James and John seek positions of sitting on Jesus' right and left in his kingdom. In their thinking, Jesus' kingship means exercising power, wielding authority, and occupying places of prestige and honor.

Perhaps, at the time when Matthew's Gospel was written, long-term members in the church were grumbling over the special care and consideration given to "newcomers" who hadn't paid their dues. Or perhaps some Jewish Christians resented the leadership being exercised by former pagans who converted to Christ. We all understand such tensions.

In the context of Jesus' ministry, I suspect some of the Pharisees and teachers of the law, who were upset with his acceptance and inclusion of "sinners," realized that Jesus had them in mind when he talked about the envious grumblers. Jesus was attracting a sizable following among the very people they excluded.

Jennifer Jones won an academy award for the title role in the movie *The Song of Bernadette*. Bernadette receives a vision of the Immaculate Conception and becomes a celebrity. An older nun, consumed by envy, prays, "Why her? No one has prayed harder, worked longer, and suffered greater than I. Why her and not me?" Later in the story Bernadette collapses while scrubbing the floor. After examining her, the doctor talks to the older nun. He asks, "Has she never complained?" "No," says the envious nun, "she just quietly does her work." The doctor responds, "That's amazing. The affliction she has, she has had a very long time and the pain is unbearable." Later, the older nun repents of her envy and prays, "God, forgive me. Thank you for the opportunity to serve the one you have chosen."[7]

Why do we struggle with envy and resentment toward those who are favored? Why must we engage in petty comparisons? Why can't we simply rejoice in the fact that we have been chosen at all? Robert Capon writes,

> Bookkeeping is the only punishable offense in the kingdom of heaven. For in that happy state, the *books* are ignored forever, and there is only the *Book* of life. And in that book, nothing stands against you. There are no debit entries that can keep you out of the clutches of the Love that will not let you go. There is no minimum balance below which the grace that finagles all accounts will cancel your credit. And there is, of course, no need for you to show large amounts of black ink, because the only Auditor before whom you must finally stand is the Lamb—and he has gone deaf, dumb, and blind on the cross.[8]

The parable contrasts two ways of thinking about life and our relationship to God. One way is rooted in the system of meritocracy, based upon rewards and punishments. Worth is determined by performance. Time invested and actual work accomplished are key factors in assessing value. Worth is earned.

The workers hired at the beginning of the day operate under this system. The owner agrees to pay them the usual daily wage. They enter a contract that stipulates a specific amount—a fair day's wage for a fair day's work. The other workers do not enter into a contract with the owner. The owner recruits them, saying, "Go work in my vineyard, and I will pay you whatever is right." No stipulation regarding the amount, no guaranteed wage, just "I will do you right." So they go to work in the vineyard, trusting that the owner of the vineyard will give them what is right. At the end of the day, "what is right" is turned upside down.

Let me offer a positive word about the concept of reward. As New Testament scholar Eduard Schweizer observes, there is "no polemic against this concept" in the story.[9] Just prior to the telling of this story, Jesus promises the disciples that they will participate in the future administration of the people of God ("the twelve tribes of Israel") and that they will be more than compensated for their sacrifices. But any reward we receive must be regarded as an expression of God's goodness, not something we deserve or earn. The moment when we begin to think we deserve a reward is the moment we start comparing our reward to that of others, which is what happens in the story.

Those who were hired first for a set wage are the last to receive payment. As they stand around waiting for their wage, they see what the others are paid and start comparing. "Here is a group that worked only one hour, and here is another group that worked only three hours, and these groups are receiving the same wage as us, who have born the burden of the work and the heat of the day." They cry, "Unfair!" But the owner says, "How is it not fair? I gave you a fair wage for your work. Now, if I want to be generous with the rest of the workers that I asked to work in my vineyard, do I not have that right? Are you envious because I am generous?"

The workers hired first received what they agreed to—a just wage. The other workers received what they didn't expect—more than what they deserved. Both groups were surprised by the generosity of the owner, but the first group wasn't happy about it at all.

Envy is the result of comparing ourselves to others, an attitude that plagues the one who lives by a system of merit and reward. Those who live by the system of meritocracy constantly look over their shoulder to see what others are getting. It's fertile breeding ground for envy, jealousy, and covetousness.

Parables do not speak to all situations. Obviously, this story says nothing about how people suffering severe oppression should respond in their unique context. This parable addresses Christ's disciples and church members who are comparing and competing for rewards and honors. It confronts us with the question, How do I want to live? Do I want to relate to God on the basis of reward and punishment, earning my way and getting what I deserve? Or do I want to entrust my life and future to God's grace?

The parable concludes, "but many who are first will be last, and the last will be first." This is one of those short, memorable one-liners that shows up in various contexts in the Gospels. It normally points to the inversion of the world's pecking order that takes place within the kingdom of God. In this context, however, it could mean that when we all stand before God and one another, we stand on the same ground. If the first become last and the last become first, then life is equalized.

The workers who were upset with the owner presumed that they would be rewarded according to the system of meritocracy. But presumption is not limited to those trying to earn their way. Christians known for a theology of grace can be presumptuous too. One might be presumptuous about getting what he thinks he deserves, and one might be presumptuous about getting better than what one deserves.

Fred Craddock tells about teaching a class on the parables some years ago. His students gravitated heavily toward these reversal parables where the offer of grace is extended to the wayward son, the publican, the servant who took big risks, and the eleventh-hour workers. The students frowned on punishing lazy stewards or slamming the door in the faces of the poor girls who forgot to fill their lamps with oil. These seminarians, says Craddock, had come to expect grace, and hence it was no longer grace, or if it was, it was cheap grace.

Craddock told them a story. There was a certain seminary professor who was strict about due dates for papers. Due dates were announced at the beginning of the semester, and failure to meet them resulted in an F for the class. In one class, three students did not meet the deadline. The first one explained, "Professor, unexpected guests from out of state came the evening before the paper was due, and I was unable to finish it." "Then you receive an F," said the professor. The second student explained, "On the day before the paper was due, I became ill with influenza and was unable to complete it." "Then you receive an F," said the professor.

The third student, visibly shaken by the news about the fate of the other two students, cautiously approached the professor's desk. Slowly he began, "Professor, our first baby was due the same day the paper was due. The evening before, my wife began having pains, and so I rushed her to the hospital and shortly after midnight she gave birth to a boy. So I couldn't complete the paper." The professor listened with interest and after a long pause said, "Then you receive an F for the course."

The news spread rapidly throughout the seminary. A large delegation of students came to the professor to protest. "Why have you been so cruel and harsh?" they asked. The professor replied, "At the beginning of the semester I gave my word concerning papers. If the word of a teacher in a Christian seminary cannot be trusted, whose word can you trust?" The students were then dismissed.

After telling the story, Craddock asked his students if they thought it was a parable. He says most of them were angry not only with the professor in the story but with Craddock for telling it. They insisted it was not a parable.[10] What do you think? Maybe when grace is expected or presumed or taken for granted, it ceases to be grace.

In one of the stories in Wendell Berry's *The Wild Birds*, Wheeler Catlett is an attorney for an old farmer named Jack Beechum. Jack dies, leaving Wheeler in charge of his affairs. The only family Jack leaves behind is his daughter, Clara Pettit, and son-in-law, Gladston Pettit, who are interested in money rather than farming. Jack and his daughter Clara never agreed on anything, but of course he still loved her.

Jack wished that his farm go to a young couple named Elton and Mary Penn, who had lived on Jack's farm for eight years, caring for the land and for Jack. Jack loved them as if they were his own children. Wheeler knows Jack's wish. The will stipulates that Jack's daughter Clara will get the land, but he left the Penns enough money to buy the land from Clara. However, Jack forgot to consider his daughter's greed.

Though he suggested that Clara sell the land for $200 an acre, he failed to establish the price in his will. Clara chooses to sell the land at public auction, anticipating a larger profit. Bidding begins at $200 an acre, and the Penns are nervous. Wheeler, however, inspired by old Jack's spirit and the desire to help, urges the Penns to keep bidding. When the auction ends, the Penns win the land. The price, though, is $300 an acre, considerably more than the Penns can afford. Wheeler covers $65 an acre, almost $10,000 out of his own pocket.

Elton Penn, a proud man, says to Wheeler, "You're saying there's not any way to get out of this friendship."

"No," says Wheeler, "you can get out of it. By not accepting it. I'm the one, so far, who can't escape it. You have it because I've given it to you, and you don't have to accept it. I gave it to you because it was given to me, and I accepted it."[11]

To be surprised by grace is a beautiful thing, and yet many of us have trouble with it. Parker Palmer writes,

> If we were to accept large areas of life as pure gift, we would be forced to acknowledge that we are not in control. Were we to live as recipients rather than makers, we might feel dependent and diminished, like clients of some cosmic welfare system that demeans our lives. If we were to affirm that we have received many gifts, that we have not earned all that we have, we might feel obliged to pass the gifts along rather than hoard our treasures to ourselves. To acknowledge that we do not and cannot make most of what

we have would strip us of too many illusions and take us too close to reality for comfort.[12]

When the illusion of our self-sufficiency is shattered and our once secure world starts to crumble, we experience the pain of loss, the confusion of being displaced, and the anxiety of an uncertain future. We may feel that life is completely out of control. The spiritual life is not about control, though; it's about relinquishment. It's about letting go of our need to determine and order life, and then trusting grace. Living by grace is God's true design. In her book *Pilgrim at Tinker Creek,* Annie Dillard writes,

> When I was six or seven years old, growing up in Pittsburgh, I used to take a precious penny of my own and hide it for someone else to find. It was a curious compulsion; sadly, I've never been seized by it since. For some reason I always "hid" the penny along the same stretch of sidewalk up the street. I would cradle it at the roots of a sycamore, say, or in a hole left by a chipped off piece of sidewalk. Then I would take a piece of chalk, and, starting at either end of the block, draw huge arrows leading up to the penny from both directions. After I learned to write, I labeled the arrows: SURPRISE AHEAD or MONEY THIS WAY. I was greatly excited, during all this arrow-drawing, at the thought of the first lucky passerby who would receive in this way, regardless of merit, a free gift from the universe. But I never lurked about. I would go straight home and not give the matter another thought, until, some months later, I would be gripped again by the impulse to hide another penny.[13]

What is the source of this impulse? Surely it comes from God, who delights in surprising us with grace. The more we reflect this impulse in our reactions and interactions with all of creation, the more clearly we reflect our true selves and the more fully we live as the daughters and sons of God in the world.

Forgiving from the Heart

In a college chapel service, Sam Moffat, a former professor at Princeton Seminary and missionary to China, shared a gripping story of his flight from Communist pursuers. He told how they seized his house and his possessions, burned the missionary compound, and killed some of his closest friends. His own family barely escaped. As he left China, he took with him a deep resentment against the followers of Chairman Mao. It led to a crisis in his faith. "I realized," he told the students, "that if I have no forgiveness for the Communists, then I have no message at all."[14]

Forgiveness was an important theme in Jesus' teaching. Consider the following parable set in the context of Peter's question about forgiveness:

> Then Peter came to Jesus and asked, "Lord, how many times shall I forgive someone who sins against me? Up to seven times?"
>
> Jesus answered, "I tell you, not seven times, but seventy-seven times. Therefore, the kingdom of heaven is like a king who wanted to settle accounts with his servants. As he began the settlement, a man who owed him billions of dollars was brought to him. Since he was not able to pay, the master ordered that he and his wife and his children and all that he had be sold to repay the debt.
>
> "The servant fell on his knees before him. 'Be patient with me,' he begged, 'and I will pay back everything.' The servants' master took pity on him, canceled the debt and let him go.
>
> "But when that servant went out, he found one of his fellow servants who owed him a few hundred dollars. He grabbed him and began to choke him, 'Pay back what you owe me!' he demanded.
>
> "His fellow servant fell to his knees and begged him, 'Be patient with me, and I will pay you back.'
>
> "But he refused. Instead, he went off and had the man thrown into prison until he could pay the debt. When the other servants saw what had happened, they were greatly distressed and went and told their master everything that had happened.
>
> "Then the master called the servant in. 'You wicked servant,' he said, 'I canceled all that debt of yours because you begged me to. Shouldn't you have had mercy on your fellow servant just as I had on you?' In anger his master handed him over to the jailers to be tortured, until he should pay back all he owed.
>
> "This is how my heavenly Father will treat each of you unless you forgive a brother or sister from your heart." (Matt 18:21-35, TNIV)

Peter had discovered in the school of Jesus that forgiveness must take the place of vengeance, but here he is still concerned about limits. It was a popular Jewish saying that a person may be forgiven up to three times but not four. Peter thinks he is being generous when he proposes to forgive seven times. Likely, he expects a commendation. Instead, he receives a response from Jesus that prompts him to marvel about life in God's new world. God's kind of forgiveness doesn't keep a running tally.

Writer Philip Yancey tells how Leo Tolstoy thought he was making the right start in his marriage when he asked his teenage fiancée to read his diaries, which spelled out the details of his past sexual dalliances. He wanted to keep no secrets from Sonya. Tolstoy's confession, however, sowed seeds of resentment and jealousy. Years later, Sonya wrote in her diary, "When he kisses me I'm always thinking, 'I'm not the first woman he has loved.'" For half a century, jealousy, resentment, and the lack of forgiveness ate away at her like a cancer, destroying any love she had for her husband. Yancey remarks, "Behind every act of forgiveness lies a wound of betrayal, and the pain of being betrayed does not easily fade away."[15]

We nurse wounds, dish out punishment, perpetuate family conflicts, nurture bitterness and resentment, and then rationalize our responses in order to avoid the unnatural act of forgiving. I read that C. S. Lewis once remarked, "Everyone says forgiveness is a lovely idea, until they have something to forgive." Forgiveness is an unnatural act because it seems unjust. If a person or persons have truly harmed us, then we reason it is only right and just for them to pay for their crime.

We can offer numerous excuses and think of a myriad of reasons not to forgive: "He needs to learn a lesson"; "I don't want to encourage irresponsible behavior"; "She needs to learn that actions have consequences"; "I was the one wronged—it's not up to me to make the first move"; or "How can I forgive if he's not even sorry?" Yancey admits,

> I never find forgiveness easy, and rarely do I find it completely satisfying. Nagging injustices remain, and the wounds still cause pain. I have to approach God again and again, yielding to him the residue of what I thought I had committed to him long ago. I do so because the Gospels make clear the connection: God forgives my debts as I forgive my debtors.[16]

In Jesus' parable from Matthew 18, the man owes the king "billions of dollars." The figure represented ten times the total annual revenue of King Herod's kingdom—an astronomical amount. Schweizer comments, "The sum is made up of the highest number used in arithmetic and the largest monetary unit employed in the ancient Near East."[17] Amazingly, the king has pity on the servant and forgives the debt. It's hard to imagine that anyone, after receiving such mercy, would be so unforgiving, demanding payment in full from a man who owed him a few hundred dollars. When the king discovers the servant's hardheartedness, he reverses his decision and throws him into prison.[18] Then this point is made: "This is how my heavenly Father will treat each of you unless you forgive a brother or sister from your heart."

We might draw the mistaken notion that forgiveness is something to be earned by our own willingness to forgive. Forgiveness, however, cannot be merited, for then it would not be forgiveness. Jesus is teaching something basic about the intrinsic nature of forgiveness. The experience of forgiveness—emotionally, psychologically, spiritually—necessitates a forgiving spirit. The man in the parable, though offered forgiveness, never really receives or experiences it for himself (perhaps he even lived with the illusion that somehow he would pay it all back). It is simply not possible to claim forgiveness for myself and not extend it to others. We must share forgiveness in order to experience it authentically.

It's not that God will not permit me to experience forgiveness; I simply cannot experience it if I do not know how to give it. For example, if I don't know how to work with equations and fractions, I can't do algebra. It's not a matter of someone not allowing me to do algebra; I simply cannot solve the problems without a working knowledge of equations and fractions, which are intrinsic to the nature of algebra. It is the same with forgiveness. We cannot experience/receive forgiveness unless we have a forgiving spirit. Such is the way forgiveness works in relationships.

It is important to understand Jesus' teaching on forgiveness in the context of a relational framework. We have already seen how Jesus imagines and relates to God as a compassionate Parent. Jesus' teaching on forgiveness must be understood within this familial setting.

A popular view sees divine forgiveness as a binding, judicial pronouncement that applies only when certain conditions are met. God is portrayed as the divine judge who must condemn humanity under the penalty of the broken law. We are forgiven (saved, justified, etc.) if we believe the right doctrine (usually understood as believing that Jesus died in our place for our sin-guilt) and if we respond in the right way (accept Jesus into our hearts, say the sinner's prayer, believe, and be baptized, etc.). Jesus, of course, has something else in mind.

A commonly asked question is, "What about the person who is not sorry for his offense or does not seek forgiveness?" I may say to someone who has hurt me, "I forgive you," only to have them say, "What do you mean? I didn't do anything." I can forgive, but the person I forgive cannot authentically receive or experience forgiveness until he or she owns his or her part in the breach. This is the meaning of Jesus' words of forgiveness from the cross: "Father, forgive them for they do not know what they are doing" (Luke 23:34). Those involved in the crucifixion of Jesus obviously were not open to receive Jesus' forgiveness, but Jesus could still forgive them. We can forgive even if the recipients are not able to receive the forgiveness we offer.

Forgiveness does not automatically result in reconciliation. These are two different issues. Consider the parable of the waiting father. The father forgives the son even before he confesses; full reconciliation, however, depends on the son's humble, sincere repentance.

The experience of forgiveness does not mean the relationship will be what it was before. It can never be what it was before. In some cases, forgiveness might lead to a restored relationship that is healthier and more truthful. In other situations, the relationship may suffer greatly, and full reconciliation or renewal of trust may be impossible. Either way, the relationship has changed.

The parable of the king settling accounts prompts us to think of forgiveness as a release from a debt and the surrender of our right for repayment. Forgiveness says, "I am not going to punish you for your offense. I am not going to make you pay for what you did (though there may be consequences that involve suffering). I refuse to be enslaved by resentment, and I let go of my right for revenge." Richard Rohr tells about his conversation with a group of black men in the Virgin Islands. They said, "We want to be Christians, but when we go back to our friends, all they say is that it was the Catholic Church that justified slavery. Jesuit priests kept slaves." Rohr replied, "I don't know my history well enough. Maybe that was true. But can't you let it go? We only have one life. Right now. We can always find a justification for our anger." One responded, "Father, we're willing to let go of it, but our culture keeps reminding us of it. Everybody says, 'Why are you going to be a Catholic? Why a Christian? Those religions don't free us. They oppress us.'" Rohr later reflected on this experience, writing, "I just want to sigh with pain for God's people. How can anyone move us forward? How can anyone free us when we constantly hold on to our hurts? And especially when most of the hurts really happened? History has become a giant glacial freeze of remembered hurts and justified retaliation."[19] The act of forgiveness is an act of letting go.

Forgiveness, however, is not forgetting. When the Scripture says God remembers our sin no more, that does not mean God eradicates our sin from his memory. It means God decides not to make us pay for it. We must not let anyone convince us that "if we haven't forgotten, then we haven't forgiven"; this idea can be psychologically and spiritually hurtful. On the other hand, we may want to ask God to help us forget, because remembering brings us pain. Even so, just because we still have pain does not mean we haven't forgiven.

Much of the need for forgiveness arises in families, who interact daily. Those who hurt us want us to stop hurting because our hurting reminds them of their offense. They may even insinuate that if we are still hurting, then we haven't forgiven. We must refuse to take on that burden. We live in a culture where we have made it sinful to hurt, and much inner pain and anxiety comes from not being able to hurt. It's okay to hurt. In fact, our acceptance of suffering and pain will cut the quantity of it immensely. Surely, part of what it means to suffer with Christ is the suffering we absorb when we decide to forgive.

Forgiveness is the fresh breeze that blows through God's new creation. James Bryan Smith says,

> For years I understood the phrase "love covers a multitude of sins" (1 Pet. 4:8) to mean that by loving others I could cover up my sins. Because I had many sins, I thought I had better try to love a lot! Then one day it hit me: love for one another leads us to cover their sins. When I am immersed in God's love and acceptance and forgiveness I am drawn to forgive the sins of the people around me. I lose my desire for revenge and find myself longing to show mercy.[20]

Forgiveness is always an act or process of faith that is enabled by the grace of God. When we decide to forgive, we are stepping out into the flow of God's Spirit, and God will certainly meet us there and bear us up. When we decide to forgive, we decide to breathe the air of God's new world and live as the daughters and sons of God.

In Due Time

The Gospel of Matthew (also Luke) connects two short parables of Jesus together that relate to the same theme,

> He put before them another parable: "The kingdom of heaven is like a mustard seed that someone took and sowed in the field; it is the smallest of all the seeds, but when it has grown it is the greatest of shrubs and becomes a tree, so that the birds of the air come and make nests in its branches."

He told them another parable: "The kingdom of heaven is like yeast that a woman took and mixed in with three measures of flour until all of it was leavened." (Matt 13:31-33)

Both stories contrast an insignificant beginning with a glorious ending. The new world ushered in by Jesus begins small, but one day it will extend into all of life. The mustard seed is the smallest of seeds and yet is "the greatest of shrubs and becomes a tree." The reference to birds nesting in the branches, drawing from an Old Testament image, probably refers to the incorporation of the Gentiles into the people of God, a mission that was well underway when these Gospels were written.[21]

The images of God's new world depicted in these brief parables are somewhat anti-apocalyptic. Whereas other parables of Jesus suggest that God's new world breaks in through a decisive, cataclysmic event, here it emerges from obscure beginnings. New Testament scholar Joachim Jeremias puts it this way: "How differently the beginnings of the Messianic Age announced by Jesus appeared than was commonly expected! Could this wretched band, comprising so many disreputable characters, be the wedding guests of God's redeemed community? 'Yes,' says Jesus, 'it is.'"[22]

These stories are stories of hope. Jerome Groopman, a professor at Harvard Medical School, has written a book titled *The Anatomy of Hope*. In an interview, he said, "I think hope has been, is, and always will be the heart of medicine and healing. We could not live without hope." He observed that even with all the medical technology available to us now, "we still come back to this profound human need to believe that there is a possibility to reach a future that is better than the one in the present." When pressed to define hope, he said, "Basically, I think hope is the ability to see a path to the future." He contended that it is the capacity to see a path ahead in spite of all that's blocking or threatening.[23] Jesus holds out the prospect of a glorious future. These parables do not tell us how God's new world will come to fulfillment; they simply assure us that in God's time the kingdom will come.

The workings of God's new world are not evident to all. This seems to be the point of the leaven mixed into the dough ("hid in the dough" is the literal Greek). The kind of kingdom Jesus inaugurated is not the kind most expected. What kind of king rides into Jerusalem on a donkey instead of a warhorse? What kind of king comes in humility and meekness instead of pomp and pageantry? What kind of king willingly submits to his captors without a fight?

The power of God's new world—the power of love and justice for all—is at work in the world, and it will, in God's time, transform the world. We don't know how or when. The teachings of Jesus in the Gospels do not resolve the tensions between our part and God's part in the fulfillment of the promise. Will it come suddenly? Will it take place gradually? Will God intervene? Will it be mainly through human instrumentality? We don't know. We do, however, see the power of this new world demonstrated through Jesus' words and deeds. Jesus' healings of the diseased and demonized bear witness to God's power at work to repair the world's alienation in all its forms. God has acted, is acting, and will act to bring in the new world.

New Testament scholar Russell Pregeant offers a perceptive, cautionary word on the pitfalls we must avoid as we struggle to understand Jesus' teaching about the kingdom of God.

> The image of the rule of God/heaven cannot be disconnected from the themes of peace and justice [recall our discussion in chapter 1], but neither can it be abstracted from the notion of God's past, present, and future action in the world. It is inherently eschatological in that it looks forward to an action of God that results in the reordering of human society, but it is also focused on the concrete realities of human life in the actual world. It is thus important to find ways to relate this image to the world we know without falling into any of these three common pitfalls: a purely futuristic reading that tends to allow the hope for divine intervention to negate the need for social activism, a "modernist" approach that reduces the announcement of God's action to a call for human endeavor, an individualism that locates God's rule in one's heart and thus ignores its collective dimension.[24]

Faith lays hold of the promise of future fulfillment while engaging the present in the pursuit of justice, peace, and the good of creation in cooperation with the Spirit of God at work in our world.

The movie *A Beautiful Mind* tells the story of John Nash, played by Russell Crowe, who is a brilliant mathematician struggling with mental instability. His marriage is a testimony to true commitment through years of illness and trial. On the evening he proposes, the following conversation ensues.

Nash says, "Alicia, does our relationship warrant long-term commitment? I need some kind of proof, some kind of verifiable empirical data."

Alicia, amused by his awkwardness, says, "Sorry, I'm just trying to get over my girlish notions of romance." Then she wonders out loud, "Hmmm . . . proof . . . verifiable data . . . okay. How big is the universe?"

"Infinite."

"How do you know?"

"I know because all the data indicates it's infinite."

"But it hasn't been proven yet?"

"No."

"You haven't seen it?"

"No,"

"How do you know for sure?"

"I don't. I just believe."

"It's the same with love, I guess."[25]

It's the same for faith. The first disciples witnessed the presence and love of God in a special way through their association with Jesus of Nazareth, and as a consequence of his resurrection they became convinced that the love they experienced through his life and ministry would one day transform the world.

A little girl approached her father, who was in his study preparing his sermon for Sunday. She asked rather timidly, "Daddy, can we play?" Her father told her that he couldn't play because he was in the middle of preparing his sermon, but he would play when he finished. She said, "Okay, when you're finished, Daddy, I am going to give you a big hug." She turned to leave, but when she got to the door she did a big U-turn, came running back to her father, and as he reached down for her she wrapped her arms around him and squeezed as hard as she could. He said, "Honey, you said you were going to give me a hug after I finished." She answered, "Daddy, I just wanted you to know what you have to look forward to." In the little expressions of love and compassion now, people of faith see signs of things to come. They give us hope and inspire us to engage our world through works of mercy and justice in anticipation of God's redemption of all creation.

These parables of Jesus hold out hope for all who see little fruit for their effort and grapple with disappointments and setbacks. There are times when it seems as if nothing will ever change; the world with its powerful economic, political, social, and religious structures negates and diminishes the pursuit of peace and justice to apparent insignificance. Disciples of Jesus must cling to the promise of these parables—that the insignificant, obscure beginnings will one day transform the planet; that the way of Christ, the way of justice and compassion, the way of grace and forgiveness, will one day be realized on earth, and it will come to pass not through independent human achievement, but through the power and work of God.

Pastor Bruce Thielemann tells about a flight to Europe where he sat next to a nervous elderly lady. When he asked if it was her first flight, she said, "No. I'm always nervous when I fly." Then she countered, "But it won't be bad this trip." He asked why, and she explained, "We're flying into the morning. We're flying toward the dawn." As followers of Christ, this is a good thing to remember when the darkness seems overwhelming and we can't see our way through. We are flying toward the morning, toward the dawn of a new world that God will cause to rise.

It is good to be reminded that the Gospel writer who passed on these Jesus stories also gave us a word of assurance that God will never abandon us. After God raised Jesus from the dead, the living Christ met with his disciples on a hill in Galilee. He entrusted them with a mission and ministry of instructing others in his way, and then he said, "And remember, I am with you always, to the end of the age" (Matt 28:20). We are not alone or on our own. In due time, God's new world, which has already broken through, will shine over all the earth with the brightness of the noonday sun.

Questions for Reflection and Discussion

1. Do you think a parable can work in our culture the same way it worked in Jesus' culture—disarming the listener so the truth of God's new world can sneak in?
2. In the parable of the day laborers, do you think the workers who bore the heat of the day and received the same wage as the others had a right to be angry? What do you think is the central message/teaching of this parable?
3. Is it possible to be presumptuous regarding God's grace? Can you think of an example?
4. Do you agree with the perspective that forgiveness cannot be received without a forgiving spirit (see Matt 6:14-15)?
5. Is there such a thing as unconditional forgiveness? How does it relate to reconciliation? What is the difference between forgiveness and reconciliation?
6. How do you define forgiveness? What are the essential components of forgiveness? Is it an act or a process?
7. How do you deal with the obvious tension in the parables and teachings of Jesus that suggests on the one hand that the fullness of God's new

world will come suddenly, and on the other hand that it will come gradually? How do you envision it coming?

8. In your own words, describe the key elements of a vital hope.

Notes

1. Marcus Borg, *Meeting Jesus Again for the First Time: The Historical Jesus and the Heart of Contemporary Faith* (New York: HarperSanFrancisco, 1994), 71.

2. Philip Gulley, *Hometown Tales: Recollections of Kindness, Peace, and Joy* (New York: Harper SanFrancisco, 2001), 9.

3. Attributed to German novelist Thomas Mann, quoted by Marcus J. Borg, *The Heart of Christianity: Rediscovering a Life of Faith* (New York: HarperSanFrancisco, 2003), 50.

4. Robert H. Stein, *The Method and Message of Jesus' Teaching*, rev. ed. (Louisville: Westminster John Knox Press, 1994), 39-40.

5. Robert Farrar Capon, *Kingdom, Grace, Judgment: Paradox, Outrage, and Vindication in the Parables of Jesus* (Grand Rapids: William B. Eerdmans, 2002), 5.

6. Eugene Peterson, *Living the Message: Daily Help for Living the God-Centered Life*, ed. Janice Stubbs Peterson (New York: HarperSanFrancisco, 1996), 13–14.

7. *The Song of Bernadette*, dir. Henry King, written by Franz Werfel, 20th Century Fox, 1943.

8. Capon, *Kingdom, Grace, Judgment*, 395–96.

9. Eduard Schweizer, *The Good News According to Matthew*, trans. David E. Green (Atlanta: John Knox Press, 1975), 393.

10. Fred Craddock, *Craddock Stories*, ed. Mike Graves and Richard F. Ward (St. Louis: Chalice Press, 2001), 18–19.

11. Wendell Berry, *The Wild Birds* (San Francisco: North Point Press, 1986), 45–73.

12. Parker Palmer, *The Active Life: A Spirituality of Work, Creativity, and Caring* (San Francisco: Jossey-Bass, 1990), 50–51.

13. Annie Dillard, *Pilgrim at Tinker Creek* (New York: Harper & Row, 1974), 14–15.

14. Philip Yancey, *What's So Amazing about Grace* (Grand Rapids: Zondervan, 1997), 90.

15. Ibid., 85.

16. Ibid., 93.

17. Schweizer, *The Good News According to Matthew*, 377.

18. "And in anger his lord handed him over to be tortured until he would pay his entire debt" (18:34). The wording here is characteristic of Matthew, who tends to embellish pronouncements of judgment, giving them a harsher and more vindictive tone.

19. Richard Rohr, *The Good News According to Luke: Spiritual Reflections* (New York: Crossroad Publishing Company, 1997), 115–16.

20. James Bryan Smith, *Embracing the Love of God: The Path and Promise of Christian Life* (New York: HarperSanFrancisco, 1995), 107.

21. Joachim Jeremias, *The Parables of Jesus,* second rev. ed. (Upper Saddle River, NJ: Prentice Hall, 1972), 149.

22. Ibid., 149.

23. Reported by Rachel K. Sobel, "The Mysteries of Hope and Healing," *U.S. News and World Report,* 26 January 2004.

24. Russell Pregeant, *Matthew,* Chalice Commentaries for Today (St. Louis: Chalice Press, 2004), 42.

25. *A Beautiful Mind,* dir. Ron Howard, written by Akiva Goldsman, Universal, 2001.

Chapter 5

Living in God's New World

Fred Craddock tells how he and his wife used to vacation in the Smoky Mountains. On one trip, they left the kids at Grandma's house and stopped to eat at a new restaurant called the Black Bear Inn. One side of the restaurant was solid glass, offering a splendid view of the mountains as they dined.

The couple relaxed, looking at the huge menu. Fred was trying to find the hamburgers. An old man, well advanced in years, came by their table.

"Good evenin'," said the old man.

"Good evenin'," responded Fred.

"Ya'll on vacation?" asked the man.

"Yes sir."

"Havin' a good time?"

Fred was beginning to think, *Well, we were*, but he said, "Yes sir."

"Ya'll gonna be here very long?" Fred thought, *Maybe not.*

"No, we won't be here but a week."

"I hope you have a good time. What do you do?" Fred thought, *That's none of his business. We're on vacation. We got rid of the kids. I'm going to get rid of this old man.*

"Well, I teach in seminary. I'm a Christian minister."

"What church?"

"The Christian church."

The old man paused for a moment, then said, "I owe a great deal to a minister of the Christian church," and with that he pulled up a chair and sat down. He told this story:

> I grew up in these mountains. My mother wasn't married, and in those days, such shame. And when we went to town, the other women looked at her and looked at me, and began to guess who I was and who my father was, and the reproach that was hers fell upon me. And it was painful. At school the children said ugly things to me, and so I stayed to myself during recess, and I ate my lunch alone.
>
> In my early teens I started going to a little church back in the mountains called Laurel Springs Christian Church. There was a preacher; a cranky, rough preacher, both attractive and frightening. He had a chiseled face and a heavy beard and a deep voice. He scared me but he fascinated me. I would go just for the sermon and then get out quick because I was afraid somebody would speak to me and say, "What's a boy like you doing in church?" And I was afraid.
>
> One Sunday after I'd been going for some time some of the people queued up the aisle and I couldn't rush out as I usually did. I couldn't get by. I began to chill. I thought, "Oh no, somebody will say something to me. I need to get out of here."
>
> Then I felt a hand on my shoulder, and I looked out of the corner of my eye and it was that preacher. I saw his beard and I saw that face, and I thought, "Oh no!" And that preacher looked at me and said, "Well boy, you're a child of . . ." and he paused and I was thinking, "Oh no, here it comes." I knew it was coming. I knew I would have my feelings hurt. He said, "Boy, you're a child of . . . a child of God. I see a striking resemblance."
>
> Then he swatted me on the bottom and said, "Now, you go claim your inheritance." I left the building a different person. In fact, that was really the beginning of my life.

Fred was so moved by the story that he asked, "What's your name?"

"Ben Hooper," said the man.

Ben Hooper, thought Fred. *Where have I heard that name before?* Fred recalled, though vaguely, his own father talking years ago about how the people of Tennessee had twice elected as governor a bastard named Ben Hooper.[1]

We are called to be God's children, claim our inheritance, and live in God's new world. In this chapter I want to consider some of the teachings of Jesus that indicate the kind of personal and practical transformation entailed by living in God's new world.

Growing Up by Growing Down

Jesus compares life in God's new world to that of becoming like children:

> People were bringing little children to Jesus for him to touch them, but the disciples rebuked them. When Jesus saw this, he was indignant. He said to them, "Let the little children come to me, and do not hinder them, for the kingdom of God belongs to such as these. Truly I tell you, anyone who will not receive the kingdom of God like a little child will never enter it." And he took the children in his arms, put his hands on them and blessed them. (Mark 10:13-16, TNIV)

A dominant attitude in that culture devalued children; they were endured, "put up with," until they could take on adult responsibility. Children existed in order to become adults. Jesus obviously did not share this prevailing outlook and expected better from his disciples. As an expression of genuine love and as a symbolic gesture conveying the joy of belonging to and participating in God's new world, Jesus gathered the little children in his arms, placed his hands on each one, and blessed them. Not perceiving the significance of Jesus' actions, the disciples reprimanded the parents, and Jesus grew angry with them. The disciples were slow to break old habits and learn new ways. Learning to live in God's new world can be a slow, difficult process full of reversals and setbacks as we "unlearn" so many things.

In Jesus' eyes, the little children were precious. What the world deems obscure, trivial, insignificant, weak, and unimportant are often the very things that Jesus esteems of tremendous value. In Jesus' tender expression of love for the little children, we have another indication of God's inclusive, unconditional love that breaks through all boundaries and embraces all persons.

Jesus is not suggesting that little children are always good, sweet, and innocent—we know better. I am told that, during our childhood, my brother was the good baby. He was trouble later. Edie, my sister, was the inquisitive one. Two episodes stand out in my mind—opening the bathroom door to find Edie dipping a hairbrush into the toilet and combing her hair, and getting up one morning to find Edie in the refrigerator, hands in the mustard jar, rubbing it like cream all over her body. Edie loved to entertain.

I was trouble—selfish and stubborn. I hoarded my toys and acted like a defensive tackle trying to stop an end-run when anyone got close to touching them. My mother disciplined me, which in those days meant I got a swat on the rear end before having a time out, though it wasn't called "time out"—it was called "you sit there until I tell you that you can get up!" Mom would swat me on the bottom, sit me down, and dare me to move. She shouldn't have dared me. When her head was turned, I would ease out of the chair ever so slowly until eventually I was sitting not in the chair, but on the floor. She would find me there, swat me another time, sit me back down, and say, "Don't you dare get up until I say so!" Inevitably I would do what she told me not to do, and the process would start again.

Little children are little sinners. Jesus is not saying a child is innocent and always good. But children are naïve and dependent, and if they are cared for they are naturally trusting. Most children believe what they hear and receive openly and confidently what is given to them. They do not earn their keep; they live off the generosity and love of caregivers. New Testament scholar Morna Hooker notes, "The Kingdom belongs to them because they have nothing on which they can base a claim, but are content to receive the Kingdom as a gift; their attitude is akin to what Paul describes as 'faith,' which humbly receives God's grace."[2]

We have nothing to offer God except ourselves; we can claim no exclusive privilege. We must acknowledge our littleness, weakness, vulnerability, and need for help. We must cease trying to earn our way and let go of our arrogance, selfish ambition, and egocentricity.[3] The proud and arrogant, the power hungry and approval driven cannot experience the dynamic reality of God's new world. Blinded by egocentricity and deaf to the still, small voice of the Spirit, they are preoccupied with the "adult" stuff of life. God's new world is a gift for little children who are not yet fully indoctrinated into the game of judging and comparing, resisting and denying, controlling and dominating. Unless we are willing to be born again, unless we are willing to become like a little child, we will miss it.

Marcus Borg tells the story of a little girl, about three years old, who gained a new baby brother. When the parents brought the baby home from the hospital, the little girl made a strange request: she wanted to be alone with her new brother in his room with the door shut. The parents were uneasy at first, but then remembered that they had installed an intercom system in anticipation of the baby's arrival, so they agreed. They listened as their daughter walked across the room, and they imagined her standing over the baby's crib. Then they heard her say to her three-day-old brother, "Tell me about God—I've almost forgotten." Borg declares,

> The story is both haunting and evocative, for it suggests that we come from God, and that when we are very young, we still remember this, still know this. But the process of growing up, of learning about this world, is a process of increasingly forgetting the one from whom we came and in whom we live. The birth and intensification of self-consciousness, of self-awareness, involves a separation from God.[4]

The process of socialization drives us more deeply into the world of self-concern and self-occupation; we cannot help being shaped to some degree by our culture and the messages we receive from our "world." Out of this shaping process emerges the "false self" in contrast to the "true self" we were meant to be. In the theological/mythical language of Genesis, what happens to us is a "fall"—we become estranged and alienated from our true self, the self created to be in relationship with God and reflect the image of God.

The potential for egotism and evil is great. The alienated, fragmented, fractured self can become "blind, self-preoccupied, prideful; worry-filled, grasping, miserable; insensitive, angry, violent; somebody great, or only okay, or 'not much.' . . . We can even be both victim and oppressor. Especially in groups, we can be brutal and oppressive. There seems no evil of which we are not collectively incapable."[5] Huston Smith, the brilliant scholar of world religions, offers the following description of the Christian view of the human condition:

> In the biblical, metaphorical narrative Adam and Eve were created sinless but made the mistake of eating forbidden fruit, and this act expelled them from paradise, outside of which their descendants continue to live. We are mixed bags, capable of great nobility and horrendous evil. Our besetting sin is to put ourselves ahead of others; egotism or self-centeredness is built into us. We cannot get rid of that handicap, but we can and must work at restraining it.[6]

Entering God's new world like a child involves an intentional process of cooperation with God through which we shed our "false self" and recover our "true self." This is not a single, once-for-all experience but a transformative process, a journey of growth that involves dying to our old identities and learning to live in new ways as daughters and sons of God. This transformative journey is expressed in the following words of Jesus: "If any want to become my followers, let them deny themselves and take up their cross and follow me. For those who want to save their life will lose it, and those who lose their life for my sake, and for the sake of the gospel, will save it" (Mark 8:34-35). The cross was the symbol of death, of execution. Jesus is talking about dying to one's old life and learning how to live in God's new world; losing life in order to find it. Luke's version of this saying makes it explicit by adding the word "daily"—"let them deny themselves and take up their cross daily" (Luke 9:23). Marcus Borg describes it this way:

> On the one hand, it is a dying of the self as the center of its own concern. On the other hand, it is a dying to the world as the center of security and identity. These—the self and the world—are the two great rival centers to centering in God, and the path of transformation thus involves a dying to both of them. The "world" to which one must die is the world of conventional wisdom, the world of "culture" with its preoccupying securities; and the self which must die is the self-preoccupied self. Then is born a self which is centered in God, in Spirit, and not in culture.[7]

Even people with a decisive, intense conversion experience are by no means changed overnight. Old habits, attitudes, feelings, and patterns of acting, reacting, and interacting that have become ingrained in the personality do not die without conflict and struggle. Often the spiritual life is a journey of twists and turns, setbacks and challenges, where progress means three steps forward and two steps back. Living in God's new world calls for a personal transformation that enables us to reflect progressively the character and values of the kingdom of God.

The Jesus Creed

An early scene in the movie *Forrest Gump* shows young Forrest waiting to get on the school bus. The bus stops and the door opens. Forrest hesitates. The bus driver growls, "Are you coming on?" Forrest says, "Mama said not to be taking rides from strangers." Impatient, the bus driver says, "This is the bus for school." Forrest thinks for a minute and says, "I'm Forrest Gump." She says, "I'm Dorothy Harris." Forrest says, "Well, now we aren't strangers anymore," and he gets on the bus.

Forrest wears braces on his legs, and none of the kids want to sit with him. As he starts toward an empty spot, one of the children says, "Seat's taken." As he turns toward another, a second child says, "Taken." Still another says, "Can't sit here." But just then a little blond girl speaks up. "You can sit here if you want." Reflecting later on this experience, Forrest says, "You know, it's funny what a young man recollects; I don't remember when I was born. I don't recall what I got for my first Christmas, and I don't remember when I went on my first outdoor picnic. But I do remember when I heard the sweetest voice in the wide world. I had never seen anything so beautiful in my life. She was like an angel."[8] Through the voice of a little girl, God called Forrest's name. Whenever we offer grace, acceptance, and love to the children of the world, to the weak and vulnerable, to the outcasts and the helpless, we become agents of God's new world.

This world can be a cruel place. Our clichés tell the story—it's dog-eat-dog, a rat race, survival of the fittest. There's no place for misfits. But the good news according to Jesus not only creates a place for misfits, but they are in fact given special recognition. Jesus embodies an alternative world with unconventional values and a radically different bottom line. Of course beauty is in the eye of the beholder. For those entrenched in the beliefs and values of this world, the life of Jesus can be offensive, his words and actions intrusive, as they shatter our assumptions and turn conventional wisdom on its head.

The heart of what God's new world is about is expressed in a Scripture passage known to some as the "Jesus Creed."

> One of the scribes came near and heard them disputing with one another, and seeing that he answered them well, he asked him, "Which commandment is the first of all?" Jesus answered, "The first is, 'Hear, O Israel: the Lord our God, the Lord is one; you shall love the Lord your God with all your heart, and with all your soul, and with all your mind, and with all your strength.' The second is this, 'You shall love your neighbor as yourself.' There is no other commandment greater than these."
>
> Then the scribe said to him, "You are right, Teacher; you have truly said that 'he is one, and besides him there is no other'; and 'to love him with all the heart, and with all the understanding, and with all the strength,' and 'to love one's neighbor as oneself,'—this is much more important than all whole burnt offerings and sacrifices." When Jesus saw that he answered wisely, he said to him, "You are not far from the kingdom of God." After that no one dared to ask him any question. (Mark 12:28-34)

Rabbis commonly discussed the question asked of Jesus. They claimed that there were 365 prohibitions and 248 positive commands in the Torah, and attempted to summarize them and find a basic principle from which the whole law could be derived. Here, Jesus begins by quoting the opening words of the *Shema*, which pious Jews recite daily. But then Jesus adds a "second" commandment alongside it and assigns it equal importance, giving the ancient commandment a fresh, new meaning.

The Gospels of Matthew, Mark, and Luke differ in how they describe this scene, but they all emphasize the connection that puts these two commands on an equal footing. Luke connects them without a break, while in Matthew Jesus says, "All the law and the prophets hang on these two commandments" (Luke 10:27; Matt 22:40). The two commandments are inseparable. Unless love for God is expressed in love for neighbor, then love for God is empty and hollow. In Luke's version this instruction is followed by Jesus' story of the Good Samaritan, making it clear that my neighbor is not the person with whom I am acquainted or share similar interests, but someone I may even be at odds with (see Luke 10:25-37).

The scribe's endorsement of Jesus' teaching mentions two common elements in Israel's worship—burnt offerings and sacrifices. To love God with the totality of one's being and to love one's neighbor as one's self is more important than all burnt offerings and sacrifices. This theme is reflected in a number of Old Testament passages. Hosea 6:6 reads, "For I desire steadfast love and not sacrifice, the knowledge of God rather than burnt offerings." The prophet is not bringing an indictment against sacrifice or worship itself, but rather against the attitude and practice that elevates ritual and a show of piety over integrity of life and service. Without love for others and justice for all, worship is meaningless.

It doesn't matter how many prayers I pray, songs I sing, sermons I preach or hear, or creeds I recite. If I can't love my neighbor (my sister or brother in the human family), then my faith lacks substance and is meaningless. Genuine worship leads us beyond ourselves into the world of need. Clean hands lifted up to God in worship must lead us to get our hands dirty in service to the world. If what the church does when it is gathered in worship doesn't compel ministry to others through acts of mercy and compassion, or the pursuit of justice for the disadvantaged, then the church is simply going through the motions of worship. It doesn't matter how strongly we believe the doctrine proclaimed, how emotionally engaged we are in worship, or how intellectually stimulating our Bible studies are. If belief, worship, and study do not translate into a loving, compassionate lifestyle that coura-geously identifies with the suffering and downtrodden of the world and acts in their behalf, then all our ecclesiastical activity and theological discussions are futile.

A rough mountaineer was known for his volatile spirit. He had been in a number of fights and once nearly killed a guy. He was known to hold grudges and retaliate against anyone he thought did him an injustice, whether it was actually true or not. Then one day he fell in love with a schoolteacher. With trepidation and fear, he asked her to marry him, and to the amazement of everyone in the town she said yes. When he got home that night, he prayed the first prayer of many to follow. He said, "God, I have ignored you all my life, but I will ignore you no longer." And then he said, "God, I ain't got nothin' against nobody."

Can love do that? It can. Love is redemptive. Love is transformational. And this is why in 1 Corinthians 13, right in the midst of a discussion about spiritual gifts that had become a source of pride, confusion, and division in the church at Corinth, Paul says, "Without love it's all nothing." Without love, he says, "I am nothing" and "I gain nothing."

When Jordan, my son, was nine years old and involved in Little League baseball, our league ran short on umpires. The home team was responsible for recruiting parents and coaches to volunteer, which is not the best scenario in a competitive sport. In one game, a parent for the other team made two controversial calls back to back. Jordan, at shortstop, tagged a kid out going from second to third, but the parent/umpire in the field said he didn't have the ball in his glove, so he called the child safe.

Next, our kids turned a double play. A ground ball was hit to our second baseman; he tagged the runner going from first to second, and then threw it over to first for the force out. The runner going to first was several steps away from the base when our first baseman caught the ball; it wasn't even a close call. After the play, however, the runner remained on first base. I called time and asked for an explanation. The umpire/parent said he didn't see the play. The opposing team's head coach was umpiring behind the plate, and he said he didn't see it either. I was thinking, *How could one not see this? It's obvious.*

I can't recall my exact words, but I may have suggested that blind per-sons should not be engaged in activities that require them to make decisions based on sight. I also remarked quite emphatically that it was difficult to compete when we, the defensive team on the field, were required to get five outs when the other team was only required to get three outs. I wasn't nice. I was angry, frustrated, nasty, and loud. I'm not suggesting that I shouldn't have protested the call or even taken action. I should have done both, but not in that manner. My actions did not reflect the values of God's new world.

Loving our neighbor doesn't mean we always give in to others. Loving an alcoholic spouse or an abusive person certainly does not mean "giving in" to their wishes. In fact, giving in would not be the loving thing to do. But love of God and love of neighbor require a certain attitude and stance. Love can be firm while simultaneously being gentle.

In Mark's account of this interchange between the scribe and Jesus, the scribe assumes he is entitled to approve or endorse Jesus' teaching, but in fact the roles are reversed, and in the end Jesus determines what is true and good. The gospel according to Jesus makes love of God and love of neighbor the essence of true religion.

God's Righteousness

In the good news according to Jesus, particularly in Matthew's version, "righteousness" is a vital characteristic of God's new world. Righteousness is a key theme in the Hebrew Scriptures and covers a wide range of meanings. It is applied to God as well as humans. With regard to God, it is used not only to speak about the character of God, but about God's saving, redeeming acts (see 1 Sam 12:7; Judg 5:11; and Mic 6:5). It is a key component of the covenant God makes with Israel, through which God demonstrates grace on behalf of his people and calls for every covenant member to "love God" and "love neighbor." A righteous person is characterized by demonstrating special concern and compassion for the poor and needy (see Ps 112:4-9). Well-known Old Testament scholar Walter Brueggemann writes,

> Every part of the Old Testament is insistent upon a covenantal, communitarian ethic that is rooted in the intention of the covenant-making God, who is the one who has ordered creation for communal well-being. The righteous are thus those people who guarantee life, and the wicked are those who bring the power of death into the community.[9]

The prophets anticipated an age of righteousness; righteousness being one, if not the primary characteristic of God's new world.[10] God will judge righteously, putting all things right, and the people of God's new world will live righteously, actively doing God's will.

This is a key theme in the body of teaching known as the "Sermon on the Mount" (Matt 5–7).[11] The Sermon on the Mount is the first of five major teaching discourses found in Matthew's Gospel; Jesus, in Matthew, is first and foremost "the Teacher." The mountain setting for the Sermon on the Mount recalls Moses' ascending the mountain to receive the Torah. Though Jesus is never called the new Moses or his disciples called the new Israel in Matthew's Gospel, clear analogies are drawn between Jesus and Moses. New Testament scholar Eugene Boring observes, "Moses imagery looms in the background, and the sermon cannot be heard without reflection on how Jesus' authoritative teaching from the mount relates to the Torah given on Sinai—a live issue in the Matthean community."[12]

The Sermon on the Mount opens with a series of beatitudes:

> Blessed are the poor in spirit, for theirs is the kingdom of heaven.
> Blessed are those who mourn, for they will be comforted.
> Blessed are the meek, for they will inherit the earth.
> Blessed are those who hunger and thirst for righteousness, for they will be filled.
> Blessed are the merciful, for they will receive mercy.
> Blessed are pure in heart, for they will see God.
> Blessed are the peacemakers, for they will be called children of God.
> Blessed are those who are persecuted for righteousness sake, for theirs is the kingdom of heaven.
> Blessed are you when people revile you and persecute you and utter all kinds of evil against you falsely on my account. Rejoice and be glad, for your reward is great in heaven, for in the same way they persecuted the prophets who were before you. (Matt 5:3-13)

The term "beatitude" is Latin for the Greek word usually translated "blessed." Some modern translations render it "happy," which is misleading, because the word is not intended to convey an emotional state of happiness but a state of spiritual well-being, a kind of wholeness broad enough to include contradictory feelings and experiences.

The beatitudes are in the indicative mood in the Greek, which means they are not commands, but declarations. They do not function to give practical advice for successful living, but as pronouncements of blessing on those who have discovered they are loved by God and have decided to allow God's love to guide their lives. They begin with a declaration of blessing in the present tense, followed by a promise in the future tense that points to an ultimate fulfillment. Two exceptions are the first and last beatitudes (I take the last beatitude to be v. 10; verse 11, though it begins with "blessed" is actually an elaboration of verse 10), where the promise is the same, and both are framed in the present tense—"theirs is the kingdom of heaven." The phrases serve as brackets to show that all these blessings are kingdom blessings, blessings related to God's new world.

The theme of righteousness that appears in the fourth and eighth beatitudes and permeates the rest of the sermon is, in my judgment, the key to the meaning of the beatitudes. The first three beatitudes (the poor in spirit, those who mourn, the meek) reflect the condition of those who are most inclined to hunger and thirst after righteousness/justice. Beatitudes five, six, and seven (the merciful, the pure in heart, the peacemakers) highlight key aspects of the righteousness of God's new world. The eighth beatitude calls attention to the opposition that comes upon those who practice God's "new world" righteousness from those who live by "old world" values. The final beatitude elaborates on the nature of this opposition, which also serves as a transition into the next part of the discourse.

The beatitudes are startling because they "invert" the world's images of blessing. These are not the kinds of people who would appear "blessed" in the world. J. B. Philips suggests that the world's beatitudes should be rendered thus:

Happy are the "pushers": for they get on in the world.
Happy are the hard-boiled: for they never let life hurt them.
Happy are they who complain: for they get their own way in the end.
Happy are the blasé: for they never worry over their sins.
Happy are the slave-drivers: for they get results.
Happy are the knowledgeable men of the world: for they know their way around.
Happy are the trouble-makers: for they make people take notice of them.[13]

Whether we hear the beatitudes as truly "blessings" or dismiss them as pious sayings unrelated to the real world largely depends on where we stand when we hear them. If we are standing on top, on the side of power, wealth, and prestige, we may not hear them as pronouncements of blessing at all; they may seem more like curses. This is certainly not the way to climb the ladder to achieve political, financial, social, or vocational success. But if we are at the bottom of the heap, crying over our losses (or the losses of others as we identify with their plight), passed-over, oppressed and suffering, then we will receive the beatitudes as good news. Barbara Brown Taylor says,

> I think Jesus should have asked the crowd to stand on their heads when he taught them the Beatitudes, because that was what he was doing. He was turning the known world upside down, so that those who had been fighting for breath at the bottom of the human heap suddenly found themselves closest to heaven, while those who thought they were on top of things found themselves flat on their backs looking up. . . .
>
> The world looks funny upside down, but maybe that is just how it looks when you have got your feet planted in heaven. Jesus did it all the time and seemed to think we could do it too. So blessed are those who stand on their heads, for they shall see the world as God sees it. They shall also find themselves in good company, turned upside down by the only one who really knows which way is up.[14]

A key text for understanding the righteousness of God's new world is Matthew 5:17-20:

> Do not think that I have come to abolish the law or the prophets; I have come not to abolish but to fulfill. For truly I tell you, until heaven and earth pass away, not one letter, not one stroke of a letter, will pass from the law until all is accomplished. Therefore, whoever breaks one of the least of these commandments, and teaches others to do the same, will be called least in the kingdom of heaven; but whoever does them and teaches them will be called great in the kingdom of heaven. For I tell you, unless your righteousness exceeds that of the scribes and Pharisees, you will never enter the kingdom of heaven.

Gospel scholars point out that the church to which this Gospel was written must have been predominantly Jewish, struggling with their connection to their Jewish heritage, especially the Torah. Here Jesus says he did not come to abolish the law but to fulfill it. There may be several different shades of meaning to this statement, but if we understand it in light of the full teaching of the Sermon on the Mount, it certainly implies that Jesus fulfills the purpose of the Torah, which was given as a gift to God's people, intended to guide them in carrying out God's good will. The practical implication is that Jesus himself and his teaching constitute the new authority for living in God's new world. From Matthew's perspective, the Torah is not cast off; it is "fulfilled" in the life and teaching of Jesus.

This has the effect of radicalizing the Torah by bringing out its broader and deeper intention. Jesus says, "You have heard that it was said to those of ancient times, 'You shall not murder . . . . But I say to you that if you are angry with a brother or sister, you will be liable to judgment . . ." (Matt 5:21-22). Jesus goes beyond outward conduct to deal with the inner springs of human action. Jesus is not abrogating the Torah; rather, he is bringing out its deeper meaning.

For example, in several places in the Gospels, Jesus brings out the true intent of Sabbath law. The Sabbath was meant to free people from the burden of work so that they could receive rest and be restored physically, emotionally, and spiritually. It was not intended to prevent them from doing good or saving life on the Sabbath. And yet some of the rabbinical interpretations that had developed to guard the Sabbath became a hindrance to true Sabbath observance. Jesus sought to restore the original intent of the Sabbath law, given by God in order to heal and restore life (see Mark 2:23–3:6).

The impression formed in the Gospels is that a group of religious leaders had obscured the real intent of the Torah as a way of asserting religious power, which in turn led to religious oppression. In a passage in Matthew's Gospel where Jesus denounces some of the scribes and Pharisees (a passage the Gospel writer heavily embellished), Jesus is reported as saying, "They [some of the scribes and Pharisees] tie up heavy burdens, hard to bear, and lay them on the shoulders of others; but they themselves are unwilling to lift a finger to move them" (Matt 23:4). Jesus accuses them of squabbling over trivialities while neglecting the weightier matters like justice, mercy, and faith (Matt 23:23).

This radicalizing of the law by Jesus in order to bring out its ultimate intent even goes so far as to negate or abolish some aspects of the Torah. Concerning the law of retaliation Jesus says,

> You have heard that it was said, "An eye for an eye and a tooth for a tooth." But I say to you, Do not resist an evildoer. But if anyone strikes you on the right cheek, turn the other also; and if anyone wants to sue you and take your coat, give your cloak as well; and if anyone forces you to go one mile, go also the second mile. Give to everyone who begs from you, and do not refuse anyone who wants to borrow from you. (Matt 5:38-42)

The Mosaic Law attempted to curb actions of revenge through the law of retaliation. In fulfilling the intent of the law against violence, Jesus annuls all provision for retaliatory violence. Jesus does this, however, not out of disrespect for the Torah, but out of deep regard for it. In the interest of broadening and fulfilling the spirit and intent of the Torah, Jesus annuls some aspects of it.

The examples Jesus gives in the above passage are not regulations set in stone; these are not new laws, but illustrations of how one might respond to an aggressor in terms of good, not evil. They are illustrations, not new legislation. They are examples of the kind of righteousness Jesus envisages for God's new world. Dallas Willard writes,

> I think it is perhaps these four statements, more than any others in the Discourse, that cause people to throw up their hands in despair or sink into the pit of grinding legalism. This is because the situations referred to are familiar, and they can only imagine that Jesus is laying down *laws* about what they *have* to do regardless of what else may be at issue.
>
> All is changed when we realize that these are illustrations of what a certain kind of person, the kingdom person, will characteristically do in such situations. They are not laws of "righteous behavior" for those personally imposed upon or injured. They are not laws for the obvious reason that they do not cover the many cases. Additionally, if you read them *as* laws you will immediately see that we could "obey" them in the wrong spirit. For example, as is often actually said, "I'll turn the other cheek, but then I'll knock your head off."
>
> Will there, then, be cases in which persons of kingdom *dikaiosune* [righteousness] will not do what is said here by way of illustration? Quite certainly, but they will be very rare, so long as it is only an individual injury that is at stake and no issues of a larger good are concerned. After all, this is *characteristic* behavior of the person with the kingdom heart and it does express who that person is at the core of his or her being. Though we are not talking about things one must do to "be Christian" or "go to heaven when we die," we are looking at how people live who stand in the flow of God's life now. We see the interior rightness of those who are living—as a matter of course, not just in exceptional moments—beyond the rightness of the scribe and Pharisee.[15]

God's new world turns our world upside down. Willard points out that within the human order, the presumption is that we return harm for harm, doing only what legal force allows us to do, and that we give only to those who have some prior claim on us. But God's new world righteousness (justice) reverses the presumption, so that we will naturally return good for evil and resist only for compelling reasons. We will give freely because there is a need.

In God's new world we do not live by a set of unbending laws; rather, we do what is right according to an ethic of divine love. Love for God and others determines the appropriate response. For example, a surgeon on his way to do a life-saving surgery must not go a second mile with someone. Or for that matter, even the first mile; the loving thing is to resist. If by turning the other cheek a friend or loved one will suffer great harm, then we have to consider carefully what the loving response is in that situation. Willard observes that those who must have a law for everything live impoverished lives and develop little in the way of kingdom righteousness. The way of law "avoids individual responsibility for decision" and "pushes the responsibility and possible blame onto God."[16] The question is never whether or not we did the specific actions in Jesus' illustrations, but rather, "Are we the kind of persons that Jesus' illustrations are illustrations of?"

God's new world righteousness transforms the dynamics of personal interactions, making possible the redemption of human relationships. Willard writes,

> Our tormentors, no doubt, count on our resistance and anger to support their continuation of the evil that is in them. If we respond as Jesus indicates, the force of their own actions pulls them off their stance and forces them to question what kind of people they are. Of course they are acting from anger, and worse. But now with our other cheek facing them, slapped already or soon to be slapped, the justification of their anger and evil that they were counting on has been removed. As anger feeds on anger, so patient goodness will normally deflate it . . . .
>
> And if it doesn't change? If they just harden themselves the more and keep on coming at us? Well, then we must act or not act as we judge best. . . . We will decide, as best we know how, on the basis of love for all involved and with a readiness to sacrifice what we simply want. And in every situation we have the larger view. We are not passive, but we act always with clear eyed and resolute love.[17]

When grace and forgiveness are applied to human relations, redemption becomes a possibility. In Victor Hugo's novel *Les Misérables*, Jean Valjean is sentenced to a nineteen-year term of hard labor for stealing bread. In prison he turns into a tough convict. No one could beat him in a fistfight and no one could break his will. At last he is released. Convicts in those days had to carry identity cards and no innkeeper would let a dangerous felon spend the night. For four days, Valjean wanders the village roads, seeking shelter against the weather, until finally a kindly bishop has mercy on him.

That night when the bishop drifts off to sleep, Jean Valjean rises from his bed, rummages through the family silver, and steals off into the night. The next morning the authorities knock on the bishop's door. Jean Valjean has been apprehended with his silver, and they are ready to put him in chains for life. The bishop, however, responds in a way no one would expect.

"So here you are!" he cries to Valjean. "I'm delighted to see you. Had you forgotten that I gave you the candlesticks as well? They're silver like the rest, and worth a good 200 francs. Did you forget to take them?" The bishop assures his captors that Jean Valjean is not a thief, that this was his gift to him.

Valjean trembles, speechless. He has never been shown such mercy. The bishop's act of forgiveness changes Jean Valjean's life. His defenses are melted, and from that day he begins a new journey dedicated to helping others in need.[18]

The righteousness Jesus embodied and taught surpasses and transcends the righteousness characteristic of many of the scribes and Pharisees because law cannot circumscribe it. The righteousness of God's new world is grounded in the ethic of divine love. Jesus says,

> You have heard that it was said, "You shall love your neighbor and hate your enemy." But I say to you, Love your enemies and pray for those who persecute you, so that you may be children of your Father in heaven; for he makes his sun rise on the evil and the good, and sends rain on the righteous and on the unrighteous. For if you love those who love you, what reward do you have? Do not even the tax collectors do the same? And if you greet only your brothers and sister, what more are you doing than others? Do not even the Gentiles do the same? Be perfect, therefore, as your heavenly Father is perfect. (Matt 5:43-48)

In the structure of the Sermon on the Mount, the words of Jesus above stand as the sixth and final antitheses between the righteousness derived directly from the Torah and the righteousness embodied and taught by Jesus. The righteousness of Jesus is derived from and directed by God's love, which even extends to those who wish our harm. The Torah was given in love to God's people, but Jesus' experience of God as Love enabled him to discern its true intent and make corrections that reflect more honestly and accurately God's real purpose.

This new world righteousness of love is grounded squarely upon the character of God. This is how God treats those who oppose him; he loves them and seeks their redemption. Jesus, as the obedient Son of God, replicates and imitates his loving Father/Abba. He calls his followers to do the same and thus to live as the daughters and sons of God.

God's righteousness as clarified and magnified through Jesus touches us in the depths of our being and transforms us there. Years ago in England, a large, beautiful clock adorned the back wall of one of the cathedrals. The preacher used it to time his sermons. This became a problem when the hands of the clock would sometimes stop and start winding backwards; it made for fairly lengthy sermons. The elders called in specialist after specialist to fix the clock, but the clock defied fixing. Finally someone hung a sign on it: "Don't blame the hands, the trouble lies deeper."

Our problem is not just with our "hands"—our overt actions and conduct—it goes deeper. Unless our righteousness goes deeper than outward, external conformity to moral and religious laws and traditions, we will not be changed in the depths of our being. Thomas Merton describes what must take place:

> This true inner self must be drawn up like a jewel from the bottom of the sea, rescued from confusion, from indistinction, from immersion in the common, the nondescript, the trivial, the sordid, the evanescent . . . saved from immersion in the sea of lies and passions which is called the "world." . . . The creative and mysterious self must be delivered from the wasteful, hedonistic and destructive ego that seeks only to cover itself with disguises.[19]

How do we become persons governed and permeated by divine love? Certainly God doesn't just zap God's love into us; at least, that has not been my experience or the experience of many others walking in the way of Jesus. We must learn to love through our discipleship to Christ. Biblical scholar Leander Keck observes,

> Moreover, the moral life is forged by the interactions (and often by lack of interaction) between persons more than by resolute application of carefully considered teachings, principles, or ideals; indeed, characteristically it is from persons that one learns these things, and it is from wise persons that

one learns how they actually function in one circumstance after another. In this light, it is not only Jesus' teachings about right behavior that shape the follower's moral life but especially Jesus' demeanor, his way of responding to situations, his way of being engaged, that determines the kind of influence he has. The Evangelists often provided the settings for Jesus' sayings, not simply because they wanted to create a more vivid narrative but also because they sensed that the sayings' impact is enhanced if one encounters them as Jesus' particular response in a particular situation rather than disembodied teaching.[20]

In this way the whole life of Jesus must be internalized. Again Keck is helpful:

> It is the deliberate, persistent appropriation of Jesus into the moral life so that he becomes its internal compass and criterion of the doer and the deed. When Jesus' word and way are assimilated, he becomes "habit forming." Then he is not simply cited as an external authority the way one quotes a rule book or eminent expert; instead his words and precedent come readily and naturally to mind because he has already shaped one's disposition, will, and way of being in the world.[21]

The actual process of transformation, however, is not all internal before it is external; it is not all change of mind, will, and disposition (heart) before it becomes expressed through our conduct. In fact, we can act our way into the way of Christ expecting God to meet us in our need with his grace.

C. S. Lewis has an excellent discussion of this in a chapter of his classic work, *Mere Christianity*, titled "Let's Pretend." He argues for two kinds of pretending. The bad kind is where the pretense is there instead of the real thing, as when a person pretends he is going to help you instead of really helping you. The good kind is where the pretense leads to the real thing, such as behaving friendly when you are not actually feeling friendly, but the more you act friendly the more you actually become friendly. Lewis says, "Very often the only way to get a quality in reality is to start behaving as if you had it already."[22] Yet we are not doing this on our own. Lewis writes,

> Christ Himself is actually at your side and is already at that moment beginning to turn your pretense into a reality. . . . He is beginning to turn you into the same kind of thing as Himself. He is beginning, so to speak, to "inject" His kind of life and thought, His *Zoe*, into you; beginning to turn

the tin soldier into a live man. The part of you that does not like it is the part that is still tin.[23]

In this way, says Lewis, God is killing off our old natural self and replacing it with the kind of self God is, "At first, only for moments. Then for longer periods. Finally, if all goes well, turning you permanently into a different sort of thing; into a new little Christ, a being which in its own small way, has the same kind of life as God; which shares in His power, joy, knowledge and eternity."[24]

As we internalize the life of Christ, the Spirit of Christ will increasingly transform our character and conduct. We will long for God's new world where everything will be put to right. We will engage issues of justice and compassion and care about such matters as the sacredness of human life, the well-being of the mentally and physically challenged, the critically ill and dying, health care for those who cannot afford it, equal rights for all people, the plight and needs of the illegal immigrant, an adequate working wage, economic justice, the care and protection of our environment, the use/misuse of imperial power, and the right to wage war.

Disciples of Jesus experience the tension of living in the overlap of the ages. The old world is passing away, but "the law of sin and death" is still an enslaving, oppressive, destructive force operative in the kingdoms of this world and in our individual lives. God's new world is here, but not yet in a final or complete form. Each day we must choose which "world" will dominate and control our lives. It helps to remember that we are loved, accepted, forgiven, and called to be God's daughters and sons in the world.

Gratitude for God's unconditional love frees us to make many new beginnings as we "seek first God's new world and God's kind of righteousness" (Matt 6:33, my translation). I love the way the late missionary Frank Laubach expresses this thought:

God forgives us instantly and eagerly. Let's forgive ourselves! To "repent" does not mean to "repine," but to "right about face and start moving in the right direction." Christ's joy is in helping men make new beginnings. He finds no pleasure in condemning. He delights only in helping us rise higher. No matter what the last hour may have been, it is past, and we live in this moment, to make it as fine as we can in thought and deed. Never let the sins or errors of the last hour poison this! "Snap out of it" instantly, and lo, a new fresh page is turned. He who adopts the philosophy of instantaneous new beginnings has the secret of peace.[25]

An Inversion of Values

Tony Campolo grew up in Philadelphia, the city of brotherly love. In his neighborhood, the night before Halloween was designated Mischief Night. On that night, the adults braced themselves against all sorts of petty "crimes" at the hands of the younger generation. Windows were soaped, air was let out of tires—all the annoying mischief an adolescent mind could conjure up.

One year Campolo and his best friend devised what they thought was a brilliant and creative plan. They imagined breaking in to the local five-and-dime store. They didn't plan to rob the place; instead, they planned to do something that, as far as the owner of the store was concerned, would have been worse. Their plan was to change the price tags on as many items as they could.

They imagined what it would be like the next morning when people came into the store and discovered that radios were selling for a quarter and bobby pins were priced at five dollars each. They wondered what it would be like when nobody could figure out the actual prices.

Campolo applies this story to the evil one, whom he personifies as the one who "has broken into our lives and changed the price tags on things." He says that too often we treat what deserves to be treated with loving care as though it were of little worth, or we find ourselves tempted to make great sacrifices for that which, in the long run of life, has no lasting value.[26] He makes a good point.

But I think the story could equally apply to Jesus. Jesus has a way of turning values that we cherish on their heads. This is particularly true regarding traditional family values. For example, in Luke's Gospel Jesus says, "Whoever comes to me and does not hate father and mother, wife and children, brothers and sisters, yes, and even life itself, cannot be my disciple" (Luke 14:26). Common sense prevents us from taking this literally; Jesus is exaggerating to evoke thought and make a point about the importance of one's commitment to God's cause in the world. Yet, he nevertheless cuts against the grain of conventional family connections and commitments.

Mark's Gospel has an interesting family story:

> Then Jesus entered a house, and again a crowd gathered, so that he and his disciples were not even able to eat. When his family heard about this, they went to take charge of him, for they said, "He is out of his mind." . . .
>
> Then Jesus' mother and brothers arrived. Standing outside, they sent someone in to call him. A crowd was sitting around him, and they told him, "Your mother and brothers are outside looking for you."

"Who are my mother and brothers?" he asked.

Then he looked at those seated in the circle around him and said, "Here are my mother and my brothers! Whoever does God's will is my brother and sister and mother." (Mark 3:20-21, 31-35, TNIV)[27]

Mary, along with her sons, think Jesus has lost his mental good sense; their intent is to take him home with them. When Jesus is notified that his mother and brothers have come, he pronounces that his true family consists of those who do the will of God.

There are other stories in the Gospels where Jesus conveys a different attitude toward family. For example, when Jesus happens on a funeral procession as they carry the body of the only son of a widow away from Nain's gates, he feels moved for this mother. He doesn't say to the widow what he says on a different occasion to a man who is hesitant about following Jesus because he wants to take care of his dying father. To him Jesus says, "let the dead bury the dead" (Luke 9:59-60 and Matt 8:21-22)—another hard saying.[28] But to the widow of Nain Jesus says, "Don't cry," and then restores her dead son to life. Luke says, "The dead man sat up and began to talk, and Jesus gave him back to his mother" (Luke 7:11-15, TNIV).

Then, at the cross, according to John's Gospel, Jesus makes arrangements for the care of his mother, commending her care to that of the beloved disciple (John 19:26-27). Jesus also forthrightly condemns the practice of some of the Jewish leaders that sought to avoid caring for aging parents. They interpreted the law in such a way that by designating their possessions "Corban" (devoted to God), they could not then be used in any secular way, such as to provide financial support to aging parents. Jesus accuses them of breaking the commandment to honor their parents (Mark 7:9-13; Matt 15:3-7).

Jesus was not antifamily, and yet he says what he says—turning traditional family values upside down. Some of Jesus' sayings and teachings regarding the family seem contradictory. Here's what I think: Jesus was absolutely and totally committed to the kingdom of God, and he wanted others to share his passion and commitment, but he also realized that the radical commitment that ordered his life would not be possible for everyone. So he lived with this tension.

Also, a certain shock factor in the sayings of Jesus was intended to jar people out of their ordinary mode of categorizing and thinking about things so that they might be open to a new way of seeing reality. There is no question that Jesus put a priority on doing God's will. Jesus was so convinced of his call and so passionate about God's new world that nothing, not even family ties and obligations, could interfere with his call or work. Some of his sayings about family may seem insensitive because they emerge from his radical commitment to God's cause in the world.

It would be a tragedy to use Jesus' teachings as a way to avoid loving and caring for our families. In fact, I think learning how to do the will of God in the context of our family relationships is a great challenge and may be the one place where we can actually make a significant difference for good. If Jesus were speaking to families in our culture, what would he say? I'm sure he would tell us that God's will must take priority over all family commitments, but I'm confident as well that he would instruct us to carry out God's will within the family structure—to love, forgive, and serve the members of our families.

Jesus seems to have encountered the kind of family tensions we all face. We may not want to be as extreme as Jesus, but then again, God's call upon each of us is unique. None of us have a right to judge anyone else. I suggest starting where you are. We can all do the will of God in the context of our families. We can love them with the love of Christ and allow God's love to enlarge our hearts to embrace all brothers and sisters in our family of faith and in the human family.

Another area where Jesus swims against the tide of conventional wisdom and inverts the values of society is that of money and finances and the honor and prestige that go with affluence. I am reminded of the pastor who convened a special meeting to call attention to the rundown condition of the church facilities. He began by asking for pledges, and he turned first to one of the more affluent members of the congregation. "Brother So-and-So, would you like to start the pledging?" The wealthy man said, "I pledge five dollars." Just then a piece of plaster fell from the dilapidated ceiling and hit this brother with such force that it knocked him to the floor. After he picked himself up and dusted himself off, he began again, "What I meant to say was that I pledge 50 dollars." The pastor looked heavenward and declared, "Hit him again, Lord, hit him again." Some of Jesus' teachings about money hit us hard.

On one occasion, Jesus told a man seeking eternal life (fullness of life in God's kingdom) to sell all his possessions, give the money to the poor, and follow him. Mark's Gospel says,

> When he heard this, he [the man] was shocked and went away grieving, for he had many possessions.

Then Jesus looked around and said to his disciples, "How hard it will be for those who have wealth to enter the kingdom of God!" And the disciples were perplexed at these words. But Jesus said to them again, "Children, how hard it is to enter the kingdom of God! It is easier for a camel to go through the eye of a needle than for someone who is rich to enter the kingdom of God." They were greatly astounded and said to one another, "Then who can be saved?" Jesus looked at them and said, "For mortals it is impossible, but not for God; for God all things are possible." (Mark 10:22-27)

The disciples were shocked by Jesus' words because typically in popular thought, wealth was considered to be a blessing from God that came from following the path of righteousness. Here Jesus regards wealth primarily as an obstacle and distraction that prevents those who possess it and pursue it from experiencing God's new world.

Wealth and possessions, then as now, were a major source of security and identity. Jesus tells his followers not to be anxious about such things and instead to seek first God's kingdom. In Luke's Gospel Jesus says,

Do not be afraid, little flock, for it is your Father's good pleasure to give you the kingdom. Sell your possessions, and give alms. Make purses for yourselves that do not wear out, an unfailing treasure in heaven, where no thief comes near and no moth destroys. For where your treasure is, there your heart will be also. (Luke 12:32-34)

Much depends on what we treasure, what we try to protect and secure. To treasure wealth, material possessions, and the honor that accompanies them is not a smart strategy for life. Again, in Luke's Gospel we read,

Someone in the crowd said to him, "Teacher, tell my brother to divide the family inheritance with me." But he said to him, "Friend, who set me to be a judge or arbitrator over you?" And he said to them, "Take care! Be on your guard against all kinds of greed; for one's life does not consist in the abundance of possessions." Then he told them a parable: "The land of a rich man produced abundantly. And he thought to himself, 'What should I do, for I have no place to store my crops?' Then he said, 'I will do this: I will pull down my barns and build larger ones, and there I will store all my grain and my goods. And I will say to my soul, Soul, you have ample goods laid up for many years; relax, eat, drink, and be merry.' But God said to him, 'You fool! This very night your life is being demanded of you. And the things you have prepared, whose will they be?' So it is with those who store up treasures for themselves but are not rich toward God." (Luke 12:13-21)

The farmer in the story is not guilty of any criminal act; there is no indication that he was unjust to his workers or mistreated his servants. For all we know he might have paid them well. He is careful, intentional, and conservative. He is also a fool for giving his possessions so much attention, for thinking he needed so much, and for trying to secure his life through his wealth. New Testament scholar Alan Culpepper observes, "The man has shut everyone else from his life and his thoughts. There is no one else in the story—just the man and his possessions—until God speaks to him."[29] This is the problem with greed of any kind; it is consuming. It shuts God and others out. The one who is full of greed or the one who is preoccupied with securing one's self in this world tends to be indifferent toward the plight and need of others. One may even be antagonistic toward the needs of others, particularly if one is prone toward feelings of guilt over one's self-indulgence. Greed destroys compassion, which is the very spirit and ethos of God's new world.

The "rich fool" has much to say to those of us who put a great deal of stock in the need to secure ourselves for the future. Culpepper remarks, "Leisure, recreation, freedom from the demands of work—the rich man's vision of the future sounds uncomfortably like the one that most of us have for our retirement years. Are we really planning prudently? What gives our life meaning now, and what will give it meaning then?"[30]

Some kids watched as a crane deposited a beautiful new Cadillac in a giant grave. A wealthy man was being buried, as he requested, in his Cadillac. One kid said, "Man, that's living!" No. It may be dying in style, but it's still dying. What any of us have we will not have for long. Someone said, "If I can't take it with me, I'm not going." We are all going. The one who gathers the most toys in this life doesn't win; rather, he or she has the most to lose.

In Jesus' parable of the dishonest manager in Luke 16, he calls money "unrighteous mammon" (v. 9, RSV). The NRSV translates the phrase "dishonest wealth" and the NIV "worldly wealth," both of which obscure the emphasis in the text. In using the Aramaic term "mammon," Jesus attributes to money a personal, spiritual character. Money is personified as a rival god. The adjective "dishonest" or "unrighteous" underscores the inherent fallenness of money. Money, when viewed in this way, is a power that seeks to win our allegiance and devotion. It is not morally neutral, but a god that must be dethroned. Spiritual writer and retreat leader Richard Foster comments,

> Money has power out of all proportion to its purchasing power. Because the children of this world understand this, they can use money for noneconomic purposes. And use it they do! Money is used as a weapon to bully people and to keep them in line. Money is used to "buy" prestige and honor. Money is used to enlist the allegiance of others. Money is used to corrupt people. . . . Rather than run from money, we are to take it—evil bent and all—and use it for kingdom purposes. We are to be absolutely clear about the venomous nature of money. But rather than reject it we are to conquer it and use it for kingdom purposes. . . . We are called to use money to advance the kingdom of God.[31]

When money is subdued, captured, and stripped of its power to corrupt, it can then be used for kingdom purposes. Instead of serving money or abandoning money, Jesus calls some disciples to use money to serve higher goals.

Lee Eclov, pastor of a church in Illinois, tells about a childhood experience that happened when he visited his grandma for a few days. His cousin Steve, who was a year or two younger, lived in the same town as his grandmother, so they spent a lot of time playing together growing up. For some reason, one week they collected bottle caps. The boy with the most was the richest; they were like currency. One day they discovered gobs of bottle caps by the softball field, and because he was the biggest and strongest, Lee collected more bottle caps than his cousin. Reflecting on that experience, he says, "I could have given some of my bottle caps to Steve just to be nice, but Steve didn't get any of my bottle caps. But if I had shared, I'm convinced that 40 years later my relationship with Steve would be enriched. It would be something different because I had spent my bottle caps on that friendship. As it is, I wasted it. Now the bottle caps are worthless—just rust and dust somewhere."[32]

Jesus challenges us to review the basic values of our lives. What are we investing in? How we relate to our money and possessions is a test of character, an indicator of what we treasure. Jesus says we cannot serve God and money (Luke 16:13).

Your Kingdom Come

In Luke's Gospel the setting for Jesus' teaching on prayer is Jesus at prayer:

He was praying in a certain place, and after he had finished, one of his disciples said to him, "Lord, teach us to pray, as John taught his disciples." He said to them, "When you pray, say:

Father, hallowed be your name.

Your kingdom come.

Give us each day our daily bread.

And forgive us our sins,

for we ourselves forgive everyone indebted to us.

And do not bring us to the time of trial."

And he said to them, "Suppose one of you has a friend, and you go to him at midnight and say to him, 'Friend, lend me three loaves of bread; for a friend of mine has arrived, and I have nothing to set before him.' And he answers from within, 'Do not bother me; the door has already been locked, and my children are with me in bed; I cannot get up and give you anything.' I tell you, even though he will not get up and give him anything because he is his friend, at least because of his persistence [better translated "shamelessness"] he will get up and give him whatever he needs.

"So I say to you, Ask, and it will be given you; search, and you will find; knock, and the door will be opened for you. For everyone who asks receives, and everyone who searches finds, and for everyone who knocks, the door will be opened. Is there anyone among you who, if your child asks for a fish, will give a snake instead of a fish? Or if the child asks for an egg, will give a scorpion? If you then, who are evil, know how to give good gifts to your children, how much more will the heavenly Father give the Holy Spirit to those who ask him!" (Luke 11:1-13)

In response to a question on how to pray, Jesus offers a set prayer, a model prayer that constitutes a legitimate pattern for prayer, commonly called the Lord's Prayer. Luke's version is shorter than Matthew's; it is likely that Luke's version is closer to what Jesus actually said, while Matthew's version expands it.

The first two lines orient the prayer. The context for prayer is a loving, caring relationship with God comparable to a relationship between a loving parent and a son or daughter. Prayer begins with a desire that all people experience this relationship. "Hallowed be your name" is a request that God's name and everything his name means and represents as the loving, compassionate God be acknowledged and regarded as such by all people.

The next petition is the central focus of prayer—the kingdom of God (God's new world). "Your kingdom come" is both a petition and a commitment to be engaged in kingdom work.

The next three petitions are requests that our physical and spiritual needs be met. We ask God to give us our daily bread, that is, to supply our daily physical and spiritual needs. We ask for forgiveness because we need it as much as bread. We seek forgiveness in a spirit of forgiveness because mercy flows through the same channel—whether it is given or received. A forgiving spirit is essential to the experience of forgiveness. The final petition is a request for deliverance from anything that threatens our participation in God's new world and/or God's provision for our physical or spiritual needs.

What follows in Luke's account is a parable, and after the parable appear sayings about prayer that ground prayer in the goodness of God. The argument is from the lesser to the greater. A friend arrives at midnight and there is no bread to give him. Offering bread was regarded as an essential part of showing hospitality. To fail to be hospitable in that shame-and-honor culture brought shame upon the family. So the individual in the story seeks help from his neighbor. Even though the whole family is asleep in their small one-room house, his neighbor gets up, in response to his friend's shameless persistence, knowing the rationale behind his friend's need.

If one's neighbor would do that, certainly God, who cares much more about us than a neighbor, will do more. And, says Jesus, if a loving parent will supply the needs of his or her child, how much more will God? Prayer is rooted in "the how much more" of God. If we who are evil, we who are selfish and flawed, know how to give good things to our children, how much more does God?

It's interesting to note that whereas Matthew's version has "good gifts," Luke substitutes the Holy Spirit—"how much more will the heavenly Father give the Holy Spirit to those who ask him." Luke is anticipating the giving of the Spirit to Jesus' followers after Jesus' death and resurrection. This is the best possible gift, namely, the continued presence of Jesus with his followers. This is fulfillment of the promise at the end of Matthew's Gospel: "I will be with you until the end of the age."

Jesus is not teaching us how to get answers to our prayers. Jesus is not saying that if we want to get what we ask for, we have to wear God down by our shameless persistence. There is something to be said for persistence and staying with our request, but Jesus is not suggesting that God has to be persuaded or cajoled to act in our behalf. Jesus is teaching that prayer is grounded in the character of a loving, compassionate, and generous God.

In Flannery O'Conner's short story "The Turkey," a little boy named Ruller has a poor self-image because nothing seems to turn in his favor. At night he hears his parents analyzing him. He hears his father say, "Ruller's an unusual one."

One day while trotting through the woods, Ruller spots a wounded wild turkey. He follows it. He thinks, "If only I can catch it and go home with that turkey slung over my shoulder, they will say, 'Look at Ruller with that wild turkey! Ruller, where did you get that turkey?'" Then he imagines saying, "Oh, I caught it in the woods. Maybe you would like me to catch you one sometime." But then a thought flashes through his mind: "God will probably make me chase that damn turkey all afternoon for nothing." He knows he shouldn't think that way about God—yet that's how he feels. And if that's how he feels, can he help it?

Ruller finally catches the turkey and he thinks maybe it's a sign of God's change of mind toward him. He even starts to feel gratitude and thinks about giving his one dime away. He prays that God will send him a beggar. Sure enough, a beggar woman shows up, and with his heart thumping up and down Ruller thrusts the dime into her hand and dashes on without looking back.

Ruller then notices a group of country boys shuffling behind him. He turns around and asks generously, "Y'all wanna see this turkey?" "Lemme see it," one boy says. Ruller hands him the turkey. The turkey's head suddenly flies into his face as the country boy slings it up in the air and over his shoulder, turning away. And the others turn with him as they saunter down the street.

They are a quarter of a mile away before Ruller moves. Finally they are out of sight. Ruller creeps toward home. He walks a bit, and then as it starts to get dark, he begins to run. O'Conner ends the tale with these words: "He ran faster and faster, and as he turned up the road to his house, his heart was running as fast as his legs and he was certain that Something Awful was tearing behind him with its arms rigid and its fingers ready to clutch."[33]

If that is how we perceive God, as "Something Awful" out to get us, then prayer will not work. We have no reason to pray. According to Jesus, prayer is grounded in the loving, generous character of God. The asking, seeking, and knocking that Jesus encourages is not a blanket promise for anything; it must be understood in the context of the model prayer. Those who are characterized by the spirit of the model prayer, those who stand in the posture of the model prayer, drawing upon their relationship with God, focused on God's new world, open to be a channel and conduit of grace— these are the ones who are told to ask, seek, and knock.

Prayer only makes sense when we put it in this larger context. If asking were only a way of getting what we want, prayer would be harmful to us rather than helpful. Our asking, seeking, and knocking must be coupled with listening, communion with God, and cooperation with God's purpose to bring about God's new world. Our posture must be one of trust, humility, forgiveness, and commitment as we share God's compassion for the needy and serve as agents of God's mercy. Only in the context of God's unconditional love and kingdom purpose does prayer make sense. I like what Dallas Willard says about prayer:

> Prayer is never just asking, nor is it merely a matter of asking for what I want. God is not a cosmic butler or fix-it-man, and the aim of the universe is not to fulfill my desires and needs. On the other hand, I am to pray for what concerns me, and many people have found prayer impossible because they thought they should only pray for wonderful but remote needs they actually had little or no interest in or even knowledge of. . . . The way to get to meaningful prayer for those good things is to start by praying for what we are truly interested in. The circle of our interests will inevitably grow in the largeness of God's love. . . . I believe the most adequate description of prayer is simply, "Talking to God about what we are doing together." . . . Prayer is a matter of explicitly sharing with God my concerns about what he too is concerned about in my life. And of course he is concerned about my concerns and, in particular, that my concerns should coincide with his. This is our walk together. Out of it I pray.[34]

Without orientation in the Lord's Prayer and the larger context of God's kingdom purpose, prayer can degenerate into an exercise in consumerism. This may explain why the prayer of Jabez has become more popular than the model prayer of Jesus in American evangelical Christianity. The prayer of Jabez is tucked away in an obscure passage in 1 Chronicles: "Jabez cried out to the God of Israel, 'Oh, that you would bless me and enlarge my territory! Let your hand be with me, and keep me from harm so that I will be free from pain'" (1 Chr 4:10, TNIV). It's all about "me"—bless me, enlarge my territory, be with me, keep me from pain. The Lord's Prayer is about "us." It is a community prayer; it's not about my territory, it's not about expanding my little kingdom. It's about God's kingdom, it's about God's story, it's about God's new world. It's about God's forgiveness and being a channel of that forgiveness to others.

Even when prayer is oriented within the context of God's kingdom purpose, there is a mystery to it that cannot be adequately explained. John Ortberg shares an interesting story about answered prayer. Bob, an insurance agent with no connection to politics, became acquainted with Doug, a man in Washington, D.C., who was part of a ministry that mostly involved people in politics. One day Bob showed up excited about Jesus' promise, "ask whatever you will in my name and I will do it." "Is that really true?" asked Bob. Doug said, "Well, it's not a blank check. You have to take it in the context of the teachings of the whole Scripture on prayer. But yes—it really is true. Jesus really does answer prayer." Bob said, "Great, I think I will pray for Africa." Doug suggested he narrow his prayer to one country. So Bob decided to pray for Kenya.

Doug challenged Bob that if he would pray faithfully for Kenya for six months, and nothing seemed to happen, then he would give Bob $500; on the other hand, if something remarkable did happen, then Bob would have to pay him $500. So Bob began to pray. For a long time nothing happened. Then one night Bob was at a dinner in Washington, D.C., where the people around the table explained what they did for a living. One woman indicated that she ran an orphanage in Kenya. Bob sprang to life and began to see his money fly away. He asked lots of questions, and the woman invited him to fly to Kenya and visit the orphanage. Nothing could have kept him away.

Bob was appalled by the poverty and the lack of basic health care. When he returned to D.C., he could not get the orphanage off his mind. So he started writing to large pharmaceutical companies, describing to them the vast need. He asked them to send their unsold supplies to Kenya. The orphanage received more than a million dollars worth of medical supplies.

The woman called Bob up. "This is amazing!" she exclaimed. "We've had the most phenomenal gifts because of the letters you wrote. We would like to fly you back over and have a big party. Will you come?" Bob went back over to celebrate with them. While he was there, the president of Kenya came to the party; this was the largest orphanage in the country. The president offered to take Bob on a tour of Nairobi, the capital. In the course of the tour, they saw a prison. Bob inquired about the prisoners. They were political prisoners. Bob said to the president, "That's a bad idea. You should let them out."

When Bob got home, he received a call from the State Department of the U.S. government. They wanted to inform him that for years they had been trying to secure the release of these prisoners, and all their maneuverings had ended in dead ends. But now they had been released, and they were told it was primarily due to . . . Bob. So the government called to say thanks.

Several months later the president of Kenya called Bob. He was going to rearrange his government and select a new cabinet. He wanted to know if Bob would be willing to come back to Kenya and pray for him for three days while he worked on his cabinet. Bob—with no political connections at all—boarded a plane, flew back to Kenya, and prayed for the president as he selected his leaders.[35]

That's a wonderful story, isn't it? But what about the stories concerning prayers as diligent and authentic as Bob's but that remain unanswered? There is a mystery to prayer that we cannot master. Marcus Borg refuses "to use interventionism as the explanation" for answers to prayers of intercession and petition, and yet he prays such prayers frequently. He writes, "To refuse to do them because I can't imagine how prayer works would be an act of intellectual pride: if I can't imagine how something works, then it can't work. To think thus involves more than a bit of *hubris*."[36]

I remember as a kid, eight or nine years old, desperately crying out to God. Not because my mother or father was seriously ill, but because I lost my ball glove. It was a Wilson A2000. Even then, it was a top-quality, high-priced glove. At the time it was about the best money could buy. My father worked at a steel mill and my mother was a homemaker, so it was no small thing for them to purchase the glove for me. And I lost it.

I recall sitting on my front porch in tears when I realized it was gone. I prayed and cried and prayed some more. I don't remember the details, where it turned up, or how I found it, but I did find it. And do you know what I believed, as a kid who prayed his heart out? I believed God cared enough to have pity on me. I didn't believe it because I read it somewhere or someone told me about it (I never paid attention in Sunday school); I believed it because I experienced it. Did God really answer my prayer, or was it mere coincidence? I don't know, but I know what I experienced at the time, and it had a significant impact on my faith as a kid.

I don't know how prayer works. I don't know why some prayers are answered and some are not. But I do believe God accommodates God's self to us in order to show us that God loves us, because primarily God wants to be with us in an intimate relationship. God is great enough and gracious enough to meet us where we are, without regard to our level of knowledge or understanding, religious beliefs or traditions, or personal holiness. God looks for ways, without being too intrusive or overpowering, to show us that God cares.

I can't explain the mystery of answered and unanswered prayer. I suspect there are all kinds of factors involved, some of which we know nothing about. But I am confident in this: God will meet us where we are to reveal to us how much God loves us. And when it comes to prayer, God is ever nudging us along so that our circle of interests and concerns are constantly expanding and extending to issues of forgiveness, justice, and mercy—the very issues and concerns that involve God's new world on earth.

Questions for Reflection and Discussion

1. Do you agree with the statement that the process of socialization moves us more deeply into the world of self-concern and self-occupation? Do you think the discussion about the "false self" adequately depicts the human condition? How do you make sense of the Genesis story of "the fall"? Why is the transformation process of shedding one's "false self" so difficult and slow? Reflect on the characteristics of the "false self" that you need to discard and replace. What characteristics, attributes, or patterns of thought and conduct need to replace them?

2. In what sense must one become like a little child in order to enter and live in God's kingdom? Reflect on childlike qualities that can nurture a transformative faith and on those that can diminish and hinder the transformational process.

3. Whenever we offer grace, acceptance, and love to the children of the world, to the weak and vulnerable, to the outcasts and the helpless, we become agents of God's new world." In so doing, we are acting to name them as children of God. In what ways might we act in our families, work relationships, and casual acquaintances to name someone a child of God and serve as an agent of God's kingdom?

4. Describe in your own words the importance of Jesus' love commands: to love God with the totality of your being and to love your neighbor as yourself. In what sense do all the law and prophets hang on these two commands?

5. In your estimation, what are the most important elements of a "righteous" life? How does our social and cultural context influence how we hear/understand the Beatitudes?

6. How does Jesus fulfill the Torah? What's the difference between interpreting Jesus' instructions regarding nonviolence as illustrations and

interpreting them as commandments? What is the most important thing we can say about the righteousness of God's new world embodied and taught by Jesus?

7. How does a nonviolent/forgiving response have the potential to break the chain of violence and offer hope of a new beginning?

8. How might we go about internalizing the life of Christ?

9. Reflect again on the apparent anti-family statements made by Jesus. How do you understand these statements in the historic context of Jesus' ministry and in the modern context of their application for today?

10. Where do you find your source of identity and security? What we actually do may reflect more accurately what we really believe. Does your lifestyle reflect your faith? Think of both positive and negative examples. What spiritual disciplines might you engage in to bring your life in line with your faith?

11. Do you agree with Richard Foster that money is a rival god and must be dethroned? Do you agree with the assessment that money has an inherent unrighteousness/fallenness to it? Why or why not?

12. It was argued that all our "asking, seeking, and knocking" in prayer only makes sense if it is permeated and directed by the spirit and posture of the Lord's Prayer. Do you agree with this? Why or why not?

13. What do you think is the purpose of prayer? How much attention should we give to personal matters in prayer? Or should we even pray about our own concerns?

Notes

1. Fred Craddock, *Craddock Stories,* ed. Mike Graves and Richard F. Ward (St. Louis: Chalice Press, 2001), 156–57. I heard some of the minor details when I personally heard Craddock tell this story, which differs slightly from the way it appears in his book. Stories are rarely told in exactly the same way twice.

2. Morna Hooker, *The Gospel According to Saint Mark,* Black's New Testament Commentaries, ed. Henry Chadwick (London: Hendrickson Publishers, 1991), 239.

3. Matthew's version (18:2) conveys clearly our need to do an about-face ("unless you change and become like little children"; the RSV translates "unless you turn").

4. Marcus J. Borg, *The Heart of Christianity: Rediscovering a Life of Faith* (New York: HarperSanFrancisco, 2003), 114.

5. Ibid., 117.

6. Huston Smith, *The Soul of Christianity: Restoring the Great Tradition* (New York: HarperSanFrancisco, 2005), 9.

7. Marcus J. Borg, *Jesus, A New Vision: Spirit, Culture, and the Life of Discipleship* (New York: HarperSanFrancisco, 1987), 113.

8. *Forrest Gump*, dir. Robert Zemeckis, written by Eric Roth (screenplay) and Winston Groom (novel), Paramount Pictures, 1994.

9. Walter Brueggemann, *Reverberations of Faith: A Theological Handbook of Old Testament Themes* (Louisville: Westminster John Knox Press, 2002), 178.

10. See Isa 9:7; 51:7; 60:17; 61:10-11; Jer 4:2; 23:5; 22:15.

11. It is doubtful that Jesus delivered all of this teaching on one occasion. Most New Testament scholars believe that this material was collected into its present form either before the Gospel was written or that the Gospel writer himself grouped the material together into a coherent whole, or perhaps both. Certainly the author shaped this material. But however it came into its present form, the structuring was intentional and well thought through.

12. Eugene M. Boring, *The Gospel of Matthew*, New Interpreter's Bible, vol. 8 (Nashville: Abingdon Press, 1995), 175.

13. Quoted by Philip Yancey, *The Jesus I Never Knew* (Grand Rapids: Zondervan Publishing House, 1995), 13.

14. Barbara Brown Taylor, *Gospel Medicine* (Boston: Cowley Publications, 1995), 145, 149.

15. Dallas Willard, *The Divine Conspiracy: Rediscovering Our Hidden Life in God* (New York: HarperSanFrancisco, 1998), 177–78.

16. Ibid., 179.

17. Ibid., 181.

18. Drawn from Philip Yancey, *What's So Amazing about Grace* (Grand Rapids: Zondervan, 1997), 101–102. Original source: Victor Hugo, *Les Misérables* (New York: Knopf, 1997).

19. Thomas Merton, *New Seeds of Contemplation* (New York: New Directions Publishing Corporation, 1972), 38.

20. Leander Keck, *Who Is Jesus? History in the Perfect Tense* (Columbia: University of South Carolina Press, 2000), 160.

21. Ibid., 166.

22. C. S. Lewis, *Mere Christianity*, rev. and amp. ed. (New York: HarperSanFrancisco, 2001), 188.

23. Ibid., 189.

24. Ibid., 192.

25. Frank Laubach, *Prayer: The Mightiest Force in the World* (Westwood NJ: Fleming H. Revell Company, 1946), 110.

26. Tony Campolo, *Who Switched the Price Tags* (Dallas: Word Publishing, 1986), 14.

27. See also Matt 12:46-50 and Luke 8:19-21.

28. For another difficult saying see Matt 10:35-39 and Luke 12:51-53.

29. R. Alan Culpepper, *The Gospel of Luke*, New Interpreter's Bible, vol. 9 (Nashville: Abingdon Press, 1995), 256.

30. Ibid., 257.

31. Richard J. Foster, *The Challenge of the Disciplined Life: Christian Reflections on Money, Sex, and Power* (New York: HarperSanFrancisco, 1985), 54.

32. Lee Eclov, *Buying Friends/Luke 16:1-13,* Preaching Today, cassette recording #193.

33. Flannery O'Conner, *The Complete Stories* (New York: Farrar, Straus, and Giroux, 1971), 42–53.

34. Willard, *Divine Conspiracy,* 242–43.

35. John Ortberg, *If You Want to Walk on Water, You've Got to Get Out of the Boat* (Grand Rapids: Zondervan, 2001), 91–94.

36. Borg, *Heart of Christianity,* 197.

Chapter 6

Tragedy and Triumph

Popular evangelical Christianity typically emphasizes the saving efficacy of Jesus' death for our sins as the central matter of Christian faith. Taking their cue from the writings of Paul, when talking about God's provision for our redemption, many evangelicals focus almost exclusively on Christ's death, making salvation primarily about the removal of sin-guilt and the promise of heaven. Theologian Hans Kung makes a perceptive observation regarding this approach to the gospel:

> For the sake of logic, Jesus' death on the cross is isolated from his message and life and at the same time also from his resurrection: essentially Jesus came simply in order to die. The concrete proclamation, conduct, suffering, and new life of the historical Jesus of Nazareth have no constitutive part in this theory. . . . Concrete human beings, for whom all this is supposed to be done, thus largely disappear behind the figure of God's Son; they are not inwardly affected and for the most part are simply put off with promises of the afterlife.[1]

If, however, we take seriously the theology of salvation expounded in the Synoptic Gospels, then we cannot speak of the redemption that Christ provides apart from the life he lived. In these Gospels the life, death, and resurrection of Jesus are woven together to form one piece.

The Way of the Cross

In the Synoptic Gospels, three times Jesus predicts his death and each time the disciples misunderstand because they are focused on their own agenda. Mark's Gospel describes the third account.

> They were on their way up to Jerusalem, with Jesus leading the way, and the disciples were astonished, while those who followed were afraid. Again he took the Twelve aside and told them what was going to happen to him. "We are going up to Jerusalem," he said, "and the Son of Man will be delivered over to the chief priests and teachers of the law. They will condemn him to death and will hand him over to the Gentiles, who will mock him and spit on him, flog him and kill him. Three days later he will rise."
>
> Then James and John, the sons of Zebedee, came to him, "Teacher," they said, "we want you to do for us whatever we ask."
>
> "What do you want me to do for you?" he asked.
>
> They replied, "Let one of us sit at your right and the other at your left in your glory."
>
> "You don't know what you are asking," Jesus said. "Can you drink the cup I drink or be baptized with the baptism I am baptized with?"
>
> "We can," they answered.
>
> Jesus said to them, "You will drink the cup I drink and be baptized with the baptism I am baptized with, but to sit on my right and left is not for me to grant. These places belong to those for whom they have been prepared."
>
> When the ten heard about this, they became indignant with James and John. Jesus called them together and said, "You know that those who are regarded as rulers of the Gentiles lord it over them, and their high officials exercise authority over them. Not so with you. Instead, whoever wants to become great among you must be your servant and whoever wants to be first must be slave of all. For even the Son of Man did not come to be served, but to serve, and to give his life as a ransom for many." (Mark 10:32-45, TNIV)[2]

The way of Jesus leads to Jerusalem, the place of rejection, suffering, and death. Paradoxically, the place of death is also the place of life. Here God vindicates Jesus by raising him up. So the way that leads to death is the way that leads to life, and it is the same for Jesus' followers.

In the story above, Jesus' third prediction of his death receives no response from the disciples. Evidently they think Jesus is speaking in parables or talking in riddles, which they do not take the time to consider. Distracted by thoughts of greatness, James and John make a bid for power, jockeying for prized positions. They obviously think the kingdom is coming soon, and they want to sit with Jesus on the throne. Jesus indicates that they do not understand the nature of God's new world and their commitment to it. In his rebuke, Jesus interjects a word of hope: "you will drink the cup I drink and be baptized with the baptism I am baptized with," implying that at a future time they will have the faith to bear it. But for now, they're pervaded by a lust for power and prestige that dulls their spiritual sensitivity and faith.

Barbara Brown Taylor comments that James and John have their minds set on Election Day, not for Galilee County but for God's kingdom, when Jesus will come into his own. She writes,

> They seem to believe that the new world will be set up just like the old world only with new leadership in place. The bad guys at the head table will be removed, their chairs will be fumigated and God's new crew will be seated, with Jesus in the number one position and the most loyal members of his campaign staff on either side of him. Once this change has been accomplished, then—finally! At last!—the good people will commence to redeem the world from top to bottom, beginning from the top. The ultimate trickle-down effect.[3]

The way of Jesus is not about wielding power and exercising authority over others or about holding prominent positions of honor and status; it's about being a "servant of all" without distinction or regard for rank, class, status, race, gender, intelligence, social standing, or anything else used to separate and divide people.

At Jesus' first mention of being rejected and killed, Mark's Gospel reads, "He called the crowd with his disciples, and said to them, 'If any want to become my followers, let them deny themselves and take their cross and follow me. For those who want to save their life will lose it, and those who lose their life for my sake, and for the sake of the gospel [of the kingdom], will save it'" (Mark 8:34-35).

Leander Keck describes the way of the cross in terms of paradigm and promise.[4] The cross as paradigm is a vivid symbol of what it means to follow Christ. The way of the cross is marked by the decision to set aside self-interest in view of a larger good (the kingdom of God) and to disregard the need for approbation in such service. It "may take the form of unabridged obedience to God that makes one vulnerable to unjust suffering or of nonreciprocal love for neighbor in accord with the God who sends sun and rain on the just and the unjust."[5] The image of "taking up one's cross" pictures the one sentenced to crucifixion carrying his cross to the place of execution. I suggested in the last chapter that the image is meant to be taken metaphorically, pointing to a pattern of dying to self, to ego, in order to serve others in humility, transparency, and love.

The promise of the way of the cross is found in the paradoxical statement that whoever tries to save his life will lose it and whoever loses his life for Christ's sake and for the sake of the gospel will gain it. Christians in Mark's church lost much for the sake of Christ and God's kingdom: status, friends, family, employment, health, security, and perhaps even their lives. The way of the cross means giving up one's selfish agenda to pursue God's cause in the world and to serve others. The irony is that in the giving up (the losing) of the ego-driven life in the service of Christ and God's kingdom, one gains life. Followers of Christ discover wholeness and peace, not only beyond death, but now in the midst of suffering and loss.

The way of the cross is the way of salvation. Mark's Gospel reads, "For the Son of Man came not to be served but to serve, and to give his life as a ransom for many." The word translated "ransom" comes from the world where prisoners, slaves, or condemned criminals could be liberated by a payment. But in the Greek translation of the Old Testament, the Septuagint (LXX), this word group/image (the verb "redeem" and the noun "redemption" come from the same Greek word for "ransom") can simply refer to God's deliverance of his people without any notion of a ransom paid.[6] It's a mistake to press the image too far and insist that Jesus' death constituted an actual ransom price paid. New Testament scholar Stephen Finlan points out that "redemption" does not mean God actually paid anyone off or paid God's self off; it just means God rescued people. Finlan argues that if we take the metaphors too literally, we can miss the forest (the point) for the trees (the details).[7] The Gospel is making the point that the self-giving of Jesus unto death has redeeming, liberating power; it is a means of liberation.

But it is not his death alone that has redeeming power; it is the self-giving of his life unto death. New Testament scholars Joel Green and Mark Baker observe,

> Just as he [Jesus] has instructed his followers to devote their lives to the service of others, so now he reveals the purpose of his own coming in the same terms, even to the point that he will embrace death on behalf of others. In his death Jesus incarnates his own message concerning the living

of life oriented toward God's purpose and thus toward the welfare of others.[8]

His death is the culmination of a life of compassion, sacrifice, and self-giving to others; his death gathers up his life, a life lived for God's cause, for God's new world.

The life of Jesus receives little consideration in most of the popular versions of evangelical Christianity; the saving power resides in his death. An article that appeared in our local newspaper reflects this position. The article attacks critics who leveled negative reviews against Mel Gibson's film, *The Passion of the Christ*. In defense of the film, the writer says,

> And some of them [the critics] complained that the movie doesn't tell enough of the story. It only focuses on 12 hours of the life of Jesus. It doesn't tell us enough about who he really was, and what he was really about. Where is Jesus the great Teacher? Where is the sweet man who came to plant seeds of love? Well, it seems to me that the movie *is* about the real Jesus. It does take us to the very heart of the story of the real Jesus. Jesus did not come to be a great religious teacher. Jesus did not come to teach us about love. He came to die.[9]

Jesus came only to die, not to teach us about love. I suspect that in the fury of arguing his point, this writer has overstated it and would surely say it differently upon realizing how foolish it sounds. Nevertheless, he did say it: "Jesus did not come to teach us about love. He came to die." The result is that we are left with a half-gospel that has no real power to transform individuals and society. By contrast, theologian Douglas Hall says this important word:

> One glimpses the God whom Jesus represents as one follows the human life that he leads, the relationships that he forms, the responses he makes to power, to weakness, to illness and death, to sin, to the demonic. In Christological doctrine, this theology assumes—as in the life of the Christ as such—that the prior concentration is upon the actual living, teaching, suffering, and death of Jesus.[10]

The liberation or redemption in this Gospel passage is not about the removal of sin-guilt; rather, it is liberation from the need to hold positions of prominence and wield power and from the lust and greed of selfish ambition. Jesus says, "This is how the world works. Tyrants wield power and rulers lord it over others. Not so with you. If you want to be great, you must become a servant of all." Albert Nolan observes that Jesus exercises a different kind of power:

> Power in the "kingdom" of God will be totally different from power as it is exercised in the "kingdom" of Satan. The power of Satan is the power of domination and oppression, the power of God is the power of service and freedom. All the monarchies and nations of this present world are governed by the power of domination and force. The structure of the "kingdom" of God will be determined by the power of spontaneous loving service which people render to one another. . . . The power of this new society is not a power which has to be served, a power before a person must bow down and cringe. It is the power which has an enormous influence in the lives of people by being of service to them. It is the power which is so unselfish that it will serve others even by dying for them.[11]

Jesus is not describing a strategy for becoming great; he is repudiating the need to become great. Jesus is not saying, "You become great by becoming a servant. The way up is down. Serve others and God will exalt you to a place of prominence above your peers." Serving others is not a kind of intermediate stage like boot camp where you prove yourself and wait for proper advancement. Jesus is not a king in disguise who will one day assume the throne and wield power; Jesus is a king who exercises power through service. Jesus is saying, "If you are occupied with the need to be great, then you misunderstand the nature of God's kingdom. God's new world is not about some who are great and others who are not. There are no great and small. All are servants of all." Serving others is not a means of climbing the ladder to assume power; it is the very power of God's new world, the power of love. Barbara Brown Taylor perceptively remarks that it is the power to turn the question of James and John upside down: "Teacher, we want to do for you whatever you ask of us."[12]

A children's Sunday school class decided to do a "reenactment" of the creation story. The children portrayed the creation of animal and plant life. A six-year-old boy was assigned the role of standing on a ladder and shining a flashlight on the unfolding of creation; he was supposed to represent God. When the creeping things began to creep over to where the swimming things were supposed to swim, the teacher felt a tug on her skirt. The little boy who was playing God wanted out. He said, "I'm just feeling too crazy to be God today." Most of us, however, don't feel that way. We like playing God. Our ego wants to call the shots and wield power. But Jesus says, "Not so with you."

How do we let go of the desire to play God? How do we experience this kind of liberation? How do we find the freedom to let go of the need to compare and compete and learn to find joy in being a servant? We experience liberation when we take up our crosses and follow Jesus. The liberating power of the cross of Jesus is experienced, not by believing in a doctrine of atonement, but by following the way of Jesus that led to the cross. The cross is the symbol that gathers up the entire teaching, way, and life of Jesus.

The way of salvation is the way of the cross. It is the way of self-surrender and sacrifice for the good of others. It is the way of service, forgiveness, unconditional love, radical grace, and compassionate justice. It means death to our egocentricity, death to the need to control others, and death to the need for honor and recognition. Most of us must die many times, and with each death our ego is put in its place, and space is made for the grace and goodness of Christ to form us into more compassionate and loving persons.

This may appear foolish to worldly wisdom and the powers-that-be because it cuts so sharply against the grain of our ego-driven society. The way of Jesus leads not to worldly power and greatness, but to suffering and death, and yet this death leads to life and liberation born and sustained by a different kind of power—the power of love.

Why Did Jesus Die?

In one sense Jesus died because he deeply angered and offended important religious and political leaders of his day. His repudiation of their hypocrisy, his prophetic call to justice, his disregard for their interpretations of the law, and his popularity with the common people were all factors that compelled some of the religious authorities to move against him. Jesus began a movement that exposed the weaknesses of and offered an alternative to much of the conventional wisdom endorsed and promoted by important religious and political authorities. Jesus scholar Marcus Borg writes,

> To a large extent, it was the conventional wisdom of the time—the "dominant consciousness" of the day—that was responsible for the death of Jesus. The high priest and his circle were both the servants and guardians of the dominant consciousness. Shaped by it and in a sense subservient to it, they were also concerned to preserve it. With its "laws" of moderation and self-preservation, and its attempt to make reality "safe" by domesticating it in a net of beliefs and rules, the dominant consciousness of conventional

wisdom is threatened by a voice of an alternative consciousness. . . . In
Jesus, the voice of the Spirit challenged the dominant consciousness.[13]

Jesus challenged the conventional wisdom of his time, which set in motion a
series of events that led to his crucifixion.

On the other hand, the Gospels interpret Jesus' death as part of God's
redemptive plan for humanity. In C. S. Lewis's *The Lion, the Witch, and the
Wardrobe*, Aslan, the great lion, is killed on a stone table by the witch and
her hordes. His execution fulfills the deal Aslan made with the witch in order
to deliver Edmund from death by her hand. The triumph of the witch, however, is short-lived; it is thwarted by a "deeper magic" at work in the death of
Aslan. When Aslan comes back to life, Susan asks what it all means.

> "It means," said Aslan, "that though the Witch knew the Deep Magic,
> there is a magic deeper still which she did not know. Her knowledge goes
> back only to the dawn of time. But if she could have looked a little further
> back, into the stillness and the darkness before Time dawned, she would
> have read there a different incantation. She would have known that when a
> willing victim who had committed no treachery was killed in a traitor's
> stead, the Table would crack and Death itself would start working back-
> wards."[14]

In the Gospels, there is a deeper significance attached to the death of
Jesus than a hostile reaction by the authorities. The triumph of the religious
leaders and the civil authorities in the crucifixion of Jesus gives way to a
greater triumph in Christ's vindication by God. God's vindication of Jesus
demonstrates that in spite of all appearances to the contrary, there is a
"deeper magic" at work; God has come near to human beings in their suffering and shame.

In the Gospel of Mark we read the following account of Jesus' death:

> They compelled a passer-by, who was coming in from the country, to carry
> his cross; it was Simon of Cyrene, the father of Alexander and Rufus. Then
> they brought Jesus to the place called Golgotha (which means the place of
> the skull). And they offered him wine mixed with myrrh; but he did not
> take it. And they crucified him, and divided his clothes among them, cast-
> ing lots to decide what each should take.
>
> It was nine o'clock in the morning when they crucified him. The
> inscription of the charge against him read, "The King of the Jews." And
> with him they crucified two bandits, one on his right and one on his left.

Those who passed by derided him, shaking their heads and saying, "Aha! You who would destroy the temple and build it in three days, save yourself, and come down from the cross!" In the same way the chief priests, along with the scribes, were also mocking him among themselves and saying, "He saved others; he cannot save himself. Let the Messiah, the King of Israel, come down from the cross now, so that we may see and believe." Those who were crucified with him also taunted him.

When it was noon, darkness came over the whole land until three in the afternoon. At three o'clock Jesus cried out with a loud voice, "Eloi, Eloi, lema sabachthani?" which means, "My God, my God, why have you forsaken me?" When some of the bystanders heard it, they said, "Listen, he is calling for Elijah." And someone ran, filled a sponge with sour wine, put it on a stick, and gave it to him to drink, saying, "Wait, let us see whether Elijah will come to take him down." Then Jesus gave a loud cry and breathed his last. And the curtain of the temple was torn in two, from top to bottom. Now when the centurion, who stood facing him, saw that in this way he breathed his last, he said, "Truly this man was God's Son!" (Mark 15:21-39)

There is a story of an old man who was known to meditate early every morning under a big tree on the bank of the Ganges River. One morning, after he had finished his meditation, he opened his eyes and saw a scorpion floating helplessly in the water. As the scorpion washed closer to the tree, the old man quickly stretched himself out on one of the long roots that branched into the river to rescue the drowning scorpion. As soon as he touched the creature it stung him. Instinctively the man withdrew his hand. A minute later, after he regained his balance, he stretched out again on the roots to save the scorpion. The scorpion stung him again, this time causing his hand to swell and bleed.

At that moment, a passerby who saw the whole thing as it unfolded shouted, "Hey, silly old man, what's wrong with you? Only a fool would risk his life for the sake of a scorpion. Don't you know you could kill yourself trying to save that ungrateful creature?"

The old man turned his head and looked into the stranger's eyes. He said calmly, "My friend, just because it is the scorpion's nature to sting, that does not change my nature to save."[15]

In the suffering of Jesus we see the capacity of human beings to harm and the capacity of God to redeem. Brennan Manning writes, "The crucified Christ is not an abstraction but the ultimate answer to how far love will go, what measure of rejection it will endure, how much selfishness and betrayal it will withstand."[16]

The title "King of the Jews" was the written notice of the charge leveled against Jesus. In Mark's story, just prior to the above passage, the Roman soldiers make sport of Jesus, draping a purple robe around him, thrusting a crown of thorns onto his brow, and scornfully crying out, "Hail, King of the Jews." They strike him, spit upon him, and mockingly bow down as if to pay homage to him. Also, the chief priests and the teachers of the law ridicule Jesus, saying, "Let this Messiah, the King of Israel, come down now from the cross that we may see and believe." They mock him by calling him the king of Israel, for they could not conceive of Israel's king hanging on a cross, humiliated, rejected, and defeated. It was scandalous for anyone to think Jesus could be Israel's king.

Yet, in this horrific scene, "the King of the Jews" was revealing the power of his kingdom, namely, the power of suffering love. In the delivering of Jesus to be crucified, the saving, redeeming power of God was at work. Jesus could not save himself if he was to save others. He would have to drink the bitter cup of suffering to the last drop in death in order to be the representative "Son of Man" who fully experiences the anguish of the human condition.

In this ultimate act of self-giving unto death, Jesus revealed the heart of God; and so Mark has the Roman centurion "who stood there in front of Jesus" and "saw how he died" declare, "Surely this man was God's Son!"[17] Morna Hooker has observed that Mark's presentation of the crucifixion is such that it reads almost like an enthronement: Jesus is hailed by the crowds as he enters Jerusalem; he is anointed by a woman; identified by the high priest; proclaimed to the people by Pilate; saluted as king by the soldiers; and now enthroned on a cross, with an inscription proclaiming to the world who he is, with two thieves occupying the places of honor at his right and his left.[18] Jesus is a different kind of king of a different kind of world.

The darkness mentioned is undoubtedly an allusion to Amos 8:9: "On that day, says the LORD God, I will make the sun go down at noon, and darken the earth in broad daylight." Normally, this apocalyptic sign is associated with judgment and may suggest God's judgment on those who crucified Jesus, or it may simply signal the distress experienced by Jesus himself. The rending of the "curtain of the temple" (most likely the outer curtain that separated the holy place from the rest of the temple) could be a foreshadowing of the temple's future destruction, or it may symbolize the proclamation to the Gentiles of access to God's presence available through Jesus' life and death.

The cry of Jesus from the cross is drawn from Psalm 22:1: "My God, my God, why have you forsaken me?" It is, on the one hand, an expression of Jesus' agonizing sense of abandonment by God; on the other hand, it is a vivid cry of radical faith. In faith Jesus clings to God, though he can no longer feel or sense God's presence. Anyone who has struggled to find God amid great tragedy and suffering can find consolation and hope in Jesus' cry of faith. Jesus refuses to forsake God, even when he feels forsaken by God.[19]

In Mark's account of the crucifixion (this is true for Matthew and Luke as well), there is no suggestion that Jesus is dying as a substitute to bear the guilt, penalty, or punishment for our sins. The only other reference to the redemptive effect of Jesus' death in the Synoptic Gospels (that is, other than the reference already mentioned regarding the giving of Jesus' life as a "ransom" or "means of liberation") is found in the context of Jesus' celebration of the Passover, where Jesus says, "This is the blood of the covenant, which is poured out for many" (Mark 14:24). The parallel passage in Matthew adds, "for the forgiveness of sins" (Matt 26:28). As I mentioned earlier, forgiveness was an important element in Jesus' teaching and proclamation of the kingdom of God.[20] The giving of Jesus' body and blood, expressed in the eating of the bread and the drinking of the cup, points simply to the giving of his total life for others.

The sacrificial imagery used here recalls Exodus 24:1-8 where the sacrifice serves to ratify the covenant between God and God's people. In Mark, the one greater than Moses ratifies a new covenant with his own blood poured out for many. It is likely that Jesus gave his death this interpretation, that he regarded his death as the sign and seal of the new covenant that would characterize the fullness of God's new world. Jesus was forming a people through whom the kingdom of God would be manifested and proclaimed to others. The sacrifice of Jesus as interpreted in the Synoptic Gospels is not a sin offering; he does not bear divine punishment or penalty for the sins of the people. Rather, his life was given up for God's cause to form a kingdom people who can spread the kingdom to the whole world. Forgiveness of sins, between the people and God and between the people themselves, is at the core of the covenant relationship.

Popular Christianity, taking its cue from the writings of Paul, typically regards Jesus' death as the sole means of our redemption. It is usually understood as follows: We are all sinners and deserve punishment. Because God is just and holy, God must punish sin, which means the sinner must bear the guilt and penalty for his sin. God sent Jesus to bear our punishment, to die in our place as our substitute, so that the sinner can be forgiven. In bearing the penalty/guilt/punishment/judgment for sin, God's justice/honor is now satisfied and God's wrath appeased so that God is now free to rain grace and forgiveness upon the sinner. The sinner is "saved" by accepting this arrangement through faith. This usually involves a prayer of acceptance and confession.[21]

Marcus Borg has an important word to say about substitutionary atonement:

> Many people think this is the orthodox and thus "official" Christian understanding of Jesus' death, including many who have difficulty with it, whether within the church or outside of it. Hence it is important to realize that it is not the only Christian understanding. Indeed, it took over a thousand years for it to become dominant.
>
> In fully developed form, it first appears in a book written in 1097 by Anselm, archbishop of Canterbury. It gradually became central in medieval Christianity and then in much of the theology of the Protestant Reformation. There it was foundational for the notion of radical grace: through Jesus' death, God has abolished the system of requirements by taking care of whatever you think separates you from God. Ironically and over time, it became for many Protestants the primary requirement in a new system of requirements: we are made right with God by believing that Jesus died as our substitute. Radical grace became conditional grace. And conditional grace is no longer grace.
>
> But seeing Jesus' death primarily within the framework of substitutionary atonement goes far beyond what the New Testament says. Strikingly, Mark's story of Jesus' death says nothing about substitutionary sacrifice. In the other gospels, it is only if one reads them within the framework of substitution that one finds the notion there.[22]

A major problem with the popular view of substitutionary sacrifice is that it binds God to a system of justice that is humanly contrived and impugns the very character of God. What kind of God would demand the sacrifice of an innocent victim to appease an offended sense of justice or pay off a penalty that God could simply remit by divine decision? Why would God need to sacrifice a human being when God can simply forgive the way a parent forgives a child? Is God subject to some sort of outside universal justice by which God must abide? If we accept the sovereignty of God, there is no justice system outside of God; God sets the standard. If God chooses to forgive sin because it is God's character to do so, there is nothing to prevent God from exercising that right.[23]

What kind of God demands the blood of an innocent person? Why would the death of an innocent, guiltless victim change God's attitude and action toward humankind? This view of the atonement makes God too similar to the pagan deities whose wrath must be placated by a sacrificial victim—in some cultures, a human victim.

According to the popular view, Jesus, in bearing our sin-guilt, does not so much save us from our sin (sin's power, influence, and control) as he saves us from God's judgment on our sin, which means Jesus saves us from God. Of course, adherents of the substitutionary atonement model would point out that God sent Jesus out of love for humanity. Nevertheless, we must ask, "What kind of God would need to save us from God's self?" Talk of God's love is idle, for if God demands innocent blood to atone for the guilty, then God is not an unconditional Lover. God's love is not free; it has its price. Talk of God's love toward sinners would be "a little like having the owner of a dog who is barking, growling, and straining at its leash say, 'Don't worry, he doesn't bite.' Maybe it is true, but the combination of messages we receive leads us to keep a safe distance from the dog."[24]

In the person of Jesus of Nazareth, God gave us a beautiful expression of what God is like, and human beings in their greed, pride, and selfish ambition found him so threatening that they crucified him. The sin that Jesus bears on the cross is not punishment inflicted by God, but the cruelty and hate of the religious, economic, and political powers that found his words and actions subversive and threatening.

In the Passion Narrative Jesus is harassed and taunted, "He saved others; he cannot save himself." It's particularly interesting how in Matthew's version the Gospel writer emphasizes that Jesus could have saved himself, but does not in order to fulfill Scripture. When Jesus is arrested and one of his disciples draws a sword and cuts off the ear of the high priest's servant, Jesus says, "Put your sword back into its place; for all who take the sword will perish by the sword. Do you think that I cannot appeal to my Father, and he will at once send me more than twelve legions of angels? But how then would the scriptures be fulfilled, which say it must happen in this way?" (Matt 26:53-54)

In Matthew, "fulfillment" of Scripture does not mean prediction and fulfillment; rather, Matthew sees the story of Israel as a story that finds its counterpart in the story of Jesus—there are points of connection. Matthew is saying Jesus is the fulfillment of Israel's purpose and hopes. Biblical scholar Donald Senior describes it this way:

> The evangelist views the total reality of Jesus as the "fulfillment" of the history of Israel and its Scriptures. . . . For Matthew, Jesus is the flowering of the history of God's people; Jesus and his mission are God's responses to the promises of salvation given to Israel. Therefore all the expectations and longings condensed within the Hebrew Scriptures find their outpouring and ultimate resolution in Jesus. Put another way, Jesus "fulfills" the Scriptures by revealing their ultimate intent and meaning.[25]

In the context of Jesus' Passion Narrative, Matthew is saying that Jesus' death is part of God's redemptive plan. Jesus could not save himself because it was not God's will that he save himself; it was important for Jesus to stand for God's cause/kingdom even unto death. Matthew doesn't explain why. There is no explicit atonement theology in the Synoptic Gospels, but there is an implicit one. Religion professor J. Denny Weaver writes,

> Is this narrative an atonement narrative? The answer is "no," if for atonement narrative one means a story that pictures Jesus' death as a divinely arranged plan to provide a payment to satisfy the offended honor of God or a requirement of divine law, or that understands Jesus as the substitute bearer of punishment that sinful humankind deserves. . . . But the answer is "yes," if one envisions a reconciliation of sinful humankind to God on the basis of the life, death, and resurrection of Jesus. . . .
>
> In carrying out that mission, Jesus was killed by the earthly structures in bondage to the power of evil. His death was not a payment owed to God's honor, nor was it divine punishment that he suffered as a substitute for sinners. Jesus' death was the rejection of the rule of God by forces opposed to that rule. . . . It poses a contrast between the attempt to coerce by violence under the rule of evil and the nonviolence of the rule of God as revealed and made visible by the life, death, and resurrection of Jesus.[26]

An implicit incarnational theology in the Gospels best serves as the backdrop for understanding the "deeper magic" at work in Christ's death. As Matthew proclaims at the beginning of his story, in Jesus, "God is with us" (Matt 1:23). God's presence/Spirit fills Jesus and permeates his life. As God's Son, Jesus experiences a special relationship and connection to God proclaimed to the reader at Jesus' baptism and transfiguration, where the voice of God affirms Jesus' sonship. In Jesus' life, words, deeds, and actions, God was present.

God, therefore, did not put Jesus to death; rather, God, in and through Jesus, made God's self available, and in making God's self available God has become expendable, susceptible to abuse and even crucifixion by human beings.

Former seminary president Roy Honeycutt tells the story about the origin of the Irish expression "chancing one's arm." On display in St. Patrick's cathedral in Dublin is a door with a rectangular opening in the center. It is known as the door of reconciliation. In 1492, two prominent Irish families, the Ormands and Kildares, were in the midst of a bitter feud. The Kildares had besieged the Ormands and the Ormands had taken refuge in the chapter house of St Patrick's cathedral, bolting themselves in. As the siege wore on, Gerald Fitzgerald, the Earl of Kildare, concluded that the feuding was foolish. Here were two families worshiping the same God, in the same church, living in the same country, trying to kill each other. He called out to Sir James Butler, the Earl of Ormand, for peace, but Butler did not respond. So Fitzgerald seized his spear, cut a hole in the door, and thrust his arm through—a vulnerable gesture. Another hand grasped it, the door then opened, and the two men embraced, thus ending the feud. From that noble gesture came the expression "chancing one's arm." God, in and through Jesus, becomes the vulnerable God, reaching out to us, "chancing God's arm"; but with Jesus the axe was not spared. He bore the animosity and wrath of humanity upon himself.

God did not crucify Jesus; we did. But God put Jesus in a crucifiable position. Jesus' life was a challenge to human pride, managed religion, political power, and our personal independence and quest for power, possessions, and prestige.

Clarence Jordan, an American Baptist who founded Koinonia Farm in 1942 as an interracial community in southwest Georgia, asked, "Did God put our sins on the back of his son on the cross? No. He made him available and we put our sins on his back."

He told about getting a phone call at 1:30 in the morning. The guy on the other end said, "Mr. Jordan, I just wanted to let you know that within seventeen minutes there's going to be a green pickup truck pull out of that dirt road there just below the bridge and it's going to be loaded with dynamite. We're going to blow your place off the face of the map. I just wanted to let you know so you would have time to get the people out of the buildings."

Jordan tried to keep the guy on the phone by asking questions, but the man who called was evidently in no mood to be conversational. He said in a huff, "Now, you have sixteen minutes," and hung up the phone.

Jordon's son woke up and wanted to know what the person needed. Jordan told him that somebody wanted to blow up the place. His son said, "Oh," and went back to bed.

Back in the bedroom, Jordon's wife inquired about the proceedings. He said, "Some guy called to say that he's going to blow the place up in sixteen minutes." She said, "Really?" and rolled over. Jordan thought, *What am I to do? My own family doesn't take this seriously.* So he went back to bed.

Jordan wrote about this incident,

> I must confess that the thoughts in my head were not conducive to sound slumber. I watched the clock tick off those minutes . . . and when it did headlights came up the road near that bridge and I thought, "Well, this is it." But we weren't going to be out there under that light, running around in our pajamas like a bunch of scared nitwits. We were going to be in our beds. And if the world wanted to have a little blowing-up party, they could have a little blowing-up party. . . .
>
> The pickup came and slowed down, and I thought he was coming in. But he didn't. We felt this taunt that they threw at Jesus' face—"Let him save himself." He couldn't. He was the one that he couldn't save. He hadn't come in the first place to save himself. He'd come to save mankind. He was the only one who couldn't save himself. . . . The taunt was true. For the world had to have a lightning rod to discharge its static, spiritual energy. And God made himself available in his son. And I think God needs in this world, available people who will bear the sins of the world.[27]

God did not put Jesus to death in order to bear the punishment of humankind or appease God's anger or satisfy God's honor; Jesus was sent to embody and proclaim God's new world and manifest God's love. God, in and through Jesus, shares the human condition; becomes the butt of insults and the victim of horrible cruelty; and suffers humiliation, betrayal, degradation, and death in order to breach the gulf separating human beings from God.

In 1960, a pastor in East Germany wrote a play called *The Sign of Jonah*. The last scene deals with the final judgment. All the peoples of the earth are assembled awaiting God's verdict, but they are not waiting passively. They are gathered in small groups, talking indignantly. One group is a band of Jews that were victims of the Nazi extermination camps. Another group consists of North American slaves who were subjugated to the suffocating holds of slave ships and cruel taskmasters. Hundreds of such groups are scattered across the plain—the victims of hatred, the poor, the afflicted, the maltreated. Each group appoints a representative to stand before the throne of God and challenge God's divine right to pass sentence. The representatives include a horribly twisted arthritic, a victim of Hiroshima, and a blind mute. They meet in council and decide that God is unqualified to sit in judgment unless God is willing to enter into the suffering, humiliated state of humanity and endure what they have undergone. Their conclusion reads, you must be born a Jew; the circumstances of your birth must be questioned; you must be misunderstood by everyone, insulted and mocked by your enemies, betrayed by your friends; you must be persecuted, beaten, and finally murdered in a most public and humiliating fashion.

Such is the judgment passed on God by the assembly. The clamor rises as they await God's response. Then a brilliant, dazzling light illuminates the entire plain. One by one those who have passed judgment on God fall silent. Emblazoned high in the heavens for the whole world to see is the signature of Jesus Christ with the inscription above it: I have served my sentence.[28]

This is not a popular interpretation of Jesus' death, for who wants to be a sin bearer? Who wants to be rejected and suffer? If we embrace Christ as the bearer of the world's hatred and evil, then we may also have to bear the hate and animosity of the world, which is what we do when we choose to forgive and love our enemies. When we forgive those who have hurt us, we choose to absorb the hurt—we bear it. It may even get us crucified! But it's the only hope for the salvation of the world. Punitive behavior is cyclical; it keeps getting passed on. People who are wounded, rejected, and hurt often pass those burdens on to others. Jesus shows us how to break the cycle by bearing it. The triumph of the cross is a triumph of love and forgiveness. This is why, I think, Matthew emphasizes forgiveness as the heart and core of God's new covenant sealed by Christ's death. Paul echoed this interpretation when he said that "in Christ God was reconciling the world to himself, not counting their trespasses against them" (2 Cor 5:19). Jesus, as the Son of Man, as the quintessential human being, in a representative way bore the anger and animosity of humanity upon himself, giving us a pattern to follow as disciples of Jesus and a way to break the cycle of evil and bring reconciliation to the world. As Jordan says, God needs available persons who are willing to be "lightning rods"; who are willing to bear the discharge of the world's hate and evil.

New Testament scholar N. T. Wright interprets Jesus' death as a representative death for Israel, the whole human race, and even the whole cosmos. He writes,

> Jesus suffers the full consequences of evil: evil from the political, social, cultural, personal, moral, religious and spiritual angles all rolled into one; evil in the downward spiral hurtling toward the pit of destruction and despair. And he does so precisely as the act of redemption, of taking that downward fall and exhausting it, so that there may be new creation, new covenant, forgiveness, freedom and hope.
>
> The Gospels thus tell the story of Jesus, in particular the story of how he went to his death, *as* the story of how cosmic and global evil, in its supra-personal as well as personal forms, are met by the sovereign, saving love of Israel's God, YHWH, the Creator of the world. This, the Evangelists are saying to us, is what the "kingdom of God" means: neither "going to heaven when you die" nor "a new way of ordering earthly political reality" but something which includes both but goes way beyond them. What the Gospels offer is not a philosophical explanation of evil, what it is or why it's there, nor a set of suggestions for how we might adjust our lifestyles so that evil will mysteriously disappear from the world, but the story of an *event* in which the living God *deals with it*.[29]

It is much easier to believe in a theory of atonement that makes Jesus the scapegoat and substitute; the one who takes away our sin-guilt and promises a happy afterlife. In traditional Christianity shaped by a penal, substitutionary theory of atonement, what is important is God's arrangement to take away our punishment. Christianity then becomes a matter of getting the doctrine right; it becomes a matter of believing the creed or confession. Why bother with Jesus' life and teachings if all that really matters is the removal of our sin-guilt? It's an easy way to avoid the sacrifice, service, forgiveness, and suffering love that Jesus asks of his disciples in bearing the sin of the world.

The unconditional love of God demonstrated through Jesus' death is a vulnerable love that could lead to rejection and suffering. It led Jesus to a cross, and Jesus tells us to take up our cross and follow. Who wants to be crucified? Who wants to suffer rejection and possible abuse? It is much easier to be right, and so we have turned Christianity into a matter of being right. N. T. Wright puts it this way:

> The call of the gospel is for the church to implement the victory of God in the world through suffering love. The cross is not just an example to be

followed; it is an achievement to be worked out, put into practice. But it is an example nonetheless, because it is the exemplar—the template, the model—for what God now wants to do by his Spirit in the world, through his people. It is the start of the process of redemption, in which suffering and martyrdom are the paradoxical means by which victory is won.[30]

Elie Wiesel, a survivor of Auschwitz, shared the following experience:

The SS hung two Jewish men and a boy before the assembled inhabitants of the camp. The men died quickly but the death struggle of the boy lasted half an hour. "Where is God? Where is he?" a man behind me asked. As the boy, after a long time, was still in agony on the rope, I heard the man cry again, "Where is God now?" and I heard a voice within me answer, "Here he is—he is hanging here on this gallows . . . ."[31]

This is what the death of Jesus reveals. The passion of Jesus is about God in Christ vicariously sharing our suffering, experiencing death, showing us that in the absurdities and cruelties of life God is with us and for us.

The suffering and death of Jesus is redemptive, not because Jesus takes our place to save us from God's judgment, but as humanity's archetypal representative Jesus makes God accessible; through Jesus we can touch and experience God, who joins us in a solidarity of suffering. Hans Kung writes,

When we look to the One sufferer [Jesus] a meaning is offered which—despite all absurdity—has only to be trustfully accepted in order to know that God is present, however bleak, meaningless, desperate the situation may be. I can encounter him, not only in light and joy, but also in darkness, sorrow, pain and melancholy. Suffering as such is not a sign of God's absence. In the light of the suffering of the One it has been clearly shown to be the way to God. . . . Nowhere did it become more clearly visible than in Jesus' life and work, suffering and death, that this God is a God for men, a God who is wholly on our side. He is not a theocratical God, creating fear, "from above," but a God friendly to men, suffering with men, "with us below." It is scarcely necessary to insist that we are talking here in metaphors, symbols, analogies. But what is meant is understandable enough and it is now clearer than ever that the God manifested in Jesus is not a cruel, despotic, legal-minded God, but a God encountering man as redeeming love, identifying himself in Jesus with suffering man.[32]

Theologian Jurgen Moltmann calls this a "theology of the pain of God, which means the theology of the divine co-suffering or compassion."[33] God, in Christ, enters into the community of suffering, sharing in the weakness and pain of the human condition. Christ becomes our brother in suffering in whom we can confide. Moltmann says, "To discover in one's own pain the pain of God means finding fellowship with God in one's own suffering and understanding one's own suffering as participation in the 'the sufferings of Christ.'"[34]

This is also a theology of hope because in our disappointments and discouragements, in our pain and losses, in our physical and spiritual sufferings, we have the opportunity to enter more fully into God's compassion and participate in God's brokenness for the world. This makes possible a sense of joyful expectation, a ray of hope that breaks into the darkness, for into our brokenness flows healing grace from the one that conquered death, and who will in time bring all creation "into the freedom and glory of the children of God" (Rom 8:21).

Easter Means Hope

Easter gave birth to the church. We might imagine what would have happened to the followers of Jesus had there been no Easter experience. For a time they may have continued as a community sharing their sorrow and disappointment. Some may have found Jesus' stories and sayings intriguing, and, revering his memory, they might have passed these down for a brief time. But, as scholar Leander Keck observes, "in due course, the group—if it had continued—would have disappeared from history, as did the followers of John the Baptist."[35] The resurrection of Jesus legitimated telling his story. Had there been no Easter encounter, there would have been no Jesus movement, no church, and hence no Gospels or New Testament.

The early followers of Jesus lived and thought in a context where Jewish eschatological and apocalyptic hopes flourished. In Persian times, after the Babylonian exile, people began to feel less satisfied with the view that all rewards and reprisals are settled in this life. More and more the idea began to take root that some kind of comprehensive fulfillment was still to come, that God's justice would settle all scores in a final judgment. In the apocalyptic literature of the second century before Christ, especially in the book of Daniel, and in the non-canonical book of Enoch, there emerged faith in either the universal resurrection of the dead or at least the resurrection of the just. Theologian Hans Kung observes,

What counted was the success of God's cause for the people and the individual in this very unjust world: resurrection was seen as part of God's self-justification, as an argument in theodicy. It is in this sense that the devout Jew confesses three times a day in the second benediction of the Eighteen Benedictions: "Blessed art Thou, O Lord, that quickenest the dead."[36]

It was natural for the early Christians to interpret the resurrection of Jesus from an eschatological and apocalyptic perspective and see in the life, death, and resurrection of Christ the beginning of the new age. It was their faith in the resurrection of Christ more than anything else that gave rise to their conviction that God's new world has pierced our present evil age and is here, though not yet in its final form.

Possibly the most interesting resurrection story is found in Luke's Gospel where two of Jesus' disciples encounter Christ on the road to Emmaus. Jesus comes alongside them and engages them in conversation, but they do not recognize him. Luke writes,

> As they came near the village to which they were going, he walked ahead as if he were going on. But they urged him strongly, saying, "Stay with us, because it is almost evening and the day is now nearly over." So he went in to stay with them. When he was at the table with them, he took bread, blessed and broke it, and gave it to them. Then their eyes were opened, and they recognized him; and he vanished from their sight. They said to each other, "Were not our hearts burning within us while he was talking to us on the road, while he was opening the scriptures to us?" That same hour they got up and returned to Jerusalem: and they found the eleven and their companions gathered together. They were saying, "The Lord has risen indeed, and he has appeared to Simon!" Then they told what had happened on the road, and how he had been made known to them in the breaking of the bread. (Luke 24:13-35)

In Luke's Gospel all the resurrection appearances take place in or near Jerusalem, and they are presented as if they all occurred on the same day. It may be that they were framed this way in celebration of Easter Sunday.

These two disciples are leaving Jerusalem, the place where Jesus was betrayed, arrested, deserted, humiliated, and crucified. It was the place where their hopes were dashed and their dreams crushed; "we had hoped," they said, "that he was the one to redeem Israel." It was a place of defeat, despair, and death. The women had come from the tomb with hopeful news, but

Luke says, "these words seemed to them an idle tale, and they did not believe them" (Luke 24:11). They were so disillusioned, fearful, and confused that their words seemed like nonsense.

As the two disciples make their way on the road to Emmaus, a stranger joins them. He expounds to them the Scriptures and their hearts are moved, but they do not recognize him until he takes the bread, blesses it, breaks it, and gives it to them. In the partaking of the sacred meal, their eyes are opened. The language deliberately recalls Jesus' final meal with the disciples before his death and his instruction to eat the bread and drink the cup in remembrance of him.

Luke is telling us that the death of Jesus, as tragic as it was, has been incorporated into God's plan. Jesus' death and resurrection are one piece. If the life of Jesus marks one side of the coin, his death and resurrection mark the other. The Gospels teach us to keep the death and resurrection together as a single event.

New Testament theologian Charles Cousar recalls a BBC series that examined various expressions of religious life. In one segment the British interviewer talked with a popular American television preacher. The footage showed his extravagant church and the throngs of people that came weekly to hear his positive and affirming sermons. The preacher came across as a warm, engaging person who dared to dream dreams of what God wanted to accomplish through him and who wanted others to dream dreams about themselves. She asked him, "What do you think about Jesus?" He said, "Jesus was the most successful religious figure of all time. Just consider it. He began in obscure surroundings amid poverty and despair; and today his followers outnumber those of any other of the world's religions. That's astounding." Then she said, "But I thought he ended up on a cross." And his response was, "Oh, no! He was raised from the dead. He overcame the cross and put all that behind him." Cousar offers this analysis:

> A theology that rings loudly the joyful note of Easter without the sobering, dissonant sounds of Good Friday inevitably tends toward triumphalism. The earthly, crucified Jesus gives way to the risen, exalted Lord. The cries of human pain, rejection, and death exposed in Jesus' passion are modulated by the exuberance of "he is risen!" As with the television preacher, negative experiences are often viewed as no more than obstacles to be overcome in the journey to something more—to success and positive living. Evangelism becomes church growth; "what works" becomes the church's operational mode. . . . At the other extreme, a Good Friday divorced from

Easter ceases to be good. The gloom and darkness that surround Jesus' death loom heavy without a transcendent power. Even the divine embrace of suffering and defeat, which the cross represents, results in no more than continued despair, because God's suffering has no resolution, no redemptive force. There can be little or no anticipation of change in the status quo nor hope for ultimate overthrow of the despotic rule of the principalities and powers. The church's ministry becomes exclusively presence; its mission to help people cope.[37]

In the Synoptic Gospels the resurrection is God's vindication of the cross; it is God's "yes" to Jesus' life, a life of love, self-giving, justice, and compassion. Jesus gave himself up, even unto death, in pursuit of God's cause, and this is God's vindication of his life that ended in suffering and death.

In contemporary American evangelical Christianity, two perspectives have surprisingly come together. One is the emphasis in traditional evangelicalism that I have discussed: God's salvation is almost exclusively centered on Jesus' death as a susbstitutionary atonement for sins. This emphasis typically ignores the life Jesus lived and the major focus of his ministry, God's new world. The other movement takes its impetus from the one noted above by Cousar, where the cross is viewed primarily as an obstacle to be overcome and therefore all attention is turned toward the resurrection. When these two perspectives unite, it sounds something like this: Jesus' death in our place takes care of the sin-guilt problem so that we can now focus on being an Easter people. The cross has turned away God's judgment, so we can now focus on successful and abundant living, which in many cases doesn't look much different than the pursuit of the American dream. Some churches are intentionally removing any sign of the cross from their sanctuaries and facilities.

I referred earlier to a story by Clarence Jordan, the founder of Koinonia Farm, an interracial community in Americus, Georgia. His brother, Robert Jordan, was a lawyer with aspirations of being governor of Georgia. Because of those aspirations, he refused to represent Koinonia Farm in the courts. In a conversation with Clarence, he said, "I can't do that. You know my political aspirations." He went on to say that he was a follower of Christ up to a point. Clarence asked, "Could that point be the cross?" He said, "That's right. I follow him to the cross but not on the cross. I'm not getting myself crucified."

Clarence told his brother he was not a disciple of Christ and that he needed to go back to his church where he was a member and tell them that he was an admirer of Jesus, but not a disciple. His brother said, "Well, now, if everyone who felt like I do did that, we wouldn't have a church, would we?" Maybe that is a good question to ask: Do we have a church today? We hear much in the contemporary church about being an Easter people, but not much about being a crucified people.

The resurrection of Christ is not justification for avoiding or bypassing the cross; it is God's vindication of the cross, God's vindication of the way of self-surrender and self-giving for the good of others. Hans Kung writes,

> Easter does not neutralize the cross but confirms it. The resurrection message therefore does not call for the adoration of a heavenly cult god who has left the cross behind him. It calls for imitation: to commit oneself in believing trust to this Jesus, to his message, and to shape one's own life in accordance with the standard of the Crucified.[38]

I love what the Rev. William Sloan Coffin says:

> Christ is risen . . . to put love in our hearts, decent thoughts in our heads, and a little more iron up our spines. Christ is risen to convert us, not from life to something more than life, but from something less than life to the possibility of full life itself. . . . Easter has less to do with one person's escape from the grave than with the victory of seemingly powerless love over loveless power. And let us also emphasize this: too often Easter comes across very sentimentally like a desert wafer—airy and sweet. But there's nothing sentimental about Easter: Easter represents a demand as well as a promise, a demand not that we sympathize with the crucified Christ, but that we pledge our loyalty to the risen One. That means an end to all loyalties, to all people, and to all institutions that crucify.[39]

The resurrection of Jesus also means that death does not have the final word. Mel Blanc is a name associated with characters in Warner Brothers' Looney Tunes. At the end of a production, when Porky Pig says, "That's all, folks!" we hear the voice of Mel Blanc. When Blanc died, his family engraved an inscription on his tombstone that reads, "That's all, folks!" The first disciples initially experienced the death of Jesus as the end of the story.

Easter means death is not the end of the story, but a chapter in an ongoing saga. There is great diversity in the resurrection appearance stories in the Gospels, but the one thing they share in common is that the same Jesus, the crucified one, was raised. I like the story about the florist who mixed up two orders on a busy day. One arrangement was to go to a new business and the other to a funeral, but they got mixed up. The next day, the guy with the new business stormed into the shop visibly upset. "What's the big idea? The flowers that arrived for our reception said, 'Rest in peace.'" The florist said, "Well, if you think that's bad you should have seen the people at the funeral who got the flowers that said, 'Good luck in your new location.'" Christ's resurrection transforms death into a transitional phase that becomes the doorway to a new form of life. We experience dying as a passing from this world into another world, but really it's all one world—all reality is God's world. Hans Kung describes this as "assumption into ultimate reality."[40] Death brings us into a completely new relationship. "Death is transition to God, is retreat into God's hiddenness, is assumption into his glory."[41]

In Lew Wallace's novel, *Ben-Hur*, Caesar assigns Quintus Arrius the task of ridding the Aegean Sea of pirates who were ruining the grain trade between Egypt and Rome and threatening Rome's lifeline. Arrius was given 100 vessels of war, the largest of which had 120 rowers, one of whom was Ben-Hur, the Jew wrongly imprisoned. The basic tactic in their fighting was to maneuver close enough to hurl burning balls of asphalt onto the enemy ship or ram their vessel.

The admiral maneuvered his ship to ram one of the pirate ships, but just as they got into position, one of the rowers screamed. They were not going to ram but be rammed. The ship broke apart. The impact thrust Ben-Hur deep into the water. Finally reaching the surface and gasping for breath, he managed to gather debris and form a makeshift raft. Suddenly, a hand came out of the water. Ben-Hur reached for it. It was the hand of Quintus Arrius, the admiral of the fleet. The two men shivered through the night. They could see in the distance the burning ships. In the morning the whole horizon was punctuated with columns of smoke from burning ships.

Then they saw one ship moving slowly, stopping, picking up survivors. Arrius asked Ben-Hur to pledge to kill him if it was an enemy ship, but Ben-Hur refused. Arrius rested with his eyes closed as Ben-Hur described the ship approaching them. When Arrius discovered it was a Roman ship, he exclaimed, "Thank thou thy God, as I do my many gods. A pirate would sink, not save, yon ship. By the act and the helmet on the mast I know a Roman. The victory is mine. Fortune hath not deserted me. We are saved."[42] Arrius then took command and went on to perfect the victory over the pirates, completely crushing them. His ship went down, and he experienced defeat, but in the overall conflict he emerged victorious.

Easter engenders hope in the midst of disappointment and defeat. Even though we may experience many defeats in life, Easter means hope because it assures us that the ultimate victory has been won; death is fatal, but not final.

Christ's Continuing Presence

On the first beautiful spring day after a long winter, a first grade teacher tried to teach her class. The children were obviously preoccupied, and it was clear that there was a conspiracy against learning that afternoon. The teacher decided to forget the lesson plans for the rest of the day. She gathered the class in a circle and said, "Let's go around the room, and when it's your turn you stand up and tell us what you want to be when you grow up." Some of the children wanted to be what their parents were. Some wanted to be athletes. Some wanted to be doctors and nurses. One child said, "I want to be a teacher like you, Miss Smith." Finally, they got to the shyest kid in the class. No one expected him to say anything. He stood up rather timidly and declared, "I want to be a lion tamer. I want to get in a cage full of lions and tigers and make them jump through hoops and do tricks and do whatever I tell them to do." About that time, the little boy noticed that all the other kids were staring at him in disbelief. Then he added, "Of course, I'll have my mommy with me."

As mentioned previously, Matthew's Gospel begins by identifying Jesus as "God with us." The Gospel concludes on the same note: "And remember, I am with you always, to the end of the age" (Matt 28:20). Jesus' resurrection meant he would continue to be with them—no longer in a visible, physical way, but spiritually.

Luke's Gospel proclaims essentially the same reality, but in a slightly different form. At the end of Luke's Gospel, Jesus tells the disciples to remain in Jerusalem until they are clothed with power from on high, a power that will embolden their witness to his death and resurrection and their proclamation of forgiveness and repentance in his name (Luke 24:49). Earlier in the Gospel, John the Baptist had announced that Jesus would be the one to baptize with the Holy Spirit and fire (Luke 3:16). In Acts, Luke's sequel, the Holy Spirit is poured out on the disciples (Acts 1:4-5; 2:1-13). In Luke-Acts, the power and presence of the Spirit is equated with the power and presence of Christ.

In both the writings of John and Paul, a connection is made between Jesus entering into participation with God's rule as Lord of the new creation and the outpouring of the Holy Spirit on Jesus' followers (John 7:39; 16:7-15; 20:22; Rom 1:4; 1 Cor 12:3). Disciples of Jesus can now experience the presence and power of the risen Christ through the Spirit as a manifestation and revelation of the world to come ahead of time. We do not encounter Jesus as a physical reality, but as a spiritual force. The assumption is that Jesus in his resurrected/glorified/exalted state shares in God's rule and glory, and being no longer bound by the limitations of mortality, he now has the capacity to be present in the way God is present.[43]

Mark's Gospel, however, expounds a different perspective and is unique among the New Testament witnesses to the resurrection. Mark's Gospel contains no resurrection appearances and ends on a rather strange note:

> When the Sabbath was over, Mary Magdalene, Mary the mother of James, and Salome bought spices so that they might go to anoint Jesus' body. Very early on the first day of the week, just after sunrise, they were on their way to the tomb and they asked each other, "Who will roll the stone away from the entrance of the tomb?"
>
> But when they looked up, they saw that the stone, which was very large, had been rolled away. As they entered the tomb, they saw a young man dressed in a white robe sitting on the right side, and they were alarmed.
>
> "Don't be alarmed," he said, "You are looking for Jesus the Nazarene, who was crucified. He has risen! He is not here. See the place where they laid him. But go, tell his disciples and Peter, 'He is going ahead of you into Galilee. There you will see him, just as he told you.'"
>
> Trembling and bewildered, the women went out and fled from the tomb. They said nothing to anyone, because they were afraid. (Mark 16:1-8, TNIV)[44]

There are no resurrection appearances, but Mark leaves no doubt about his conviction that Jesus is alive: the women are told that Jesus has risen, he is going ahead of them into Galilee, and there they will see him. Galilee is the disciples' home land, and possibly Mark is thinking in terms of a new beginning, a place to start fresh with a new mission. Perhaps this is why Peter is particularly singled out. Though all the disciples deserted and abandoned Jesus, Peter is noted in the Gospels for his denial. The young man's word of promise at the tomb is also a word of grace and forgiveness to Peter and the rest; it proclaims the prospect of a new beginning.

The silence of the women is an interesting feature of Mark's account that contrasts with both Matthew and Luke (see Matt 28:8; Luke 24:9). Luke mentions that the women were terrified, and Matthew couples their fear with their joy, but only in Mark does their fear result in silence. According to Mark, "they said nothing to anyone, for they were afraid." Throughout Mark's Gospel, fear is often viewed as a demonstration of the lack of faith. For example, when the disciples, terrified, are on the Sea of Galilee amid a violent storm and Jesus is asleep, they wake him, fearing for their lives. After Jesus brings calm to the situation, he says to them, "Why are you so afraid? Have you still no faith?" (Mark 4:35-41; also 6:50-52; 9:6, 32; 10:32)

Up to this point in Mark's story, the women have done quite well; they are commended for their faithfulness on several occasions (see 5:34; 7:29; 12:41-43; 14:3-9), and they stand alone with Jesus, witnessing his death and burial. The failure of the women in this context, however, is no different than the response of the disciples throughout Mark. The encouraging word is that in spite of repeated misunderstanding, disobedience, dullness, and lack of faith, the promise is given to them that they will all see Jesus again. Christ does not abandon his disciples even when they show no signs of progress and faith, and that is no small thing. New Testament scholar Pheme Perkins remarks, "There are no heroes among Jesus' followers. The hostility that puts Jesus on the cross has reduced them all to flight and fearful silence. Nevertheless, God brings faith out of just such weakness and failure. Jesus did not need to come once again and choose a new team in some grand lottery for better disciples."[45]

The promise of seeing Jesus again in Galilee could be taken as a promise of Christ's return. Theologian and ethicist Richard Hays argues that Mark's church encountered a "vocation of suffering discipleship without the immediate presence of the Lord. . . . There will be consolation when the Son of Man comes in glory, but for the present there is only the sober call to take up the cross and follow."[46] Perhaps the persecuted and bedraggled Markan community experienced the risen Christ more as the absent one than the present one. Mark's account reminds us that not everyone encounters Christ in the same way, and even when there is no sense of Christ's presence, hope can still flourish and sustain the community. For Mark's community it was a matter of patient waiting and enduring.

Henry Nouwen, not long before his death, in a book called *Sabbatical Journeys*, wrote about his friends who were trapeze artists. Nouwen commented on the special relationship between the flyer and the catcher. As the flyer swings high above the crowd on the trapeze, the moment comes when he must let go. He arcs out into the air. His job is to remain as still as possible and wait for the strong hands of the catcher to pluck him from the air. One of the trapeze artists told Nouwen, "The flyer must wait in absolute trust. The catcher will catch him, but he must wait. His job is not to flail about in anxiety. In fact, if he does, it would kill him. His job is to be still. To wait. And to wait is the hardest work of all."[47]

The abrupt ending of Mark's story without any reference to the obedience of the disciples or an actual appearance of Jesus puts the ball in the reader's court. We must decide how the story is to turn out. In breaking off the story at this point, Mark leaves it up to us to take the crucial step of faith for ourselves and follow Christ into Galilee. The way is still the way of the cross. The radical faith that leads to following Jesus in the way of the cross gives birth to the joyful expectation of seeing Jesus again. Present-day disciples of Jesus may not know when or where they shall see him, or how they might encounter him, but they know they cannot escape him. The good news is that he comes to us not as a raging warrior, but as a suffering servant who has poured out his life in compassion and love, even unto death.

The often-quoted words of Albert Schweitzer, taken from his classic work titled *The Quest of the Historical Jesus,* are appropriate here. Schweitzer wrote this famous work while he was a medical student. At the peak of his fame as a theological scholar, he left for Africa to establish a medical outpost. He was the recipient of the Nobel Peace Prize in 1952. He wrote,

> He comes to us as one unknown, without a name, as of old, by the lakeside, he came to those men who did not know who he was. He says the same words: "Follow me!" and sets us to those tasks which he must fulfill in our time. He commands. And to those who hearken to him, whether wise or unwise, he will reveal himself in the peace, the labours, the conflicts and the suffering that they may experience in his fellowship, and as an ineffable mystery they will learn who he is.[48]

Questions for Reflection and Discussion

1. What constitutes the central message in most versions of popular Christianity? How do you think "the way of the cross" as expounded in this chapter fits into the common system of faith and practice? Or does it fit at all?

2. Do you agree or disagree with the interpretation that Jesus is not just redefining greatness but calling for an abandonment of the pursuit of

greatness altogether? Why or why not? Can you think of how this teaching could be turned around and used to support one's own agenda and ambition?

3. How is salvation primarily understood in the context of the substitutionary model of atonement? How is salvation understood in the context of the representative model developed in this chapter? How does one appropriate salvation according to each model? Do you agree or disagree that the substitutionary model presents an inadequate picture of God? Why?

4. How would you respond to the newspaper article quoted in this chapter that suggests that Jesus' main or perhaps only purpose was to die in order to provide salvation? Why was Jesus crucified? What do you see as the most important redemptive aspect of the death of Christ?

5. Clarence Jordan likens the death of Jesus to a lightning rod where the negative energy of the world was discharged. Do you agree with his view that God needs available people who will bear the sins of the world? How does this relate to forgiveness of sins?

6. What does it mean for disciples to walk in the "way of the cross"? How might you live this idea in the network of your relationships and responsibilities?

7. Believing that God, in and through Christ, has vicariously entered into our suffering and pain is one thing, but actually experiencing "God with us" in human suffering is another. What might we do to open our hearts to God's suffering love?

8. In what sense is the resurrection of Christ an eschatological and apocalyptic event?

9. Why is it important to interpret/understand the death and resurrection of Christ as a single event (two sides of the same coin)?

10. From the theological perspective of the Synoptic Gospels, what was the main significance of the resurrection of Christ?

11. Reflect on the author's explanation of why there were no resurrection appearances and promises of continued presence in Mark's Gospel. Do you agree with this interpretation? If not, how do you explain it?

12. How does the assurance of ultimate victory signified by Christ's resurrection give one hope in the face of the many defeats of life? Identify the influences in your life that hinder your experience of new life in Christ. What can you do to access the presence and grace of the risen Christ that would enable you to overcome these "principalities and powers"?

Notes

1. Hans Kung, *On Being a Christian,* trans. E. Quinn (New York: Doubleday, 1976), 423.

2. The other two predictions are found in Mark 8:31-38 and 9:30-37.

3. Barbara Brown Taylor, *Bread of Angels* (Cambridge MA: Cowley Pub., 1997), 43.

4. Leander Keck, *Who Is Jesus? History in the Perfect Tense* (Columbia: University of South Carolina Press, 2000), 147.

5. Ibid., 148.

6. Hugh Anderson, *The Gospel of Mark,* New Century Bible Commentary (London: Marshall, Morgan & Scott, 1976), 257.

7. Stephen Finlan, *Problems with Atonement: The Origins of, and Controversy about, the Atonement Doctrine* (Collegeville MN: Liturgical Press, 2005), 107.

8. Joel B. Green and Mark D. Baker, *Recovering the Scandal of the Cross: Atonement in the New Testament and Contemporary Contexts* (Downers Grove IL: InterVarsity Press, 2000), 42.

9. *State Journal,* Frankfort KY, 21 March 2004.

10. Douglas John Hall, *The Cross in Our Context: Jesus and the Suffering World* (Minneapolis: Fortress Press, 2003), 124.

11. Albert Nolan, *Jesus Before Christianity* (Maryknoll NY: Orbis Books, 1976), 84–85.

12. Taylor, *Bread of Angels,* 45.

13. Marcus J. Borg, *Jesus, A New Vision: Spirit, Culture, and the Life of Discipleship* (New York: HarperSanFrancisco, 1987), 182–83.

14. C. S. Lewis, *The Lion, the Witch, and the Wardrobe,* 1st American ed. (New York: HarperCollins Publishers, 2001), 185.

15. Brennan Manning, "The Signature of Jesus," in *Bread and Wine: Readings for Lent and Easter* (Farmington PA: Plough Publishing Co.), 222–23.

16. Ibid., 226.

17. The translation "a son of God" adopted in some readings is technically correct, but it cannot be what Mark intended. Even if it could be demonstrated that the centurion actually said these words and meant by them a divine man or demi-god, for Mark the centurion's declaration is a proclamation of the truth about Jesus. In Mark's view, Jesus, God's Son, reveals that connection and manifests God's will through his death.

18. Morna Hooker, *The Gospel According to Saint Mark,* Black's New Testament Commentaries, ed. Henry Chadwick (London: Hendrickson Publishers, 1991), 371–72.

19. Luke's account of the passion offers a perspective different from Mark. Mark's story emphasizes the emotional and spiritual suffering of Jesus. At Gethsemane Jesus is in great sorrow and anguish, asking God three times for the cup of death to pass from him. In Luke's Gospel Jesus is confident and calm, asking only once. (The blood-sweating passage in Luke 22:43-44 is a later addition and was not part of the original text.) In Mark Jesus is silent, speaking only once from the cross, crying out in anguish. In Luke Jesus is presented as an innocent martyr. Three times in Luke Pilot pronounces Jesus innocent, and the centurion who watches Jesus die says, "Certainly this man was a righteous man," whereas in Mark he says, "Surely this was the Son of God." In Luke Jesus calmly and confidently surrenders and submits to death. In Luke Jesus talks to the women who are weeping, prays for the forgiveness

of his tormentors, tells a dying thief, "Today, you will be with me in Paradise," and his final words are not words of a man feeling forsaken, but confident: "Father, into your hands I commit my spirit." In Mark Jesus suffers intense spiritual and emotional agony, feeling abandoned by God while clinging to God in faith; in Luke Jesus is a courageous, faithful martyr who faces death calmly, confidently, almost serenely. Yet in both accounts Jesus is acting as the representative human being, "the Son of Man" who identifies and vicariously enters the human condition.

20. See Matt 6:12-15=Luke 2:4; Mark 2:5=Matt 9:6, Luke 5:20; Matt 18:21=Luke 17:3-4; Matt 18:23-33; Mark 11:25; Luke 6:37.

21. The current popular form of the doctrine of substitutionary atonement is somewhat of an amalgamation of the satisfaction model of Anselm and the penal, substitutionary model of Charles Hodge. See Green and Baker, *Recovering the Scandal of the Cross*, 126–36, 140–52. There is no doubt that Paul, along with Christians before him (see 1 Cor 15:1-3), interpreted Christ's death in terms of sacrifice. In Gal 1:4 Paul speaks of Christ "who gave himself for our sins." In Rom 5:6 Paul says Christ "died for the ungodly" and in Rom 5:8 he "died for us." In Rom 8:3 God sent his Son "to deal with sin" and God through Christ "condemned sin in the flesh." In Gal 3:13 Paul says Christ became "a curse for us." In 1 Thess 5:10 Christ is the one who "died for us." In 2 Cor 5:21 he was "made sin for us." The Greek preposition used in these references could mean "in our behalf," "in our place," or simply "for our advantage" or "for our good." Paul personalizes this in Gal 2:20 where he speaks of the Son of God, "who loved me and gave himself for me." Paul inherited the sacrificial imagery of Christ's death from Christians before him, but it makes sense that Jewish believers would interpret the saving significance of Christ's death using sacrificial/cultic metaphors and images. The background for the imagery is variously argued and debated by interpreters. Some think it comes out of Temple Judaism and the priestly sacrificial system. Others find a parallel in the way the deaths of the righteous martyrs of the Maccabean period were believed to have a cleansing effect on Israel. Their deaths were interpreted vicariously (see 4 Macc 17:22). Others see connections with the Suffering Servant passages in Isaiah. We can't pinpoint the background, but sacrificial language and thought was common among the Hebrews. While Paul uses sacrificial imagery to communicate the saving effects and influence of Christ's death, he never tells us how it works. He says Christ died for us, became a curse for us, became sin for us; that God through the death of Christ judges sin and takes away sin; that his death accomplishes justification, redemption, and reconciliation, but he never gets specific about how all of this works.

22. Marcus J. Borg, Jesus: *Uncovering the Life, Teachings, and Relevance of a Religious Revolutionary* (New York: HarperSanFrancisco, 2006), 268–69.

23. "Within a penal substitution model, God's ability to love and relate to humans is circumscribed by something outside of God—that is, an abstract concept of justice instructs God as to how God must behave . . . God who wants to be in relationship with us but is forced to deal with a problem of legal bookkeeping that blocks that relationship. The solution is having God the Father punish God the Son." (Green and Baker, *Recovering the Scandal of the Cross,* 147)

24. Green and Baker, *Recovering the Scandal of the Cross,* 150. All through human history it has been a common experience to conceive of the divine as terrifying and condemning, a God who must make humans pay for their sins. It is an interesting anthropological fact that people all over the world have practiced animal and even human sacrifice. Somehow this notion of offering up our best and brightest to placate the offended deity has had universal appeal. Whenever the deity breaks into the human sphere, one had better run for cover

because it can't be good. This may explain why, in Scripture, whenever God breaks into human affairs, God or the angelic representative of God must say, "Do not fear!" It is a common human reaction to be afraid of God. The doctrine of substitutionary atonement imagines a God that needs to be placated.

25. Donald Senior, *The Gospel of Matthew*, Interpreting Biblical Texts (Nashville: Abingdon Press, 1997), 36.

26. J. Denny Weaver, *The Nonviolent Atonement* (Grand Rapids MI: William B. Eerdmans Pub. Co., 2001), 43–44.

27. Clarence Jordan, "At God's Expense," in *Bread and Wine*, 371–76.

28. Brennan Manning, *The Signature of Jesus*, rev. ed. (Sisters OR: Multnomah Books, 1996), 182–83.

29. N. T. Wright, *Evil and the Justice of God* (Downers Grove IL: InterVarsity Press, 2006), 92–93.

30. Ibid., 98–99.

31. Elie Wiesel, in *Night*, quoted by Dorothee Soelle, "On this Gallows," in *Bread and Wine*, 175.

32. Kung, *On Being a Christian*, 434–35.

33. Jurgen Moltmann, *The Way of Jesus Christ: Christology in Messianic Dimensions*, trans. Margaret Kohl (Minneapolis: Fortress Press, 1993), 178.

34. Ibid., 180.

35. Keck, *Who Is Jesus?* 128.

36. Kung, *On Being a Christian*, 356–57.

37. Charles B. Cousar, *A Theology of the Cross: The Death of Jesus in the Pauline Letters* (Minneapolis: Fortress Press, 1990), 88–91.

38. Kung, *On Being a Christian*, 382.

39. William Sloan Coffin, *Letters to a Young Doubter* (Louisville: Westminster John Knox Press, 2005), 169–70.

40. Kung, *On Being a Christian*, 358.

41. Ibid., 358. The God of the beginning is the God of the end. "The Creator and Conserver of the universe and of man can be trusted, even at death and as we are dying, beyond the limits of all that has hitherto been experienced, to have still one more word to say: to have the last word as he had the first" (ibid., 360).

42. Lew Wallace, *Ben-Hur*, Oxford World Classics, ed. David Mayer (Oxford: University Press, 1998), 158.

43. Moltmann talks about the "process of resurrection" that has "its foundation in Christ, its dynamic in the Spirit, and its future in the bodily new creation of all things" (*The Way of Jesus Christ*, 241). He writes, "Resurrection is not a deferred consolation—'the opium of the next world.' It is the power which enables this life to be reborn. The hope is directed, not towards a different world but towards the redemption of this one. In the Spirit, resurrection happens every day. In love we experience many deaths and many resurrections. We experience resurrection by being born again to a living hope through love, in which we already, here and now, wake from death to life, and through liberation: 'Where the Spirit of the Lord is, there is freedom' (II Cor. 3:17)." (Ibid., 242)

44. This abrupt ending in Mark so puzzled some early Christians that they figured the real ending must have been lost, so they took upon themselves the liberty of adding what they considered to be an appropriate ending to the story. In the manuscript tradition, there is a history of both a "shorter" and "longer" ending. Some translations include these endings, either in brackets, italics, or in the footnotes. Gospel scholars are confident that the original text ended at verse 8, with the women fleeing the tomb, fearful and silent.

45. Pheme Perkins, *Mark,* New Interpreter's Bible, vol. 8 (Nashville: Abingdon Press, 1995), 733.

46. Richard B. Hays, *The Moral Vision of the New Testament: A Contemporary Introduction to New Testament Ethics* (New York: HarperSanFrancisco, 1996), 88.

47. Referenced by John Ortberg, *If You Want to Walk on Water, You've Got to Get Out of the Boat* (Grand Rapids: Zondervan, 2001), 182.

48. Albert Schweitzer, *The Quest of the Historical Jesus* (Minneapolis: Fortress Press, 2001), 487.

Chapter 7

The Final Chapter

There are many different opinions among evangelicals regarding "the end times." Most assume that Christ will return to this earth physically and visibly to usher in a new stage in God's redemptive plan. Some evangelicals have developed elaborate schemes and prophetic timetables of "signs" that will signal the end. Dispensational evangelicals believe in a literal seven-year tribulation period, beginning with the rise of the Antichrist and the signing of a peace pact with Israel, and climaxing with the Battle of Armageddon and the personal return of Christ to the earth. Most dispensational evangelicals believe that the church will be "raptured" (taken up to heaven to be with Christ) before the tribulation begins. At the end of the seven-year period, they believe that Christ will return with the church to usher in the millennium, a one-thousand-year reign of Christ on earth, which will give way to a new heaven and new earth when the one thousand years is complete.

It is not my intention to enter into a full-scale evaluation of this scenario, but I must critique the foundation on which the above view is based. The above view is a modern-day "apocalyptic" interpretation.

Scholars of ancient Jewish and Christian literature use the term *apocalyptic* to denote both a particular kind or genre of literature and the worldview (a set of beliefs and ideas) that inspired the literature and emerged from it. Apocalyptic beliefs and ideas flourished during the time of Jesus. Some of the features of an apocalyptic perspective are as follows:

- Time is divided into two ages—the old age ends with some great crisis and the new age begins with a decisive victory of the righteous over the forces of evil.
- Supernatural powers are at work behind the good and evil in the world.
- It is both dualistic and deterministic; history is moving toward an inevitable consummation.
- There are usually severe portrayals of judgment culminating in the punishment of the unrighteous and the eternal salvation of the righteous.
- Typically a period of great tribulation precedes the climax.
- The writer uses special "insider" code language, numerology, and cryptic symbols. Hidden knowledge is often communicated by dreams, visions, and angels.
- Often the writer is transported to some transcendent realm where he sees and hears things otherwise unknown.
- There is frequent mention of the opening, closing, and sealing of heavenly books containing secrets about human destiny.
- Practically, it is aimed at encouraging the faithful to endure present trials, and theologically, it demonstrates that everything is under God's control despite all appearances to the contrary.[1]

New Testament scholar Craig Hill, from whom the above list was drawn, offers this insight:

> Apocalypses might not offer a nuanced view of the world, but they are extraordinarily adept at exposing the evils perpetrated by unrestricted human power and at staking out a place for faith in the face of injustice. It is easy for modern readers to disdain the wild and even violent imagery and the expansive and mostly unfulfilled hopes of the apocalyptic writers. A fairer and more charitable attitude compels us to honor their courage, respect their sense of justice, and emulate their trust in God.[2]

In the time of Jesus, a number of apocalyptic ideas came to be associated with the prophetic hope of Israel for a new world. Jesus himself seems to have believed in the imminent arrival of God's new world. A key discourse in the Synoptic Gospels points to this conclusion. Here is Mark's version:

> As Jesus was leaving the temple, one of his disciples said to him, "Look, Teacher! What massive stones! What magnificent buildings!"

"Do you see all these great buildings?" replied Jesus. "Not one stone here will be left on another; every one will be thrown down."

As Jesus was sitting on the Mount of Olives opposite the temple, Peter, James, John, and Andrew asked him privately, "Tell us, when will these things happen? And what will be the sign that they are all about to be fulfilled?"

Jesus said to them: "Watch out that no one deceives you. Many will come in my name, claiming, 'I am he,' and will deceive many. When you hear of wars and rumors of wars, do not be alarmed. Such things must happen, but the end is still to come. Nation will rise against nation, and kingdom against kingdom. There will be earthquakes in various places, and famines. These are the beginning of birth pains.

"You must be on your guard. You will be handed over to the local councils and flogged in the synagogues. On account of me you will stand before governors and kings as witnesses to them. And the gospel must first be preached to all nations. Whenever you are arrested and brought to trial, do not worry beforehand about what to say. Just say whatever is given you at the time, for it is not you speaking, but the Holy Spirit.

"Brother will betray brother to death, and a father his child. Children will rebel against their parents and have them put to death. Everyone will hate you because of me, but those who stand firm to the end will be saved.

"When you see 'the abomination that causes desolation' standing where it does not belong—let the reader understand—then let those who are in Judea flee to the mountains. Let no one on the housetop go down or enter the house to take anything out. Let no one in the field go back to get their cloak. How dreadful it will be in those days for pregnant women and nursing mothers! Pray that this will not take place in winter, because those will be days of distress unequaled from the beginning, when God created the world, until now—and never to be equaled again.

"If the Lord had not cut short those days, no one would survive. But for the sake of the elect, whom he has chosen, he has shortened them. At that time if anyone says to you, 'Look, here is the Messiah!' or, 'Look, there he is!' do not believe it. For false messiahs and false prophets will appear and perform signs and wonders to deceive, if possible, even the elect. So be on your guard; I have told you everything ahead of time.

"But in those days, following that distress, 'the sun will be darkened, and the moon will not give its light; the stars will fall from the sky, and the heavenly bodies will be shaken.'

"At that time people will see the Son of Man coming in clouds with great power and glory. And he will send his angels and gather his elect from the four winds, from the ends of the earth to the ends of the heavens.

"Now learn this lesson from the fig tree: As soon as its twigs get tender and its leaves come out, you know that summer is near. Even so, when you see these things happening, you know that it is near, right at the door. Truly I tell you, this generation will certainly not pass away until all these things have happened. Heaven and earth will pass away, but my words will never pass away.

"But about that day or hour no one knows, not even the angels in heaven, nor the Son, but only the Father. Be on guard! Be alert! You do not know when that time will come. It's like a man going away: He leaves his house and puts his servants in charge, each with an assigned task, and tells the one at the door to keep watch.

"Therefore keep watch because you do not know when the owner of the house will come back—whether in the evening, or at midnight, or when the rooster crows, or at dawn. If he comes suddenly, do not let him find you sleeping. What I say to you, I say to everyone: 'Watch!'" (Mark 12:1-37, TNIV)

This discourse cannot rightly be called an "apocalypse," but it is peppered with apocalyptic symbols and images. Gospel scholars point out that it is virtually impossible to dissect the various layers of the gospel tradition in this discourse. What goes back to Jesus? What entered the tradition as "the word of the Lord" given through the prophets and teachers of the church? What was added by the Gospel writers themselves? Mark's, Matthew's, and Luke's versions each have their own flavor and emphasis. Morna Hooker, commenting on the discourse as it appears in Mark says,

> What we can say with certainty is that, whether Mark took over an already existing outline or is himself responsible for its plan, the discourse in its present form is clearly composite and shows signs of Markan editing. It contains a number of sayings from different sources, some possibly Jewish, some of them going back to Jesus himself, and others reflecting the concerns of the Christian community in the middle of the first century.[3]

The saying, "this generation will certainly not pass away until all these things have happened," most likely goes back to Jesus himself. Jesus seems to have expected the kingdom to come in connection with a crisis. Jesus may have anticipated this crisis in connection with his death and resurrection or, as this discourse in Mark suggests, with the destruction of Jerusalem and the temple—or with both. Some of the passages that the early church later associated with the return of Jesus may have originally been intended by Jesus to refer to his vindication through resurrection, which he connected to the full arrival of God's new world. For example, Jesus, at his trial before the high priest, is asked, "Are you the Messiah, the Son of the Blessed One?" Jesus responds in the affirmative and then says, "'you will see the Son of Man sitting at the right hand of the Power,' and 'coming with the clouds of heaven'" (Mark 14:61-62).[4] In the original context, Jesus would have been referring to his vindication/resurrection. Early Christians probably altered and adapted the wording to reflect their application of it to Christ's coming back.

In all three of the passages in the Gospels where Jesus predicts his death, he also anticipates his vindication/resurrection (Mark 8:31-32; 9:30-32; 10:32-34). The language of these texts reflects a post-Easter context, but undoubtedly Jesus anticipated his death and resurrection.

Craig Hill writes,

> Jesus expected to be put to death and yet continued to believe that his purpose would succeed, that he would be vindicated by God, even if such vindication came only beyond the grave. Had Jesus imagined that his ministry could be thwarted by death, he could have taken steps to avoid it. Instead, he stayed the course, wishing that some other path were available (Mark 14:32-42), but resolute in his conviction that he was doing God's work and fulfilling God's will. Believing that he would die, he interpreted the meaning of his death to his followers at the Last Supper. It is of no small significance that the Synoptic account of the Last Supper tradition includes the expectation of eschatological vindication: "Truly I tell you, I will never again drink of the fruit of the vine until that day when I drink it new in the kingdom of God" (Mark 14:24 par.).
>
> Jesus' acceptance of Calvary was made possible by his belief in resurrection and by his identification with the Son of Man, who must suffer before glorification. Many commentators believe that Daniel's Son of Man came to be seen (or was even meant to be seen originally) as a corporate symbol for the suffering people of Israel, who would rise again and rule. Thus, the themes of suffering, resurrection, and vindication may already have been associated with the Son of Man. In identifying himself with that figure, Jesus might even have thought that he acted on behalf and in the place of Israel.[5]

In another context where Jesus talks about the coming of the Son of Man, he says to the disciples, "Truly I tell you, there are some standing here who will not taste death until they see that the kingdom of God has come with power" (Mark 9:1). Jesus probably connected his vindication in resurrection to the full arrival of the kingdom of God. He would have thus anticipated the coming destruction of the Jerusalem temple as part of the end-time woes, the distress and upheaval that would be a prelude to Israel's repentance and the final realization of God's new world. Most likely, Jesus envisaged in close succession, his death and vindication, the destruction of the temple, the end-time woes, and the arrival of God's kingdom it its complete form.

The early Christians, deriving their sense of expectancy from Jesus, also believed in an imminent end or conclusion to the story. They interpreted the redeeming significance of Jesus in light of a two-age scenario, most likely taking their cue from Jesus himself, who believed that the gracious, redeeming power of God's new world was present in and through his life and ministry. These early Christ followers believed that the new age, God's new world, had broken into the old age in the person of Jesus. They interpreted the death and resurrection of Jesus as an apocalyptic event signaling the ultimate victory of Christ over evil, believing he would soon come back to complete what he began. They expected the final chapter to end in their lifetime.

In the development and articulation of this hope, some rather fanciful apocalyptic images and ideas became incorporated into the scheme. This is particularly reflected in the book of Revelation and in some of Paul's writings, as well as in the Jesus discourse above.

This brings us to where we are now. Many Christians take this hope quite concretely and literally; Jesus will come back personally, bodily, and visibly to bring to fulfillment God's plan for the world. In the opening chapter of the book of Acts, as the disciples watch Jesus ascend into heaven, two men in white robes (an apocalyptic image) say to the disciples, "Men of Galilee, why do you stand looking up toward heaven? This Jesus, who has been taken up from you into heaven, will come in the same way as you saw him go into heaven" (Acts 1:11). Many Christians throughout the church age have held to this belief. Many Christians today, perhaps most, believe Christ will return in this manner. Maybe he will. But the early Christians also believed that Christ would return soon, in their lifetime, but of course it didn't happen. Now, almost two millennia later, the church is still waiting. I am inclined to take a different perspective. Theologian Harvey Cox suggests,

> Rather than seeing the *parousia* [coming] as the "coming again" of an
> absent one, we can see it as the manifesting of the one who has been pres-
> ent with us all the time, albeit often unrecognized, like the Jesus on the

road to Emmaus whose disciples did not recognize him until they ate together at the end of the journey. We experience the God who "returns" as having been with us all along, especially among the misfits and losers in the great race—among whom we might least expect to find him or her.[6]

The Greek word that is translated "coming" can have other translations: "appearing" or even "presence." Instead of thinking of Christ as having left and now returning or coming back, we could think of Christ, who is already here, as *manifesting his presence* in a fresh way. The task, then, is not to escape the world by living in anticipation of Christ taking us out of it, but to engage the world in works of justice and compassion. Our mission is to join Christ who is at work in the world in order to help Christ create a better world. A world where weapons of mass destruction are all laid to rest before they can destroy all the peoples of the earth in a Battle of Armageddon. A world where sisters and brothers in the human family respect each other, care for each other, and serve each other. A world where Christ becomes the cosmic Christ of the nations, present in many ways, traditions, forms, and expressions, not just the Christ of the United States or Israel or even Christians. A world that eliminates hunger, homelessness, and a substandard living that is the norm for more than half the world's population. A world where hate and greed are no more.

Many Christians who believe in a bodily return of Jesus take the other apocalyptic images and symbols literally as well, and hence are preparing for the Battle of Armageddon and looking for the rise of the Antichrist. It is doubtful, though, that even the early Christians, who filtered their under-standing of the Jesus story (or as theologians like to say, "the Christ Event") through an apocalyptic imagination and mindset, believed that all these apocalyptic images and symbols had a corresponding historical reality. I like to think of the apocalyptic imagination as sacred fantasy; a medium to convey truth through the mythical characters and images of the apocalyptic story world. The apocalyptic story, while not literally true, may indeed convey truth about God, our world, and the human condition.

Apocalyptic Spirituality

One aspect of truth in the apocalyptic story is that most of us must go through a "falling apart" before we can experience a "coming together." Restoration assumes a prior condition of dissipation. Deconstruction pre-cedes reconstruction. Before God's kingdom can come, our kingdoms have to go. Is it not true that most of us must have our old world shaken before we are open to the possibilities of a new world? Chaos and confusion, disorder and disruption, tumult and turbulence precede and prepare the way for peace, wholeness, salvation, and new creation. Great tribulation may be necessary before great transformation.

The film *Regarding Henry* is a story about reconstruction from deconstruction. Henry Morris (played by Harrison Ford) is a successful lawyer in New York City who holds the world by the tail, leaving little time for his family. Henry will do whatever it takes to win, to climb the corporate ladder, and to maintain his affluent lifestyle.

His life is suddenly changed late one night at a convenience store, when he becomes the victim of a shooting. He is shot in the chest and head. Doctors save his life, but he requires months of hospitalization and therapy. He enters into an intensive program to reclaim his identity, though he has no memory of his past. He finds himself wearing clothes that now feel uncomfortable and eating food, like eggs and steak, that he no longer likes. The process of learning how to walk again is difficult, as well as recapturing his love for his family, who are strangers to him. Eventually he reclaims both.

After many months of rehabilitation, he resumes his life again, still without a memory of his past, and discovers troubling things. He learns that his wife was unfaithful to him, and he is devastated by the news. But then he learns that he was unfaithful to her as well. Henry also discovers that he withheld evidence in court that prevented a critically ill patient from obtaining a settlement from the hospital Henry was defending. After promising to make things right with this family, Henry returns home deeply troubled by his past. His wife, Sarah, meets him at the door and begins to cry.

"I'm sorry," Sarah says.

"No, I'm sorry," says Henry. "You were right. Things were different. I have something I need to tell you."

"What is it?" she asks.

"I don't like my clothes. . . . Maybe they used to be my favorite, but I don't feel comfortable in them anymore."

"We'll get new clothes," says his wife. She reaches to embrace him.

"I'm not done," says Henry. "Eggs. I don't like eggs, or steak. And Sarah, I hate being a lawyer. I quit, and told Charlie goodbye."

"Whatever you want is fine," Sarah assures him.

"I want us to be a family for as long as we can, Sarah," Henry quietly whispers. "For as long as we can."

"I love you," she says.

"I love you, too," Henry says as they embrace.[7]

Henry experienced a conversion, but he had to deconstruct before he could reconstruct. His deconstruction was the window through which grace entered, making possible a more loving, compassionate life.

Jesus made it his practice to overturn people's kingdoms. He opened table fellowship to sinners and tax collectors. He broke piety rules and sacred taboos. He turned traditional religious, social, and familial values upside down. He said things like, "Blessed are the poor" and "Woe to the rich." As Jesus went about the business of embodying, proclaiming, and manifesting the reality of God's new world, stars fell from the heavens and the moon became dark; there was a shaking of the foundations. Christ shakes up our world so that we can see the possibilities of an alternative world, God's world.

Another vital aspect of a healthy spirituality, as strange as it may at first seem, is the apocalyptic call to watchfulness. I love the story of the little boy who wanted a special watch for Christmas. He pestered his parents for the watch to the point that his father finally said, "Son, if you say one more word about a watch, if you even bring up the subject again, you're not going to get it." That evening the family sat down to dinner together. It was the first time they had all been able to eat together in several days. They were well into the Christmas season, so the father asked each member of the family to share a special part of the holidays. When it was the little boy's turn to share, he said, "I like the Advent readings at church, and my favorite passage is Mark 13:37: 'What I say to you, I say to everyone: Watch!'" The call to watch is as relevant to us today as it was to Christians who believed Jesus was going to return in their lifetime.

Barbara Brown Taylor reminds us that the "end of the world" is relative, and any one of us at any given time may find ourselves at the brink of despair. She observes,

> When Jesus died, his disciples believed the world had ended. When Jerusalem fell and Nero swooped down on the young church like a mad vulture, they believed the world had ended. In a manner of speaking, the world can end any day of the week with a declaration of war, or the death of a child, or a grim diagnosis, and watching for Christ's coming again in power and great glory can become the only light in such time, when sun and moon and stars have all been snuffed out.[8]

Perhaps a better way of saying it is, "Stay awake." A healthy Christian spirituality enables us to be awake to God in the present moment. The "now" is never as empty as it first appears. If God's nature is unconditional love, then God is present in the "now" in a non-blaming way. By being awake, we may be able to discern God's presence at work regardless of our present circumstances.

There is a wonderful story about a monk who was walking through a desolate area. A hungry tiger spotted him and began a pursuit. The monk found himself at the edge of a cliff, where he noticed a rope dangling from the side. He quickly leaped over the edge and grabbed the rope, just as the tiger's ferocious claws whipped past his face. As he started to make his way down, the monk soon realized that directly below him were large, sharply pointed rocks and that his rope only extended halfway to the bottom. As he hung there pondering what to do, two mice about ten feet above him started nibbling at the rope. Just then, he became aware that immediately in front of him, growing out of the side of the cliff, was the largest, most luscious strawberry he had ever seen. He plucked it and turned it over in his hand ever so slowly as he breathed in the aroma. Then he bit into it, savoring the taste. He said to himself, "Undoubtedly this is the very best strawberry I have ever tasted."

I suspect most of us find it difficult to enjoy the present moment because of the tigers in our past or the rocks in our future. We allow the painful memories of our past to haunt us and the uncertainties of the future to make us anxious. We want predictability; we strive to control people and circumstances in order to secure ourselves in the world, and are thus rarely awake to the wonder, joy, mystery, beauty, aroma, and taste of the present moment.

There is no need to deny, dismiss, or ignore the wounds of our past or the uncertainties of our future. "What is" is, and there is no reason to run from it. But the good news is that God is present in the "what is," and God is good. The world is a temple and everything is sacred. The key is awareness. God is here, in the "now," and God is unconditional love.

Many Christians keep looking to the heavens for Christ to return, and yet in a real sense Christ has not left. Christians can get caught up in watching for Christ's body to appear and forget that we are the body of Christ in whom and though whom Christ manifests his presence on earth.

Redemptive Justice

It is a common belief among Christians that Jesus will judge the world; that Christ as "the Son of Man," God's representative human being, will make all things right. As part and parcel of this belief, Christians believe they will give an account to Christ. Leander Keck notes, "When Jesus had the audacity to invite people to become his disciples he tacitly asserted his right to be the authority in their moral lives, to authorize their character and direction."[9] In other words, to acknowledge Jesus as Lord is to recognize him as the moral judge of our lives.

In Mark 8:38, judgment is rendered on the basis of one's confession or denial of Jesus: "Those who are ashamed of me and of my words in this adulterous and sinful generation, of them the Son of Man will also be ashamed when he comes in the glory of his Father with the holy angels." This saying presupposes a context of persecution, and it appears in the other Gospels with variations in form and meaning, so it is difficult to know what Jesus may have actually said (see also Luke 9:26; 12:8-9; Matt 10:32-33). To acknowledge or confess Jesus is to side with the way of love, forgiveness, and compassionate justice; to deny him is to opt for the power, pride, and possessions of the world. To confess Jesus is to give allegiance to God's kingdom and God's cause in the world; to deny Jesus is to comply with the domination system, the principalities and powers that crucified Jesus. It is not difficult to imagine people from other religious traditions and some perhaps from no tradition at all, while not explicitly confessing Christ, nevertheless standing with Christ against the domination systems of the world and for the way of love, peace, and justice for all people.

A fascinating judgment text is Luke 22:28-30: "You are those who have stood by me in my trials. And I confer on you a kingdom, just as my Father conferred one on me, so that you may eat and drink at my table in my kingdom and sit on thrones, judging the twelve tribes of Israel" (see Matt 19:28 for another form). In Luke this saying occurs just after Jesus corrects the disciples for aspiring after positions of power and instructs them in the way of service, pointing to himself as an example—"I am among you as one who serves." Jesus scholar E. P. Sanders argues that Jesus anticipated the restoration of Israel as a prelude to the arrival of God's new world.[10] Jesus intended Israel to be the locus of God's presence on earth that would spread and encompass all people. This explains the interim mission of the disciples emphasized in Matthew's Gospel, where the disciples are charged with announcing the nearness of God's new world and manifesting its power only to and among Israel (Matt 10:5-8). The interesting thing about this passage is that judgment is shared with his followers.

John the Baptist announced an impending judgment, and we can be almost certain that Jesus too proclaimed this aspect of God's new world. What is not clear, however, is how Jesus himself conceived of that judgment or, for that matter, even how his first followers imagined it.

Traditional evangelicalism has typically believed in a literal hell. The word translated "hell" is *gehenna*, which was a valley near Jerusalem where people once offered human sacrifices to the god Molech. King Josiah put an end to the practice and designated the area accursed. Later it was used as a city rubbish dump, where fires burned continuously. In some rabbinic teaching, the word came to be used as a symbol for the future destruction of the wicked.

The word occurs once in Mark's Gospel in a passage employing shockingly hyperbolic language:

> If your hand causes you to stumble, cut if off. It is better for you to enter life maimed than with two hands to go into hell, where the fire never goes out. And if your foot causes you to stumble, cut it off. It is better for you to enter life crippled than to have two feet and be thrown into hell. And if your eye causes you to stumble, pluck it out. It is better for you to enter the kingdom of God with one eye than to have two eyes and be thrown into hell, where their worm does not die, and the fire is not quenched. (Mark 9:43-48, TNIV)

Jesus draws strikingly somber images to stress the importance of being freed from anything that would hinder our obedience to God. This passage, however, gives no warrant for understanding "hell" in any literal sense. Albert Nolan comments,

> It should be noted that according to this imagery it is the worms that never die and the fire that is perpetual or eternal. Everything and everybody else in *Gehenna* dies, decomposes, and is destroyed. *Gehenna* is the image of complete destruction, the extreme opposite of life. If Jesus used this image at all, this was what he would have in mind.[11]

The only reference in Luke is found in a saying where Jesus tells the crowd not to be afraid of those who can only kill the body, but rather fear the One who has the authority to destroy both body and soul in hell (Luke

12:5). But Jesus immediately follows this by pointing out that a small, insignificant sparrow is cared for by God and is not forgotten. Then he says, "Indeed, the very hairs of your head are all numbered. Don't be afraid; you are worth more than many sparrows" (Luke 12:7). Jesus is saying that while God is the One to be feared, there is no need to fear God since God cares so much for us.

Luke does give us Jesus' interesting story about a rich man and a beggar:

There was a rich man who was dressed in purple and fine linen and who feasted sumptuously every day. And at his gate lay a poor man named Lazarus, covered with soars, who longed to satisfy his hunger with what fell from the rich man's table; even the dogs would come and lick his sores. The poor man died and was carried away by the angels to be with Abraham. The rich man also died and was buried. In Hades, where he was being tormented, he looked up and saw Abraham far away with Lazarus by his side. He called out, "Father Abraham, have mercy on me, and send Lazarus to dip the tip of his finger in water and cool my tongue; for I am in agony in these flames." But Abraham said, "Child, remember that during your lifetime you received your good things; but now he is comforted here, and you are in agony. Besides all this, between you and us a great chasm has been fixed, so that those who might want to pass from here to you cannot do so, and no one can cross from there to us." He said, "Then, father, I beg you to send him to my father's house—for I have five brothers—that he many warn them, so that they will not also come into this place of torment." Abraham replied, "They have Moses and the prophets; they should listen to them." He said, "No, father Abraham; but if someone goes to them from the dead, they will repent." He said to them, "If they do not listen to Moses and the prophets, neither will they be convinced even if someone rises from the dead." (Luke 16:19-31)

In Luke's narrative, Jesus has just said that we cannot serve God and money. The Pharisees scoff at this view; their faith perspective comfortably joins the two. In response, Jesus tells the story of Lazarus, Abraham, and the rich man. The story fits Luke's emphasis regarding the eschatological reversal that will take place with the final coming of the kingdom of God.

The story falls into two parts: the first speaks of the fate of the rich man and Lazarus, while the second speaks of not believing the law and the prophets. The connection of these two parts makes sense because some of the Pharisees used the Scriptures to support their view of wealth—the righteous prosper and the wicked suffer. Jesus regarded their position as a misreading of the law and the prophets.

It would probably be improper to call this story a parable. Most parables have a true-to-life sense about them; this is pure allegorical fiction. A similar story appears in other literature and cultures. According to scholar Fred Craddock, at least seven versions of the story are to be found in the rabbis, though the characters vary.[12] Some scholars trace it back to Egypt, a land with an abundance of stories about the dead.

The fictitious story is adapted by Jesus (and/or Luke) and employed to critique the Pharisees' misuse of the law, particularly in the way they interpreted the law to justify their love of money. It says nothing about the actual fate of the righteous or the unrighteous. The word for hell (*gehenna*) does not appear in the text; instead, the word is *hades*, meaning the "abode of the dead." Literalizing the details of the story robs it of its power and reduces it to the ridiculous.

All other references to *gehenna* are found in Matthew's Gospel (Matt 5:22, 29, 30; 10:28; 18:9; 23:15, 33). It is difficult to know which, if any, of these references originate with Jesus because of Matthew's tendency to embellish the judgment texts. Matthew's Gospel speaks of judgment with a severity, harshness, and vindictiveness not found in Mark or Luke, using phrases like "gnashing of teeth" (8:12; 13:42, 50; 22:13; 24:51; 25:30; outside of Matthew only in Luke at 13:28), "everlasting fire" (5:22; 7:19; 13:40, 42, 50; 18:8; 25:41-46), "eternal punishment" (25:30), and "outer darkness" (8:12; 22:13) to describe the judgment of the Son of Man.

Anyone familiar with Matthew's Gospel should be able to observe how these images of divine vengeance contradict Matthew's own portrait of Jesus. It is hard to imagine that the Jesus who shares table fellowship with tax collectors and sinners, who speaks of God as *Abba,* who teaches and embodies unlimited forgiveness, who teaches his followers to pray for their enemies, who brings healing and wholeness to the diseased and demonized, and who condemns condemnation would so mercilessly dismiss, condemn, and punish the unrighteous. Theologian Walter Wink comments, "Matthew's use of the judgment theme is particularly vindictive. . . . The unconditional loving Abba of the Sermon on the Mount (5:45) now wants to settle some scores. Matthew's heart will not be happy until 'all evildoers' have been thrown 'into the furnace of fire, where there will be weeping and gnashing of teeth.'"[13]

Matthew, it would appear, has an axe to grind. Would Jesus, who teaches us how to love our enemies, be responsible for their eternal torture? Would Jesus, who gives his life for the liberation of others, cast people out of his presence into a fiery forever? I cannot imagine Jesus envisaging judgment in such horrifying, vindictive ways. If he used this language, as noted earlier, it would have certainly been in a metaphorical, exaggerated sense. There is no justice in punishing a lifetime of sin with an eternity of suffering. If Christ, as Judge, sentenced humans to eternal punishment, he would be violating his own character and mission, both of which embodied the compassion and justice of God. The Christ who proclaimed and manifested God's compassionate justice would then be guilty of the greatest injustice of all.

Jesus stands in the tradition of the prophets of Israel in announcing the salvation and judgment of God. The prophets proclaimed judgment and salvation in the context of God's covenant relationship with God's people. Against this backdrop, the salvation of God takes center stage. Judgment is a sub-theme, serving as a means of repentance and restoration. Its function is redemptive, intended to set God's people on the path of renewal and obedience. Walter Wink remarks, "If we remove the apocalyptic framework, with its residue of power lust, judgment can be seen as a perpetual feedback loop aimed, not at condemnation, but at correction."[14] Theologian Jurgen Moltmann observes, "Only when the apocalyptic expectation of judgment is completely Christianized does it lose its terror and become a liberating hope, in which we go to meet the future with heads held high. . . . Then the fear of judgment will no longer hinder and paralyze the expectation of the parousia."[15]

Jesus' experience and understanding of God as *Abba*, a loving parent, would have certainly shaped his understanding of judgment. Punishment from a loving parent is never intended to inflict pain and suffering as a means of retribution; its purpose is to correct, redeem, and restore. When punishment is excessive, it is abuse. God would never abuse God's children. The very idea of eternal punishment contradicts Jesus' revelation of God as a loving, merciful parent. Every caring parent understands the need for punishment as a means of correction, but there is a huge difference between punishment by a loving parent and the concept of eternal punishment or banishment. As Gulley and Mulholland remark, "No loving parent would send their child to their room forever."[16]

The righteousness by which Jesus will judge the world is surely no different than the righteousness he himself proclaimed in his gospel and embodied through his table fellowship with sinners and through his works of healing the diseased and demonized. God's creative justice is not retributive justice that rewards the good and punishes the wicked; it is, rather, redemptive justice that puts all things right, both the victims and perpetrators of injustice. The crucified Christ will redeem them together. Moltmann writes,

> The victims of injustice and violence are first judged so that they may receive justice. The perpetrators of evil will afterwards experience the justice that puts things to rights. They will thereby be transformed inasmuch as they will be redeemed only together with their victims. They will be saved through the crucified Christ, who comes to them together with their victims. They will "die" to their evil acts and the burden of their guilt in order to be born again to a new life together with their victims. . . . As the coming judge of victims and perpetrators, the risen Christ will do away with the suffering of the one and the burden of the other, and will bring both out of the dominion of evil into the community of God's righteousness and justice. The purpose of his judgment is not reward or punishment, but the victory of the divine creative righteousness and justice, and this victory does not lead to heaven or hell but to God's great day of reconciliation on this earth. . . . Judgment is not the last thing of all. It serves the new creation of all things. It is therefore not last but penultimate. What is last and final is the new word of creation: "Behold, I make all things new" (Rev. 21.5).[17]

The metaphorical fire of God's judgment need not be a fire that torments or destroys the person; rather, it may be a fire that destroys the evil in the person. If the fire is God's consuming love, then what is consumed is hate, greed, pride, selfish ambition, and all that is hurtful or destructive—anything that stands in contradiction and opposition to God's loving purpose for creation. Individually, this means the false self, the ego-driven self, will be purged so that the true self, the God-like self, can emerge more fully. God's purpose in judgment, then, is not to condemn or banish, but to purify and purge the spirit, so that the individual self can develop more freely and completely into the truly human self, the Christ self.[18] Barbara Brown Taylor says, "It is the fire of a potter who wants to make useful vessels out of damp clay. It is the fire of a jeweler who wants to refine pure gold from rough ore . . . a fire that both lights us up and changes us, melting us down and reforming us more nearly into the image of God."[19] Theologian and scientist John Polkinghorne suggests,

Perhaps then, judgment is not simply a retrospective assessment of what we have been but includes the prospective offer of what we might become. Perhaps judgment is a process rather than a verdict. Perhaps its fire is the cleansing fire that burns away the dross of our lives; its sufferings the consequences of the knife wielded by the divine Surgeon who wounds to heal.[20]

Should we expect anything less from the self-giving Son of Man, who as the representative human being suffered and gave his life for our redemption? United Methodist bishop Will Willimon tells about the time his father-in-law attempted to comfort a grieving family whose son had just died while committing a crime. The family was not only in grief that their son had died, but in greater grief at the way he had died and what people were saying about him. "Just remember," Willimon's father-in-law said, "that when your son is judged, neither I nor anyone else in this town will be making the judgment. The judge will be Christ, the one who is the embodiment of mercy."[21]

The best way to approach the language of "hell" is to understand it as symbolic, religious language for a state of separation, alienation, and fragmentation. It is an apt description of the condition of a person or society driven by hate, self-destruction, and despair. Anyone who has ever felt unloved, overwhelmed by shame or guilt, or helplessly caught up in an addiction knows what it is like to be in "hell." In like manner, we might think of heaven, not as a literal place, but where we are embraced in love, welcomed home, and reconciled to God and those from whom we were estranged.

We don't know what the future will hold, but the One who is ultimately in control is unconditional love, so we have a solid, credible basis for believing that God will never abandon the world or give up on us. God wills the reconciliation of all people and the good of all creation.[22] I love the way Walter Wink assesses the human condition and expresses hope:

We live in a remarkable time, when entire nations have been liberated by nonviolent struggle; when miracles are openly declared, such as the fall of the Berlin Wall, the collapse of communism in the Soviet Union and Eastern Bloc, and the transformation of South Africa; when for the first time people are beginning to resist domination in all its forms. Yet these are also times of endemic violence, ethnic hatred, genocide, and economic privation around the world, as the super-rich hoard increasing shares of the

world's wealth and the poor drown in poverty. It is a time of hope; it is a
time of despair. I have seen enough of God's wily ways with the Powers to
stake my life on the side of hope. I believe that even these rebellious Powers
can be transformed in the crucible of God's love.[23]

I believe that love will have the final word; that love will win the day. In
the movie *The Lord of the Rings: The Two Towers*, based on the second
volume of Tolkien's *Lord of the Rings* trilogy, Frodo and Sam encounter
Gollum. Gollum, the previous possessor of the ring, is a dirty, scheming,
pitiful creature, obsessed with possessing the ring once again. For Gollum
nothing else matters.

Sam and Frodo find themselves traveling in circles in the Misty
Mountains as they make their way to Mount Doom. Gollum agrees to help
them, secretly planning to steal the ring back. Sam despises Gollum and is
harsh and demeaning toward him. Finally Frodo confronts Sam.

"Why do you do that—call him names and run him down all the time?"

"Because that's what he is, Mr. Frodo. There's naught left in him but lies
and deceit. It's the ring he wants. It's all he cares about."

Looking sadly at Gollum, Frodo says, "You have no idea what it did to
him. I have to help him, Sam."

"Why?" asks Sam.

"Because I have to believe he can come back."[24]

That is my hope. Most traditional Christians do not share this hope.
They believe in the apocalyptic dualism that dominated the thought world
of first-century Judaism, namely, that the wicked will be banished and condemned, excluded from God forever, and the righteous will be rewarded
with eternal life. It would be interesting to know how many traditional
Christians still believe that "the lost" will dwell in misery and torment. Most
evangelicals who no longer literalize the fire of hell still believe that those
who die without Christ are lost forever. They imagine them separated from
God in endless unhappiness. Some have softened this by imagining that the
judgment of the lost is destruction in hell, that is, annihilation, a ceasing to
exist.

Many traditional Christians would call my hope in universal reconciliation "wishful thinking"; others would simply call it heresy. I'm convinced it
is a solid hope because it is grounded in the unconditional love of God. It is
an expression of trust in God's goodness and grace. This is the only way love
can actually win. Love doesn't win by losing a person forever. Love wins
when the evil person is won over by love to be a different kind of person, a

Christ-like, loving person. Martin Luther King, Jr., reflects this spirit in his sermon, "Loving Your Enemies," written in a Georgia jail and preached just after the bus protest in Montgomery, Alabama. He says,

> To our most bitter opponents we say: "We shall match your capacity to inflict suffering by our capacity to endure suffering. We shall meet your physical force with soul force. Do to us what you will, and we shall continue to love you. We cannot in all good conscience obey your unjust laws, because noncooperation with evil is as much a moral obligation as is cooperation with good. Throw us in jail, and we shall still love you. Bomb our homes and threaten our children, and we shall still love you. Send your hooded perpetrators of violence into our community at the midnight hour and beat us and leave us half dead, and we shall still love you. But be ye assured that we will wear you down by our capacity to suffer. One day we shall win freedom, but not only for ourselves. We shall so appeal to your heart and conscience that we shall win *you* in the process, and our victory will be a double victory."[25]

Then the prophetic hope will be fulfilled: "They will not hurt or destroy on all my holy mountain; for the earth will be full of the knowledge of the Lord as the waters cover the sea" (Isa 11:9). The universal knowledge of God will be the knowledge of love written on the minds and hearts of all people.

The Heart of the Matter

Three judgment parables are unique to Matthew's Gospel: the parable of the weeds (13:24-30, 36-43); the parable of the net (13:47-52); and the parable of the sheep and goats (25:31-46). Matthew's hand is all over these parables, and some scholars argue that they are Matthew's works in their entirety. Other interpreters think, and I concur, that while Matthew has clearly embellished these parables with his own allegorical interpretations, their core elements come from Jesus. The most well-known of these judgment stories is the one in Matthew 25. Some interpreters refuse to call this story a parable, describing it rather as an apocalyptic drama.[26] It reads,

> When the Son of Man comes in his glory, and all the angels with him, then he will sit on the throne of his glory. All the nations will be gathered before him, and he will separate people from one another as a shepherd separates the sheep from the goats, and he will put the sheep at his right hand and the goats at the left. Then the king will say to those at his right hand, "Come, you that are blessed by my Father, inherit the kingdom prepared

for you from the foundation of the world; for I was hungry and you gave me food, I was thirsty and you gave me something to drink, I was a stranger and you welcomed me, I was naked and you gave me clothing, I was sick and you took care of me." Then the righteous will answer him, "Lord, when was it that we saw you hungry and gave you food, or thirsty and gave you something to drink? And when was it that we saw you as a stranger and welcomed you, or naked and gave you clothing? And when was it that we saw you sick or in prison and visited you?" And the king will answer them, "Truly I tell you, just as you did it to one of the least of these who are members of my family, you did it to me." Then he will say to those at his left hand, "You that are accursed, depart from me into the eternal fire prepared for the devil and his angels; for I was hungry and you gave me no food, I was thirsty and you gave me nothing to drink, I was a stranger and you did not welcome me, naked and you did not give me clothing, sick and in prison and you did not visit me." Then they also will answer, "Lord, when was it that we saw you hungry or thirsty or a stranger or naked or sick or in prison, and did not take care of you?" Then he will answer them, "Truly I tell you, just as you did not do it to one of the least of these, you did not do it to me." And these will go away into eternal punishment, but the righteous into eternal life.

This story does its work by utilizing the elements of surprise and shock. Both groups are surprised—surprised that Jesus knew what they were up to when he wasn't around and surprised that they didn't recognize him when he was around. Both groups declare, "Lord, when did we ever see you?" Jesus says he was present in those who were impoverished—those who were hungry, lonely, destitute, sick, and imprisoned, the "least of these who are members of my family" ("the least of these brothers and sisters of mine," TNIV). While some interpreters identify "the least of these" as Christians or Christian missionaries, most likely it's a reference to the disadvantaged and unfortunates of the world.[27]

Tony Campolo tells the story of being on a landing strip just outside the border of the Dominican Republic in northern Haiti. A small airplane was supposed to pick him up and fly him back to the capital city. As he waited, a woman approached him holding her child in her arms. The baby was emaciated—his arms and legs were like sticks and his stomach swollen from lack of food. She held up her child and began to plead with him, "Take my baby! Take my baby! If you don't take my baby, my baby will die. Please take my baby!"

Campolo tried to explain why he couldn't take her baby, but she wouldn't listen. No matter which way he turned, she was in his face, crying, "Please, mister, take my baby!" She kept saying, "Take my baby to a hospital. Feed my baby. Save my baby. Please take my baby!" He breathed a sigh of relief when the Piper Cub airplane came into sight. The minute it touched down he ran to meet it. But the woman kept running after him, screaming, "Take my baby! Please, take my baby!" He boarded the plane as fast as he could. The woman ran alongside the plane as it started to take off, the child in one arm and the other arm banging on the plane.

Halfway back to the capital, Campolo says it hit him. He thought of this passage of Scripture in Matthew 25. "It was Jesus! The baby was Jesus."[28]

This story in Matthew had a major influence on the ministry of Mother Teresa. She considered her work with the outcasts of Calcutta to be work done for, with, and to Jesus. She remarked once, "We serve Jesus in the neighbor, see him in the poor, nurse him in the sick; we comfort him in his afflicted brothers and sisters."[29] At her funeral she was eulogized for having exemplified Matthew 25 in ministering to the needs of the outcasts and unfortunates. She could see Christ in the disfigured faces of the despised and rejected, the sick and destitute. In her book, *No Greater Love*, Mother Teresa wrote,

Hungry for Love, He looks at you.
Thirsty for kindness, He begs from you.
Naked for loyalty, He hopes in you.
Sick and imprisoned for friendship, He wants for you.
Homeless for shelter in your heart, He asks of you.
Will you be that one to Him?[30]

The criterion for judgment in this parable, for distinguishing the sheep and the goats, the righteous and the unrighteous, is not at all what we would expect. Barbara Brown Taylor observes that the goats are not judged for doing bad things; they are judged for doing nothing. They are judged not for what they did, but for what they did not do. They may have borne no malice at all toward "the least of these," but they didn't show them any compassion either. They saw no connection, no relationship between their lives and the lives of the needy and the destitute.[31]

The criterion for judgment has nothing to do with the purity or holiness laws that occupied such an important place in Palestinian Judaism. Nor does it have anything to do with what traditional, evangelical Christianity today affords such high value, namely, believing the right things, assenting or confessing to a statement of doctrine, or "inviting Jesus into our hearts." There is nothing here about believing Jesus died for our sins or accepting Christ as Savior.

All that matters here is how we treat Jesus, who is present in the least of these, the needy and destitute. It's all about showing compassion to those who desperately need compassion. But simple charity is not sufficient either. Barbara Brown Taylor reminds us, "Charity is no substitute for kinship. We are not called to be philanthropists or social workers, but brothers and sisters. We are called into relationship, even when that relationship is unlikely, momentary, or sad."[32] You see, the least are not charity cases; they are our brothers and sisters. The age-old question comes back: "Am I my brother's keeper?" The answer of course is "Yes."

John Ortberg talks about a friend whom he says would not do well in a contest of high piety. His deep wounds still affect him in many ways. He had virtually no father growing up, and his mother was a difficult person. She married five times, with none of the relationships lasting long. She had little time for her children and gave them little encouragement. His mother developed a degenerative muscular disease and gradually lost almost every physical capacity. None of her children would have anything to do with her, none of the men she had married, no one except this son. Ortberg says,

> My friend decided to love. He took her into his home and cared for her, feeding her by hand, combing her hair, and cleaning up after her messes . . . about all she could do was cry and moan incessantly. I thought to myself, "How can he stand this? I've been given blessings—the church, Scripture, family—exponentially greater than this guy, and I don't know if I could love like this."

When she died, sixteen people came to the funeral. None of her other kids came. The son who cared for her had a toy tape recorder she had gotten him one Christmas; with it he played a tape of he and his mother singing a Christmas carol. He talked about how she loved Christmas and said when he was a kid, he would play the guitar and she would sing with him. Ortberg says, "He didn't love her perfectly, not by a long shot. But he loved her when loving was hardest. He loved her when no one else would love her, and he remembered her with kind words."[33] I have no idea what Ortberg's friend believes about God or Jesus or anything else, but I suspect, that according to this story, he would be numbered with the righteous.

This leaves me wondering where I would stand. I have to admit that this story makes me feel uneasy, which is what the life and teaching of Jesus is designed to do—to unsettle us, challenge us, and cause us to rethink life.

The good news according to Jesus challenges the faith and practice of much of what we find today in traditional Christianity. Some of us may need a fresh conversion, not from a pagan way of life, but from some of our conventional Christian beliefs and practices. If the good news of Jesus is to break into our lives with transformative power, then we must prepare to be shocked, unsettled, and taken by surprise, because Jesus intends to turn our world upside down in order to create a new world.

If we can imagine how Jesus might have used the parables of the wheat and the tares, the net with the good and bad fish, and the story of the goats and sheep, before they were shaped by Matthew and before the harsh, vindictive elements were added, then these parables can have a redemptive and transformative influence in our lives.

Dennis, Sheila, and Matthew Linn presented a redemptive interpretation of God's judgment to a group of retired Roman Catholic nuns. One sister raised her hand and said, "But what about the story of the sheep and the goats? It says right there that the sheep go to heaven and the goats go to hell."

Dennis responded by asking the group, "How many of you, even once in your life, have done what Jesus asks at the beginning of that passage and fed a hungry person, clothed a naked person, or visited a person in prison?" All the sisters raised their hands. Dennis said, "That's wonderful! You're all sheep." Then Dennis asked, "How many of you, even once in your life, have walked by a hungry person, failed to clothe a naked person, or not visited someone in prison?" Hesitantly, all the sisters raised their hands. Dennis said, "That's too bad. You're all goats."

The sisters looked worried and perplexed. Then suddenly one of the sisters' hands shot up. She blurted out, "I get it! We're all good goats!"[34]

We are all both sheep and goats; we have within us both wheat and tares, good and bad. God will sort it all out in the end, but the God of Jesus is not looking to condemn those who have more bad than good. The God of Jesus is a purifying fire; his passion is to heal and restore. God doesn't want to banish us from his presence; rather, God's purpose is to redeem us along with all creation.

N. T. Wright declares that the New Testament invites us "to imagine a new world as a beautiful, healing community . . . vibrant with life and energy, incorruptible, beyond the reach of death and decay; to hold it in our mind's eye as a world reborn, set free from the slavery of corruption, free to be truly what it was made to be."[35] The Spirit of love and redemption, the Spirit of the new creation, is even now vibrantly at work in our lives and communities. The good news according to Jesus invites us to participate with the Spirit as partners and agents in the healing and wholeness that is God's new world.

Questions for Reflection and Discussion

1. It was suggested that Jesus expected the fullness of the kingdom to come shortly after his death and vindication/resurrection. He probably viewed the destruction of the temple, the spiritual restoration of Israel, and the end-time woes as a prelude to the kingdom's arrival. Obviously, things did not develop exactly as he thought. Does your faith perspective permit Jesus to be wrong? Why or why not?

2. Many Christians entertain the hope that Jesus will come back personally and visibly to usher in the future kingdom. Can one still have faith and hope in the future kingdom without belief in Christ's personal return to earth as a cataclysmic event? Can you imagine how this might happen and what this might look like? (Eschatological imagination spawned apocalyptic thought in the first place.)

3. Consider viewing the film *Regarding Henry* for a powerful example of how deconstruction can open the way for reconstruction, how "falling apart" can lead to wholeness and new life. Have you experienced this in your own life? In what ways?

4. Reflect on the story of the monk and the strawberry. What might we do to quiet our hearts, still our anxieties, and dispel our worries and uncertainties so that we are truly free to "taste" the present moment?

5. Reflect on the discussion of "restorative justice." How does this perspective differ from the traditional view of punitive retribution? Do you agree or disagree with the writer's interpretation? How do the view of restorative justice/redemptive judgment and the view of punitive judgment differ in the way they understand God? How do you understand the language of "hell"?

6. If Matthew did indeed embellish the judgment texts, what might have motivated him? Can you sense these same forces at work in the church today? Are they healthy or unhealthy? How do we balance the severity of judgment with the magnanimity and forgiveness of love?

7. What do you think is the central message in the judgment story of Matthew 25?

Notes

1. See Craig C. Hill, *In God's Time: The Bible and the Future* (Grand Rapids: William B. Eerdmans Pub. Co., 2002), 60–63.

2. Ibid., 64.

3. Morna Hooker, *The Gospel According to Saint Mark,* Black's New Testament Commentaries, ed. Henry Chadwick (London: Hendrickson Publishers, 1991), 298. Hugh Anderson writes, "It is probably best therefore to think of Mk 13 as an amalgam of authentic sayings of Jesus, like the prophecy of the Temple's ruin (verse 2) or the denial of knowledge of the day or hour of the end (verse 32), and the pronouncements of a Jewish or Christian prophet or prophets, worked together and developed gradually by the Church and given its final shape by the Evangelist himself" (Hugh Anderson, *The Gospel of Mark,* New Century Bible Commentary [London: Marshall, Morgan & Scott, 1976], 290).

4. The Son of Man sayings in the Synoptic Gospels generally fall into three broad categories, though there's certainly some overlap: statements where Jesus refers to himself and his current ministry; sayings that relate to Jesus' impending rejection and death; and sayings relating to a heavenly figure that will come to judge the earth. There is much debate regarding the background of these sayings. In the poetic sections of the Psalms, the phrase simply means "human being" and is used as a synonym for humankind. In Ezekiel God frequently addresses the prophet as "Son of Man." In the apocalyptic Similitudes of Enoch, the expression has Messianic connotations. The heavenly "Son of Man" sayings most likely have some connection to Daniel 7:13-14. The number and range of these sayings in the Gospels make it almost certain that Jesus used the phrase in one sense or another, most likely in multiple senses.

5. Hill, *In God's Time,* 167.

6. Harvey Cox, *When Jesus Came to Harvard: Making Moral Choices Today* (New York: Houghton Mifflin Company, 2004), 292.

7. *Regarding Henry,* dir. Mike Nichols, written by Jeffrey Abrams, Paramount Pictures, 1991.

8. Barbara Brown Taylor, *Gospel Medicine* (Boston: Cowley Publications, 1995), 137.

9. Leander Keck, *Who Is Jesus? History in the Perfect Tense* (Columbia: University of South Carolina Press, 2000), 164.

10. E. P. Sanders, *Jesus and Judaism* (Philadelphia: Fortress Press, 1985), 95–106.

11. Albert Nolan, *Jesus Before Christianity* (Maryknoll NY: Orbis Books, 1976), 107.

12. Fred Craddock, *Luke,* Interpretation: A Bible Commentary for Teaching and Preaching (Louisville: John Knox Press, 1990), 195.

13. Walter Wink, *The Human Being: Jesus and the Enigma of the Son of Man* (Minneapolis: Fortress Press, 2002), 177.

14. Ibid., 190.

15. Jurgen Moltmann, *The Way of Jesus Christ: Christology in Messianic Dimensions,* trans. Margaret Kohl (Minneapolis: Fortress Press, 1993), 315.

16. Philip Gulley and James Mulholland, *If Grace Is True: Why God Will Save Every Person* (New York: HarperSanFarnacisco, 2003), 81.

17. Jurgen Moltmann, *In the End—The Beginning: The Life of Hope* (Minneapolis: Fortress Press, 2004), 142–43.

18. Paul employs this redemptive image of fire in 1 Cor 3:15: "If the work is burned up, the builder will suffer loss; the builder will be saved, but only as through fire."

19. Taylor, *Gospel Medicine*, 130.

20. John Polkinghorne, *The God of Hope and the End of the World* (New Haven: Yale University Press, 2002), 130.

21. William H. Willimon, "Our Kind of Crowd," in *Reflections on Forgiveness and Spiritual Growth,* ed. Andrew J. Weaver and Monica Furlong (Nashville: Abingdon Press, 2000), 83.

22. In the letter to the Ephesians the writer says that when time reaches its fulfillment, all things in heaven and earth will be united and gathered up in Christ (Eph. 1:10). Paul, in his letter to the Philippians, says that every knee will bow and tongue confess that Jesus Christ is Lord to the glory of God the Father (Phil 2:10-11). And a majestic passage in Colossians says that in and for Christ all things were created, in Christ all things hold together, and in and through Christ God will reconcile all things, in heaven and on earth, to God's self (Col 1:15-20).

23. Walter Wink, *The Powers That Be: Theology for a New Millennium* (New York: Doubleday, 1998), 10.

24. *The Lord of the Rings: The Two Towers*, dir. Peter Jackson, written by J. R. R. Tolkien (novel) and Fran Walsh et al. (screenplay), New Line Cinema, 2002.

25. Martin Luther King, Jr., *Strength to Love*, memorial ed. (New York: Harper and Row, 1963), 48–49.

26. M. Eugene Boring argues, "Parables begin with familiar, this-worldly scenes, which then modulate into a new dimension of meaning. This scene, in contrast, begins with an other-worldly depiction of the parousia—the coming of the Son of Man with his angels and the gathering of all the nations before the throne—and modulates into affirmations of the ultimate importance of ordinary, this worldly deeds." (M. Eugene Boring, *Matthew,* New Interpreter's Bible, vol. 8 [Nashville: Abingdon Press, 1995], 455)

27. See the excellent discussion in Arland J. Hultgren, *The Parables of Jesus: A Commentary* (Grand Rapids: William B. Eerdmans Pub. Co., 2000), 318–23.

28. Tony Campolo, *Let Me Tell You a Story* (Word Publishing Group, 2000), 24–25.

29. Quoted by Hultgren, *Parables of Jesus,* 326.

30. Mother Teresa, *No Greater Love,* ed. Becky Benenate and Joseph Durepos (Novato CA: New World Library, 1989), 86.

31. Barbara Brown Taylor, *The Preaching Life* (Cambridge: Cowley Publications, 1993), 137.

32. Ibid., 138.

33. John Ortberg, "Spiritual Growth—My Job or God's?" *Preaching Today* Tape 190, a sermon resource produced by Leadership Resources and *Christianity Today.*

34. Dennis Linn, Sheila Fabricant Linn, and Matthew Linn, *Good Goats: Healing Our Image of God* (Mahwah NY: Paulist Press, 1994), 49.

35. N. T. Wright, *Evil and the Justice of God* (Downers Grove IL: InterVarsity Press, 2006), 118.

Recommended Reading

Autry, James A. *Looking Around for God: The Oddly Reverent Observations of an Unconventional Christian.* Macon GA: Smyth & Helwys, 2007.

Borg, Marcus J. *Jesus: A New Vision.* New York: HarperSanFrancisco, 1987.

———. *Meeting Jesus Again for the First Time: The Historical Jesus and the Heart of Contemporary Faith.* New York: HarperSanFrancisco, 1994.

———. *The Heart of Christianity: Rediscovering a Life of Faith.* New York: HarperSanFrancisco, 2003.

———. *Jesus: Uncovering the Life, Teachings, and Relevance of a Religious Revolutionary.* New York: HarperSanFrancisco, 2006.

Chalke, Steve, with Alan Mann. *The Lost Message of Jesus.* Grand Rapids MI: Zondervan, 2003.

Coffin, William Sloan. *Letters to a Young Doubter.* Louisville: Westminster John Knox Press, 2005.

Dunn, James D. G. *Jesus' Call to Discipleship.* Understanding Jesus Today series. Cambridge: Cambridge University Press, 1992.

Green, Joel B., and Mark D. Baker. *Recovering the Scandal of the Cross: Atonement in New Testament & Contemporary Contexts.* Downers Grove IL: InterVarsity Press, 2000.

Gulley, Philip, and James Mulholland. *If Grace Is True: Why God Will Save Every Person.* New York: HarperSanFrancisco, 2003.

———. *If God Is Love: Rediscovering Grace in an Ungracious World.* New York: HarperSanFrancisco, 2004.

Hall, John Douglas. *The Cross in Our Context: Jesus and the Suffering World.* Minneapolis: Fortress Press, 2003.

Hill, Craig C. In *God's Time: The Bible and the Future.* Grand Rapids/Cambridge: William B. Eerdmans Publishing Company, 2002.

Keck, Leander E. *Who Is Jesus? History in Perfect Tense.* Studies on Personalities of the New Testament. Edited by D. Moody Smith. Columbia: University of South Carolina Press, 2000.

Knitter, Paul F. *Introducing Theologies of Religion.* Maryknoll NY: Orbis Books, 2002.

Kung, Hans. *On Being a Christian.* Translated by Edward Quinn. New York: Doubleday, 1976.

Lewis, C. S. *Mere Christianity.* Revised and amplified edition. New York: HarperSanFrancisco, 2001.

Linn, Dennis, Sheila Fabricant Linn, and Matthew Linn. *Good Goats: Healing Our Image of God.* Illustrations by Francisco Miranda. Mahwa/New York: Paulist Press, 1995.

————. *Understanding Difficult Scriptures in a Healing Way.* Illustrations by Francisco Miranda. Mahwa/New York: Paulist Press, 2001.

Manning, Brennan. *The Ragamuffin Gospel: Embracing the Unconditional Love of God.* With a foreword by Rich Mullins. Sisters OR: Multnomah Books, 1990.

————. *The Signature of Jesus.* Revised edition. Sisters OR: Multnomah Books, 1996.

————. *Ruthless Trust: The Ragamuffin's Path to God.* With a foreword by Richard J. Foster. New York: HarperSanFrancisco, 2000.

————. *A Glimpse of Jesus: The Stranger to Self-Hatred.* New York: HarperSanFrancisco, 2003.

McLaren, Brian. *The Secret Message of Jesus: Uncovering the Truth that Could Change Everything.* Nashville: W Publishing Group, 2006.

————. *Everything Must Change: Jesus, Global Crises, and a Revolution of Hope.* Nashville: Thomas Nelson, 2007.

Moltmann, Jurgen. *The Way of Jesus Christ: Christology in Messianic Dimensions.* Translated by Margaret Kohl. Minneapolis: Fortress Press, 1990.

————. *In the End—The Beginning: The Life of Hope.* Translated by Margaret Kohl. Minneapolis: Fortress Press, 2004.

Nolan, Albert. *Jesus Before Christianity.* 25th anniversary edition. Maryknoll NY: Orbis Books, 2001.

Nouwen, Henri J. M. *The Return of the Prodigal Son: A Story of Homecoming.* New York: Doubleday, 1992.

Ortberg, John. *Love beyond Reason: Moving God's Love from Your Head to Your Heart.* Grand Rapids: Zondervan, 1998.

Polkinghorne, John. *The God of Hope and the End of the World.* New Haven/London: Yale University Press: 2002.

Rohr, Richard, with John Bookser Feister. *Jesus' Plan for a New World: The Sermon on the Mount.* Cincinnati: St. Anthony Messenger Press, 1996.

————. *Hope against Darkness: The Transforming Vision of Saint Francis in an Age of Anxiety.* Cincinnati: St. Anthony Messenger Press, 2001.

————. *Everything Belongs: The Gift of Contemplative Prayer.* Revised edition. New York: The Crossroad Publishing Company, 2003.

Rollins, Peter. *How (Not) to Speak of God.* Brewster MA: Paraclete Press, 2006.

Smith, James Bryan. *Embracing the Love of God: The Path and Promise of the Christian Life.* With a foreword by Richard J. Foster. New York: HarperSanFrancisco, 1995.

Weaver, J. Denny. *The Nonviolent Atonement.* Grand Rapids/Cambridge: William B. Eerdmans Publishing Company, 2001.

Willard, Dallas. *The Divine Conspiracy: Rediscovering Our Hidden Life in God.* With a foreword by Richard J. Foster. New York: HarperSanFrancisco, 1997.

Wink, Walter. *The Powers That Be: Theology for a New Millennium.* New York: Doubleday, 1998.

Wright, N. T. *Simply Christian: Why Christianity Makes Sense.* New York: HarperSanFrancisco, 2006.

————. *Evil and the Justice of God.* Downers Grove IL: InterVarsity Press, 2006.

Yancey, Philip. *What's So Amazing about Grace?* Grand Rapids: Zondervan, 1997.

Printed in the United States
146043LV00002B/1/P